DATA
QUALITY
ASSESSMENT

Arkady Maydanchik

Technics Publications

New Jersey

Published by:

Technics Publications, LLC

Post Office Box 161

Bradley Beach, NJ 07720 U.S.A.

Orders@technicspub.com

www.technicspub.com

Edited by Susan Wright and Owen Genat

Cover design by Mark Brye

Cartoons by Abby Denson, www.abbycomix.com

Layout by Owen Genat

All rights reserved. No part of this book may be reproduced or transmitted in any form or by any means, electronic or mechanical, including photocopying, recording or by any information storage and retrieval system, without written permission from the publisher, expect for the inclusion of brief quotations in a review.

The author and publisher have taken care in the preparation of this book, but make no expressed or implied warranty of any kind and assume no responsibility for errors or omissions. No liability is assumed for incidental or consequential damages in connection with or arising out of the use of the information or programs contained herein.

The publisher offers discounts on this book when ordered in quantity for special sales. For more information, please contact:

Technics Publications Corporate Sales Division

Post Office Box 161

Bradley Beach, NJ 07720 U.S.A.

CorporateSales@technicspub.com

This book is printed on acid-free paper.

© 2007 by Technics Publications, LLC. All rights reserved.

ISBN, print ed.   978-0-9771400-2-2

First Printing 2007

Printed in the United States of America

Library of Congress Control Number: 2007902970

To my parents.

Table of Contents

INTRODUCTION

It was the year 1991 and I had just arrived in the United States as an immigrant from Russia. My specialty was pattern recognition and statistical modeling, and my first contract was to build a mathematical model for cash circulation in the USA. A governmental agency that sponsored the project provided me with over a gigabyte of data – a huge volume by the standards of 1991 – containing 25 years of inter-bank transactions and a variety of other information about cash circulation. They had a great idea that statistical analysis could identify unusual patterns of cash movement and eventually lead to the discovery of illegal financial activities.

I worked hard for three months and built the best models I could imagine. They absolutely had to work… but the results made no sense whatsoever. After a week of sleepless nights in search for a flaw in the logic or bug in the program, I finally got to the point of trying to work the logic by hand for a small subset of the data. The results still defied logic, but so did the data itself. The numbers did not add up; the amount of money going out did not equal the amount of money coming in. Some numbers were outrageously large, while others ridiculously small. This was my first exposure to bad data quality. Of course something had to be done, and so over the next six months I did my first data quality assessment and data cleansing project. It taught me several lessons.

First, data quality is very important. My clients would not get the results they wanted, and I would not get paid, all because some tiny pieces of data in the database were inaccurate. Secondly, data quality can get really bad, especially in large historical databases. According to my clients, their data were managed with utmost care, and they were certain its quality would be far above average. I kept wondering: What would be the quality of data in an average database? Thirdly, with some effort, data quality can be measured, analyzed, and improved. Even though it was my first effort, in six months I was able to fix 98% of the data problems and get the desired results. Finally, nobody had a clue about what data quality was and how to deal with it. There was no data quality profession, no textbooks for practitioners, and no training courses. There was really nowhere to turn to get advice.

The experience intrigued me so much that I decided to dedicate my career to data quality. It took longer to get the ball rolling, but in 1997 I finally started a data quality services company. Now, there is a huge difference between being a consultant and a services provider. As a consultant, when a client asks your opinion about a solution that seems unreasonably difficult, you can simply advise them against trying it, and if they do not listen, you wash your hands and quietly watch the suffering. As a service provider, you are asked to solve the problems, no matter how difficult or impossible the solutions, and clients rarely take "no" for an answer. So I had to deal with all kinds of problems and figure out how to deal with all practical aspects of data quality in the most efficient manner. I did not complain though; it was fun.

Something else has happened over the last 15 years. In early 1990s, not many people had heard the words "data quality." Even in late 1990s, when I occasionally stepped up to the podium to speak at a conference, I always expected rotten tomatoes flying in my face. Data quality was a taboo topic. Even the companies that successfully completed a data quality initiative did not want to talk about it in public. Over time the tide has changed and data quality has become one of the hottest topics. It almost seems like everybody wants to know about data quality these days. More and more, data quality departments are formed, and many data quality improvement initiatives are started every year.

Yet, the data quality profession is still in its infancy. There are very few truly seasoned practitioners and existing training courses. Data quality books mostly focus on the "what" and "why" of data quality, not the "how." And so data quality remains a major IT problem. I have seen databases of all kinds at many large companies – HR, payroll, financial, marketing, and data warehouses. They varied in size, architecture, and complexity, but they had one thing in common – poor data quality. According to some estimates, the cost of poor data quality can reach as high as 15% to 25% of operating profit. The problem must be solved, and I believe that can only be accomplished if the data quality professionals have access to practical textbooks describing data quality solutions in all details. Without proper methodology and techniques, data quality projects can only succeed by accident.

That was the impetus behind my decision to switch from being a full-time services provider to becoming an educator. Over the last two years I created and taught a series of training course – "Practical Skills for Data Quality". Among several hundreds of attendees, the majority gave very high assessment to the value of my classes. Someone carelessly advised me to write a book based on my courses so that I can reach a broader audience. And so I did.

This book is intended as the first in a data quality series. It is a textbook from a practitioner to other practitioners. For the last 15 years, I was a data doctor – I studied, diagnosed, and treated data. My objective now is to teach you what I have learned about how to solve data quality problems from A to Z.

This book consists of 14 chapters. The first two chapters give a broad overview of data quality problems and the key components in a comprehensive data quality program. It provides the roadmap for the entire book series. The rest of the book is dedicated to data quality assessment – the process of identifying data problems and measuring their magnitude and impact on various data-driven business processes. After a brief overview in Chapter 3, I will roll up my sleeves and delve into the details.

Even though the topic is technical, I tried to do my best to make it a light reading. It proved to be harder than I thought, and my respect for great authors has grown day by day. The problem is it takes months to write a book: day, after day, after day. Some days I was happy, and other days I was sad. Sometimes I felt I could do stand-up comedy, and other days I would be better off teaching advanced calculus, so different parts of the book have inherited different personalities. Hopefully you will still take pleasure from reading this book, and at the same time will find it practically useful in everyday work.

I am looking forward to any feedback and suggestions. Those will certainly influence future volumes of this project. You can visit my website at www.dataqualitygroup.com where you will find a forum dedicated to the discussion of data quality problems in general and this book in particular.

ACKNOWLEDGEMENTS

I cannot even describe how much I owe this book to my wife and partner in many years of work, Olga. She suffered through the years when I worked 12 hours a day, weekends included. She shared the workload with me, and I could always rely on her ability to solve the most difficult problems. She tried to stop me from making wrong turns and consoled me after I did not listen. She put together a better half of my training materials and read and critiqued every page of this book. She also managed to raise our 9 year-old son, Max, and give birth to another boy, Nathaniel, as I was finishing this book. And through all these years she remained my beautiful, loving wife. For this I am infinitely grateful.

I also want to thank my good friend and colleague, Dave Wells. Over the years Dave and I discussed data quality matters many times and his insights always proved to be on the mark. In fact we were even thinking about writing a data quality book together, and I am sure it would be a much better book than what I was able to accomplish myself. Dave also read this book three times in attempts to find every possible flaw.

Gian Di Loreto, my old friend and business partner, has also contributed to this book. While I now spend more time in education, he stays down in the trenches fighting data quality battles every day and only brings me to see the new and interesting parts.

I thank Susan Wright for editing this text. I could certainly learn better grammar and punctuation if I could take some lessons from her, but she is busy in the noblest profession of a schoolteacher.

I thank my son, Max, for always trying to help. Setting an example for him has been my greatest inspiration.

I thank my dad for teaching me to believe in myself and strive to be the best I could possibly be, and my mom for showing me how to be happy with who I am. I thank my older brother for endless hours of teaching me math and the mysteries of numbers. I wish everyone had such a great brother. I thank my late math teacher, Vladimir Sapozhnikov, for instilling in me perfectionism – the trait that distinguished his life, which was dedicated to making better people of all he taught.

PART I – DATA QUALITY OVERVIEW

The corporate data universe consists of numerous databases linked by countless real-time and batch data feeds. The data continuously move about and change. The databases are endlessly redesigned and upgraded, as are the programs responsible for data exchange. The typical result of this dynamic is that information systems get better, while data quality deteriorates. This is very unfortunate since it is the data quality that determines the intrinsic value of the data to the business and consumers. Information technology serves only as a magnifier for this intrinsic value. Thus, high quality data combined with effective technology is a great asset, but poor quality data combined with effective technology is an equally great liability.

Yet we tolerate enormous inaccuracies in the databases. It has been widely accepted that most databases are riddled with errors. These errors are the cancer of information systems, spreading from place-to-place and wreaking operational and financial havoc. Corporations are losing million of dollars due to inaccurate data. What is even more disheartening is that the magnitude of the data quality problems is continuously growing, fostered by exponential increase in the size of the databases and further proliferation of information systems. This certainly qualifies data quality management as one of the most important IT challenges in this early part of the 21st century.

The big part of the challenge is that data quality does not improve by itself or as a result of general IT advancements. Over the years, the onus of data quality improvement was placed on modern database technologies and better information systems. I remember well an HR executive confidently telling me over lunch that now that his company has implemented a modern HR and payroll system, it will no longer have data quality problems. "PeopleSoft does not have data quality problems," he said. How could I respond? I said, "I cannot tell you whether or not PeopleSoft has data quality problems, but your company certainly does, and they are not going away. In fact they are about to get much bigger." He did not believe me; people do not like those who predict rain on a sunny day. A few years later the recently appointed new HR executive of that company called me for advice about their data quality strategy.

In reality, most IT processes affect data quality negatively. Thus, if we do nothing, data quality will continuously deteriorate to the point where the data will become a huge liability. In fact I have seen many databases that are living proof (or I'd rather say, fossils) of this statement. The only way to address the data quality challenge is by a systematic, ongoing program, which would assess and improve existing data quality levels, as well as continuously monitor data quality and prevent its future deterioration as much as possible.

It is most important to understand that data quality is not a mountain that you can climb, raise the flag, and live happily ever after, proud of your accomplishment. It is rather like a garden that must be taken care of continuously. With effort and patience, it can be made stunningly beautiful; but left unattended for just a short while, and the weeds will overrun it like seven-headed monsters, whose heads grow back faster than you can slash them.

In the first chapter I will discuss various processes that affect data quality. I will outline the structure of a comprehensive data quality program and briefly discuss its components in Chapter 2. The challenge of implementing the data quality program is so monumental that it would be naive to tackle it in a single book. I am planning to accomplish this in steps through this book series. In this first book I will only address data quality assessment, the first step in most data quality initiatives. Chapter 3 offers an introduction to the topic, while the remaining eleven chapters of the book will discuss the details.

CHAPTER 1
CAUSES OF DATA QUALITY
PROBLEMS

Data is impacted by numerous processes, most of which affect its quality to a certain degree. I had to deal with data quality problems on a daily basis for many years and have seen every imaginable scenario of how data quality deteriorates. While each situation is different, I eventually came up with a classification shown in Figure 1-1. It shows 13 categories of processes that cause the data problems, grouped into three high-level categories.

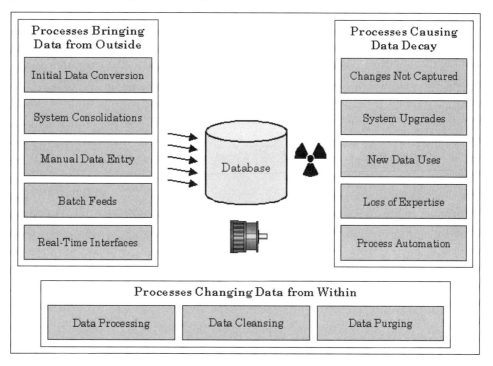

Figure 1-1: Processes Affecting Data Quality

The group on the left shows processes that bring data into the database from outside – either manually or through various interfaces and data integration techniques. Some of these incoming data may be incorrect in the first place and simply migrate from one place to another. In other cases, the errors are introduced in the process of data extraction, transformation, or loading. High volumes of the data traffic dramatically magnify these problems.

The group on the right shows processes that manipulate the data inside the databases. Some of these processes are routine, while others are brought upon by periodic system upgrades, mass data updates, database redesign, and a variety of ad-hoc activities. Unfortunately, in practice most of these procedures lack time and resources, as well as reliable meta data necessary to understand all data quality implications. It is not surprising, then, that internal data processing often leads to numerous data problems.

The group on the bottom shows processes that cause accurate data to become inaccurate over time, without any physical changes made to it. The data values are not modified, but their accuracy takes a plunge! This usually happens when the real world object described by the data changes, but the data collection processes do not capture the change. The old data turns obsolete and incorrect.

In this chapter we will systematically discuss the 13 processes presented in Figure 1-1 and explain how and why they negatively affect data quality.

1.1. INITIAL DATA CONVERSION

Databases rarely begin their life empty. More often the starting point in their lifecycle is a data conversion from some previously exiting data source. And by a cruel twist of fate, it is usually a rather violent beginning. Data conversion usually takes the better half of new system implementation effort and almost never goes smoothly.

When I think of data conversion, my first association is with the mass extinction of dinosaurs. For 150 million years, dinosaurs ruled the earth. Then one day – BANG – a meteor came crashing down. Many animals died on impact, others never recovered and slowly disappeared in the ensuing darkness. It took millions of years for flora and fauna to recover. In the end, the formerly dominant dinosaurs were completely wiped out and replaced by the little furry creatures that later evolved into rats, lemurs, and the strange apes who find nothing better to do than write data quality books.

The data conversion is no different. Millions of unsuspecting data elements quietly do their daily work until – BANG – data conversion comes hurling at them. Much data never makes it to the new database; many of the lucky ones mutate so much in transition that they simply die out slowly in the aftermath. Most companies live with the consequences of bad data conversions for years or even decades. In fact, some data problems can be traced to "grandfathers of data conversions," i.e. conversion to the system from which the data were later converted to the system from which the data is converted to the new system…

I still vividly remember one of my first major data conversion projects. I was on a team implementing a new pension administration system. Among other things, we needed to convert employee compensation data from the "legacy" HR database. The old data was stored in much detail – by paycheck and compensation type. The new database simply needed aggregate monthly pensionable earnings. The mapping was trivial – take all records with relevant compensation types (provided as a list of valid codes), add up amounts for each calendar month, and place the result into the new bucket.

The result was disastrous. Half of the sample records I looked at did not match the summary reports printed from the old system. The big meeting was called for the next morning, and in the wee hours of the night, I had a presence of mind to stop looking for bugs in the code and poke into the source data. The data certainly did not add up to what was showing on the summary reports, yet the reports were produced from these very data! This mathematical puzzle kept me up till dawn. By then I had most of it figured out.

Half a dozen compensation codes included in the aggregate amounts were missing from our list. In fact they were even missing from the data dictionary! Certain codes were used in some years but ignored in other years. Records with negative amounts – retroactive adjustments – were aggregated into the previous month, which they technically belonged to, rather than the month of the paycheck. Apparently the old system had a ton of code that applied all these rules to calculate proper monthly pensionable earnings. The new system was certainly not programmed to do so, and nobody remembered to indicate all this logic in the mapping document.

It took us eight weeks of extensive data profiling, analysis, and quality assessment to complete this portion of the project, whereas one week was budgeted for. We were lucky, though, that the problem was relatively easy to expose. In many conversion projects, the data is converted based on the mapping specifications that are ridiculously out-of-sync with reality. The result is predictable – mass extinction of the data and the project teams.

So what is it that makes data conversion so dangerous? At the heart of the issue is the fact that every system is made of three layers: database, business rules, and user interface. As a result what users see is not what is actually stored in the database. This is especially true for older "legacy" systems. During the data conversion it is the data structure that is usually the center of attention. The data is mapped between old and new databases. However, since the business rule layers of the source and destination systems are very different, this approach inevitably fails. The converted data, while technically correct, is inaccurate for all practical purposes.

The second problem is the typical lack of reliable meta data about the source database. Think about it, how often do we find value codes in the data that are missing from the mapping documents? The answer is: All the time. But how can we believe any meta data when even such a basic component is incorrect? Yet, over and over again, data conversions are made to the specifications built on incomplete, incorrect, and obsolete meta data.

To summarize, the quality of the data after conversion is directly proportional to the amount of time spent to analyze and profile the data and uncover the true data content. In an ideal data conversion project, 80% of time is spent on data analysis and 20% on coding transformation algorithms.

So far I have talked about the data problems introduced by the conversion process; however, the source data itself is never perfect. Existing erroneous data tends to mutate and spread out during conversion like a virus. Some bad records are dropped and not converted at all. Others are changed by the transformation routines. Such changed and aggregated errors are much more difficult to identify and correct after conversion. What is even worse – the bad records impact conversion of many correct data elements.

To conclude, data conversion is the most difficult part of any system implementation. The error rate in a freshly populated new database is often an order of magnitude above that of the old system from which the data is converted. As a major source of the data problems, data conversion must be treated with the utmost respect it deserves.

1.2. SYSTEM CONSOLIDATIONS

Database consolidations are the most common occurrence in the information technology landscape. They take place regularly when old systems are phased out or combined. And, of course, they always follow company mergers and acquisitions. Database consolidations after corporate mergers are especially troublesome because they are usually unplanned, must be completed in an unreasonably tight timeframe, take place in the midst of the cultural clash of IT departments, and are accompanied by inevitable loss of expertise when key people leave midway through the project.

An old man once rode his Pontiac three miles in the oncoming traffic before being stopped. He was very surprised why everybody was going the wrong way. That is exactly how I feel when involved in a data consolidation project.

Instead of two small cars we have one big pile of iron, plastic, and rubber.

Data consolidation faces the same challenges as initial data conversion but magnified to a great extent. I have already discussed why conversions cause data quality problems. The idea of consolidation adds the whole new dimension of complexity. First of all, the data is often merged into an existing non-empty database, whose structure can be changed little or none whatsoever. However, often the new data simply does not fit! The efforts to squeeze square pegs into round holes are painful, even to an outside observant.

More importantly, the data in the consolidated systems often overlap. There are duplicates, there are overlaps in subject populations and data histories, and there are numerous data conflicts. The traditional approach is to setup a winner-loser matrix indicating which source data element is picked up in case of a conflict. For instance, date of birth will be taken from System A if present, from System B otherwise, and from System C if it is missing in both A and B. This rarely works because it assumes that data on System A is always correct – a laughable assumption. To mitigate the problem, the winner-loser matrix is usually transformed into a complex conditional hierarchy. Now we take the date of birth from System A for all males born after 1956 in California, except if that date of birth is January 1, 1970, in which case we take it from System B, unless of course the record on System B is marked as edited by John Doe who was fired for playing games on the computer while doing data entry, in which case we pull it from Spreadsheet C…

At some point the winner-loser matrix is so complex, that nobody really understands what is going on. The programmers argue with business analysts about the exact meaning of the word "unless," and consumption of antidepressants is on the rise. It is time to scrap the approach and start over.

I will discuss the proper methodology for data consolidation in the next chapter. For now we just conclude that data consolidation is one of the main causes of data problems and must be treated with great fear. Walking a tightrope is child's play in comparison.

1.3. Manual Data Entry

Despite high automation, much data is (and will always be!) typed into the databases by people through various forms and interfaces. The most common source of data inaccuracy is that the person manually entering the data just makes a mistake. To err, after all, is human! People mistype; they choose a wrong entry from the list or enter right data value into the wrong box. I had, at one time, participated in a data-cleansing project where the analysts were supposed to carefully check the corrections before entering them – and still 3% of the corrections were entered incorrectly. This was in a project where data quality was the primary objective!

Common error rate in data entry is much higher. Over time I collected my personal indicative data from various databases. My collection includes eight different spellings of my first name, along with a dozen of my last name, and four dates of birth; I was marked as male, female, and even the infamous 'U'.

Convoluted and inconvenient data entry forms often further complicate the data entry challenge. The same applies to data entry windows and web-based interfaces. Frustration in using a form will lead to exponential increase in the number of errors. Users often tend to find the easiest way to complete the form, even if that means making deliberate mistakes.

A common data entry problem is handling missing values. Users may assign the same blank value to various types of missing values. When "blank" is not allowed, users often enter meaningless value substitutes. Default values in data entry forms are often left untouched. The first entry in any list box is selected more often than any other entry.

Good data entry forms and instructions somewhat mitigate data entry problems. In an ideal fantasy world, data entry is as easy to the user as possible: fields are labeled and organized clearly, data entry repetitions are eliminated, and data is not required when it is not yet available or is already forgotten. The reality of data entry, however, is not that rosy (and probably won't be for years to come). Thus we must accept that manual data entry will always remain a significant cause of data problems.

1.4. BATCH FEEDS

Batch feeds are large regular data exchange interfaces between systems. The ever-increasing number of databases in the corporate universe communicates through complex spiderwebs of batch feeds.

In the old days, when Roman legions wanted to sack a fortified city, they hurled heavy stones at its walls, day after day. Not many walls could withstand such an assault. In the modern world, the databases suffer the same unrelenting onslaught of batch feeds. Each batch carries large volumes of data, and any problem in it causes great havoc further magnified by future feeds. The batch feeds can be usually tied to the greatest number of data quality problems. While each individual feed may not cause too many errors, the problems tend to accumulate from batch to batch. And there is little opportunity to fix the ever-growing backlog.

So why do the well-tested batch feed programs falter? The source system that originates the batch feed is subject to frequent structural changes, updates, and upgrades. Testing the impact of these changes on the data feeds to multiple independent downstream databases is a difficult and often impractical step. Lack of regression testing and quality assurance inevitably leads to numerous data problems with batch feeds any time the source system is modified – which is all of the time!

Consider a simple example of a payroll feed to the employee benefit administration system. Paycheck data is extracted, aggregated by pay type, and loaded into monthly buckets. Every few months a new pay code is added into the payroll system to expand its functionality. In theory, every downstream system may be impacted, and thus each downstream batch feed must be re-evaluated. In practice, this task often slips through the cracks, especially since many systems, such as benefit administration databases, are managed by other departments or even outside vendors. The records with the new code arrive at the doorsteps of the destination database and are promptly dropped from consideration. In the typical scenario, the problem is caught after a few feeds. By then, thousands of bad records were created.

The other problem with batch feeds is that they quickly spread bad data from database to database. Any errors that somehow find their way into the source system will usually flow immediately through the batch feeds like viruses and can blend well enough with the rest of the batch data to come unnoticed and cause the greatest damage.

The batch feeds are especially dangerous because newly arrived records do not sit quietly. The incoming transactions usually trigger immediate processing in the target database. Even during loading, existing data might be changed to reflect new transactions. Thus more data is immediately corrupted. Additional processing can be triggered, creating more and more errors in an avalanche of bad data. For example, erroneous employee termination records arriving to a benefit administration system will initiate a sequence of benefit calculations. The results will be forwarded to the benefit payment system, which will create more wrong data and initiate more wrong activities. The cost of a single bad record can run in to thousands of dollars. It is hard to even visualize the destructive power of a batch feed full of erroneous data.

1.5. REAL-TIME INTERFACES

More and more data is exchanged between the systems through real-time (or near real-time) interfaces. As soon as the data enters one database, it triggers procedures necessary to send transactions to other downstream databases. The advantage is immediate propagation of data to all relevant databases. Data is less likely to be out-of-sync. You can close your eyes and imagine the millions of little data pieces flying from database to database across vast distances with lightning speed, making our lives easier. You see the triumph of the information age! I see Wile E. Coyote in his endless pursuit of the Road Runner. Going! Going! Gosh!

The basic problem is that data is propagated too fast. There is little time to verify that the data is accurate. At best, the validity of individual attributes is usually checked. Even if a data problem can be identified, there is often nobody at the other end of the line to react. The transaction must be either accepted or rejected (whatever the consequences). If data is rejected, it may be lost forever!

Further, the data comes in small packets, each taken completely out of context. A packet of data in itself may look innocent, but the data in it may be totally erroneous. I once received an email from a Disney World resort thanking me for staying there. The text was grammatically perfect and would have made me feel great, except I did not go to Disney that year.

The point is that "faster" and "better" rarely go hand-in-hand. More often quality is the price paid for faster delivery. Real-time data propagation is no exception – it is a liability from the data quality perspective. This does not make it any less valuable. Real-time interfaces save millions of dollars and significantly improve efficiency of the information systems. But data quality suffers in the process, and this has to be recognized. When an old batch feed is replaced by a new real-time interface, the potential cost of data quality deterioration must be evaluated and weighed against the benefit of faster data propagation.

1.6. DATA PROCESSING

Data processing is at the heart of all operational systems. It comes in many shapes and forms – from regular transactions triggered by users to end-of-the-year massive calculations and adjustments. In theory, these are repetitive processes that should work "like a clock." In practice there is nothing steady in the world of computer software. Both programs and underlying data change and evolve, with the result that one morning the proverbial sun rises in the West, or worse yet, does not rise at all.

The first part of the problem is the change in the programs responsible for regular data processing. Minor changes and tweaks are as regular as normal use. These are often not adequately tested based on the common misconception that small changes cannot have much impact. Of course a tiny bug in the code applied to a million records can create a million errors faster than you can read this sentence.

On the flip side, the programs responsible for regular processing often lag behind changes in the data caused by new collection procedures. The new data may be fine when it enters the database, but it may be different enough to cause regular processing to produce erroneous results.

A more subtle problem is when processing is accidentally done at the wrong time. Then the correct program may yield wrong results because the data is not in the state it is supposed to be. A simple example is running the program that calculates weekly compensation <u>before</u> the numbers from the hours tracking system were entered.

In theory, documenting the complete picture of what is going on in the database and how various processes are interrelated would allow us to completely mitigate the problem. Indeed, someone could then analyze the data quality implications of any changes in code, processes, data structure, or data collection procedures and thus eliminate unexpected data errors. In practice, this is an insurmountable task. For that reason, regular data processing inside the database will always be a cause of data problems.

1.7. DATA CLEANSING

The data quality topic has caught on in recent years, and more and more companies are attempting to cleanse the data. In the old days, cleansing was done manually and was rather safe. The new methodologies have arrived that use automated data cleansing rules to make corrections *en masse*. These methods are of great value and I, myself, am an ardent promoter of the rule-driven approach to automated data cleansing. Unfortunately, the risks and complexities of automated data cleansing are rarely well understood.

The reader might ask in surprise, "How come that data cleansing that strives to correct data errors may instead create new ones?" Those who, like me, in their college years mixed whites and colors in the laundry machine will know how hopelessly "dirty" the white shirts become after such cleansing. And so, despite the noble goal of higher data quality, data cleansing often creates more data problems than it corrects. This situation is further complicated by the complacency that commonly sets in after the cleansing project is "completed."

Data cleansing is dangerous mainly because data quality problems are usually complex and interrelated. Fixing one problem may create many others in the same or other related data elements. For instance, employment history is tightly linked with position history, pay rate history, and many other employment data attributes. Making corrections to any one of these data categories will make the data inconsistent with all other categories.

I also must mention that automated data cleansing algorithms are implemented by computer programs, which will inevitably have bugs. Bugs in these algorithms are very dangerous because they often impact thousands of records.

Another problem is that data quality specifications often do not reflect actual data requirements. As a result, data may be brought in compliance with some theoretical model but remain incorrect for actual use. For example, in one of my early projects the client – a large corporation with a history of acquisitions – requested to cleanse employment history on their HR system. One of the major problems was missing or incorrect original hire date for many employees, used to calculate amount of retirement pension benefits. I had access to several "legacy" data sources and was able to devise a series of algorithms to correct the problem for over 15,000 employees. Unfortunately, many of the employees were not originally hired by my client but came through numerous acquisitions. The pension calculations performed by the HR system were not supposed to use the period of employment with the acquired companies prior to the acquisition. Therefore, what the system really expected in the original hire date field for the employees from acquired units was the acquisition date. However, the data quality specifications I was given did not reflect that. As a result, many corrections were wrong. Since I had a complete audit trail of all data changes, it was not too difficult to fix the problem. Many data cleansing projects do not have the happy ending, and newly created errors linger for years.

To summarize, data cleansing is a double-edged sword that can hurt more than help if not used carefully. I will discuss the proper methodology for data cleansing in the next chapter.

1.8. DATA PURGING

Old data is routinely purged from systems to make way for more data. This is normal when a retention limit is satisfied and old data no longer necessary. However, data purging is highly risky for data quality.

When data is purged, there is always a risk that some relevant data is purged by accident. The purging program may simply fail. More likely, the data structure may have changed since the last purging due to a system upgrade, data conversion, or any of the other discussed above processes. So now the purging may accidentally impact the wrong data. More data than intended can be purged. Or alternatively less data than intended might be purged, which is equally bad since it leaves incomplete records in the database.

Another factor that complicates things is the presence of erroneous data in the database. The erroneous data may accidentally fit the purging criteria and get removed when it should be left alone, or vice versa. For example, if the HR system is setup to purge data for all employees that were terminated over five years ago, then it will wipe out records for some employees with incorrectly entered termination dates.

Since purging often equals destruction, it has to be exercised with great care. The fact that it worked reasonably well last year does not guarantee that it will work again this year. Data is too volatile a compound to be fooled around with. This requires more sophisticated design of the purging programs than is often used for such a trivial technical task. After all, it seems quite easy to just wipe out a few millions of records. So we live with the data quality consequences of data purging in almost every database.

1.9. CHANGES NOT CAPTURED

Data can become obsolete (and thus incorrect) simply because the object it describes has changed. If a caterpillar has turned into a butterfly but is still listed as a caterpillar on the finch's menu, the bird is in her right to complain about poor data quality.

This situation is very commonplace in human affairs, too, and inevitably leads to gradual data decay. The data is only accurate if it truly represents real world objects. However, this assumes perfect data collection processes. In reality, object changes regularly go unnoticed to computers. People move, get married, and even die without filling out all necessary forms to record these events in each system where their data is stored. This is actually why, in practice, data about same person may be totally different across systems, causing pain during consolidation.

In this age of numerous interfaces across systems, we rely largely on the fact that a change made in one place will migrate to all other places. This obviously does not always happen. As a result, changes are not propagated to all concerned databases and data decays. For instance, interfaces often ignore retroactive data corrections. Alternatively, IT personnel may make changes using a backdoor update query, which, of course, does not trigger any transactions to the downstream systems.

Whether the cause is a faulty data collection procedure or a defective data interface, the situation of data getting out of sync with reality is rather common. This is an example of data decay inevitably leading to deterioration of the data quality.

1.10. SYSTEM UPGRADES

Most commercial systems get upgraded every few years. Homegrown software is often upgraded several times a year. While upgrades are not nearly as invasive and painful as system conversions and consolidations, they still often somehow introduce data problems. How can a well tested, better version negatively impact data quality?

The culprit here is the assumption that the data complies with what is theoretically expected of it. In practice, actual data is often far different from what is described in data models and dictionaries. Data fields are used for wrong purposes, and some data is missing while other was massaged into a form acceptable to the prior version. Yet more data just exists harmlessly as an artifact of past generations but should not be touched.

Upgrades expose all these problems. More often than not, they are designed for and tested against what data is expected to be, not what it really is. Once the upgrades are implemented, everything goes haywire. People lose their hair trying to figure out why the system worked in the past, and the new version did beautifully in the testing environment, yet all of the sudden it breaks on every step.

System upgrades usually impact data quality through the described above process of data decay. However, they often require real restructuring and mass updates of the existing data. Such changes coupled with lack of reliable meta data lead to huge quantities of data errors.

1.11. NEW DATA USES

Remember that data quality is defined as "fitness to the purpose of use." The data may be good enough for one purpose but inadequate for another. Therefore, new data uses often bring about changes in perceived level of data quality even though underlying data is the same. For instance, HR systems may not care too much to differentiate medical and personal leave of absence – a medical leave coded as a personal leave is not an error for most HR purposes. But start using it to determine eligibility for employee benefits, and such minute details become important. Now a medical leave entered as a personal leave is plain wrong.

The new uses may also put greater premium on data accuracy even without changing the definition of quality. Thus, a 15% error rate in customer addresses may be perfectly fine for telemarketing purposes, but try to survive with that many inaccurate addresses for billing!

Besides accuracy, other aspects of data quality may differ for various uses. Value granularity, or data retention policy, may be inadequate for the new use. For example, employee compensation data retained for three years is adequate for payroll administration but cannot be used to analyze compensation trends.

1.12. LOSS OF EXPERTISE

On almost every data quality project I worked, there is Dick or Jane or Nancy whose data expertise is unparalleled. Dick was with the department for the last 35 years and is the only person who really understands why for some employees date of hire is stored in the date of birth field, while for others it must be adjusted by exactly 17 days. Jane still remembers times when she did calculations by hand and entered the results into the system that was shut down in 1985, even though she still sometimes accesses the old data when in doubt. When Nancy decided to retire, she was offered hourly work from home at double her salary. Those are true stories.

Much data in databases has a long history. It might have come from old "legacy" systems or have been changed several times in the past. The usage of data fields and value codes changes over time. The same value in the same field will mean totally different thing in different records. Knowledge of these facts allows experts to use the data properly. Without this knowledge, the data may be used literally and with sad consequences.

The same is true about data quality. Data users in the trenches usually know good data from bad and can still use it efficiently. They know where to look and what to check. Without these experts, incorrect data quality assumptions are often made and poor data quality becomes exposed.

Unfortunately much of the data knowledge exists in people's minds rather than meta data documents. As these people move on, retire, or simply forget things, the data is no longer used properly. How do we solve this problem? Besides erecting monuments honoring Dick, Jane, and Nancy, what we need is obviously a well-designed and maintained meta data repository and data quality meta data warehouses. This is a great dream to have, and maybe with luck, some day, our names will be etched on the monuments too. In the meantime, we must deal with the consequences of lost expertise in the form of data decay.

1.13. PROCESS AUTOMATION

With the progress of information technology, more and more tasks are automated. It starts from replacement of data entry forms with system interfaces and extends to every layer of our life. Computer programs process and ship orders, calculate insurance premiums, and even send spam – all with no need for human intervention. Where in the past a pair (or several pairs) of human eyes with the full power of trained intellect protected the unsuspecting customers, now we are fully exposed to a computer's ability to do things wrong and not even feel sorry.

A human would automatically validate the data before using it. Computer programs take the data literally and cannot make a proper judgment about the likelihood of it been correct. Some validation screens may be implemented in the automated processes, but these will often fail to see all data peculiarities, or are turned off in the interest of performance. As a result, automation causes data decay!

Another aspect of technology development is greater data exposure to broader group of users. For instance, over the last 15 years it has become possible to publish HR data for employee access via voice response systems and later intranet. Employees can check their eligibility for benefits, various educational programs, and query other information. All of the sudden erroneous HR data became exposed, causing floods of employee complaints. The data did not change, but its perceived quality deteriorated.

SUMMARY

We have discussed various processes that affect data quality. In some cases, bad data comes from outside of the database through data conversions, manual entry, or various data integration interfaces. In other cases, data deteriorate as a result of internal system processing. Yet in many situations, data quality may decline without any changes made to the data itself – the process we referred to as data decay. Each of these problems must be addressed if we are to assume the data quality management responsibility. The next chapter will discuss how it can be done through a comprehensive data quality program.

CHAPTER 2
DATA QUALITY PROGRAM
OVERVIEW

Data quality program is a collection of initiatives with the common objective of maximizing data quality and minimizing negative impact of the bad data. It is made up of several components as shown in Figure 2-1.

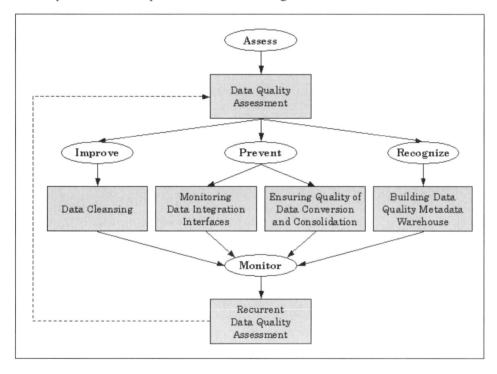

Figure 2-1: Components of the Data Quality Program

The first step is to assess the magnitude of the problem. It is accomplished through a process called data quality assessment. The objective of the data quality assessment is to identify data errors and measure their impact on various business processes. Once assessment is complete we can decide what to do about data quality. First of all, we may want to improve the data quality level of existing data. This noble initiative is achieved through a process called data cleansing. The objective of data cleansing is to correct as many existing errors as practically feasible and thus to turn the bad data into useable and trustworthy data. Keep in mind that 100% data quality is not realistic, and so the objective of data cleansing is never set at the absolute. Rather, it is defined as the quality level that provides optimal return on investment into data cleansing.

Once we achieve a certain acceptable level of data quality, the next step is to maintain the status quo by preventing new errors from being introduced into the data. This proves to be extremely difficult, actually far more difficult than identifying and correcting existing problems. The two preventive measures that provide the biggest immediate return on investment are monitoring data integration interfaces and ensuring quality during data conversion and consolidation. These measures address the two most common external sources of data problems. Also, using the findings of the data quality assessment by itself helps prevent data quality from deterioration in more ways than one. For example, it helps improve data collection procedures and seriously limits potential data decay.

While we might attempt to identify and correct most data errors, as well as try to prevent others from entering the database, the data quality will never be perfect. Perfection is practically unattainable in data quality as with the quality of most other products. In truth, it is also unnecessary since at some point improving data quality becomes more expensive than leaving it alone. The more efficient our data quality program, the higher level of quality we will achieve, but never will it reach 100%. However, accepting imperfection is not the same as ignoring it. Knowledge of the data limitations and imperfections can help use the data wisely and thus save time and money. The challenge, of course, is making this knowledge organized and easily accessible to the target users. The solution is a comprehensive integrated data quality meta data warehouse.

Finally, once we have gone through all of the above steps, there remains just one more important aspect of a comprehensive data quality program – ongoing monitoring. Without monitoring even the best preventive measures might eventually begin to fail. We may not notice data quality deterioration until it is too late. Also, even more perfect measures will not completely eliminate new data problems. To monitor data quality, we must perform data quality assessment recurrently, compare the results, and observe the dynamics. The results can then be used to perform more data cleansing, improve preventive measures, and sharpen our understanding of data imperfections. Thus we have come full circle.

In this chapter we will outline various components of a comprehensive data quality program and discuss their role in data quality management. The rest of this book will be dedicated to data quality assessment. The other components will be presented in future volumes of this book series.

2.1. DATA QUALITY ASSESSMENT

The objective of data quality assessment is to identify erroneous data elements and estimate their impact on various data-driven business processes. In an ideal world, it would be possible to determine whether or not each data element in the database is correct and, if incorrect, where it came from and what had caused the error. Had we accomplished that, we could understand the source of each and every data problem. Then (again in theory) we could correct the existing errors and make sure that future problems are prevented.

In practice this proves an insurmountable challenge. Indeed, the only way to be sure that a piece of data is correct is to compare it with some "trusted" source, that is, a source which is correct 100% of the time. Such source may not always exist or at least may not be readily available. For example, imagine we want to validate the date of birth for all 1,000 employees of a mid-size corporation. To verify someone's date of birth we could use a birth certificate if a copy was available in the employee file. But what if we do not have one? Then we would have to contact that person. The process of contacting each of 1,000 employees is quite lengthy.

Another dimension of complexity is added when we deal with historical data. Say we wanted to validate the employment history for each employee. It would include original date of hire, any leaves of absence, resignations, and rehire events. Employee paper files are often kept but may not always be complete and accurate. Contacting employees may not help either, as they may not remember all these details or be unwilling to provide the information.

The bottom line is that the trusted source is often not easily available. Another problem is the time constraint on data quality assessment. Consider a relatively small HR database for 1,000 employees. It may contain about 1 million individual data pieces, a rather small size in today's world of gigabytes and terabytes. Imagine further that we have access to a trusted source of each data element (say a paper file), and we want to validate each one manually. Assuming that a data expert can validate one data element in 15 seconds, we come up with 15 million seconds required to do the job, the equivalent of about two person-years of full-time work. And frankly, this estimate is rather conservative.

This approach is unreasonably expensive and totally impractical for larger databases. But even for relatively small ones, it makes little sense because most databases change over time. Even assuming that we are willing to dedicate money and a year of work by two data experts to manually validate the data, by the time they were done a year later, the data would have changed by at least 15-20%. Thus we would be chasing our tails and continuously spending more time and money.

Despite the obvious flaws in this approach, I have seen it employed in practice on many occasions. One of the companies I consulted had a team of 38 people (including two project managers, nine managers, and 27 data analysts) working day and night to validate data in their HR database. After nine months, they were about 12% done, which was probably why I was brought into the picture.

And so the inevitable conclusion is that outside of the very small databases, total manual data validation is impractical. Then how do we assess data quality? Sampling approaches were suggested, mostly drawing on the experience of quality management in other industries. Indeed, measuring quality of most mass-production products (e.g. automobiles) relies on a comprehensive investigation of sample products. You take random sample of automobiles coming off production line and study them to find any defects. You also collect information about car breakdowns from repair shops. Based on the results, you can extrapolate the overall quality of all produced automobiles.

This is not bad. We could validate the data for a random sample of 100 employees in a mere three months, and then try to draw conclusions about the entire database based on the findings. This scales the problem down a bit, but the solution remains impractical for larger databases or on an enterprise-wide scale. We simply have way too much data! The endless gigabytes are incomprehensible – the number of pieces of data in use by an average company dwarfs the volume of any other resource. Besides, data is heterogeneous, and so it takes a larger sample to represent all different elements and situations. Our task can be compared to an attempt to check the health of every flower and every blade of grass on Earth by sending a few botanists to check out a few plants here and there. No sample is small enough to be looked at in a reasonable amount of time, yet also large enough to provide comprehensive conclusions about the overall state of affairs.

Without a better way, the data quality profession would never come to exist. Luckily there is a better way. Modern databases have two important characteristics that distinguish data from all other products. First, they allow the data to be accessed and processed with dramatic speeds. Secondly, myriads of data elements stored in them are tied by equally huge numbers of data relationships. The combination of these two factors allows validating the data *en masse* by computer. This is far more efficient than doing it manually one data element at a time.

The main tool of a data quality assessment professional is a data quality rule – a constraint that validates a data element or a relationship between several data elements and can be implemented in a computer program. Of course, I use the term data relationship here in the broadest sense – ranging from simple entity relationships found in data models to complex business rule dependencies. The solution relies on the design and implementation of hundreds and thousands of such data quality rules, and then using them to identify all data inconsistencies. Miraculously, a well-designed and fine-tuned collection of rules will identify a majority of data errors in a fraction of time compared with manual validation. In fact, it never takes more than a few months to design and implement the rules and produce comprehensive error reports. What is even better, the same setup can be reused over and over again to reassess data quality periodically with minimal effort.

Using data quality rules brings comprehensive data quality assessment from fantasy world to reality. However, it is by no means simple, and it takes a skillful skipper to navigate through the powerful currents and maelstroms along the way. Considering the volume and structural complexity of a typical database, designing a comprehensive set of data quality rules is a daunting task. The number of rules will often reach hundreds or even thousands. When some rules are missing, the results of the data quality assessment can be completely jeopardized. Thus the first challenge is to design all rules and make sure that they indeed identify all or most errors.

It is also very hard to design perfect data quality rules. The ones we come up with will often fail to spot some erroneous records and falsely accuse others. They may not tell you which data element is erroneous even when the error is identified. They may identify the same error in many different ways. Error reports produced by such rules tend to suffer from the same malady as the data itself – poor quality. This imperfection, if not understood and controlled, will overrun and doom any data quality assessment effort. Minimizing the imperfection in the data quality rules and accounting for it in the assessment results is the second challenge.

Data quality rules produce endless reports of data errors. Each error applies to one or several data elements from one or several tables. Making any sense out of the error reports is overwhelming. The sight of a 500-page printout or even of an electronic listing with 20,000 lines of error messages will make most data quality professionals duck for cover. And the error reports are just the tip of the iceberg. Data quality assessment uses and creates many other types of meta data, such as data models, data catalogues, data profiles, rule definitions, and aggregate quality metrics. Organizing all of these meta data in a manageable data quality meta data warehouse with a built-in dimensional data quality scorecard is the third challenge.

In this book I will address these and other challenges of data quality assessment and show how it can be successfully performed in practice. It is not by accident that I chose to start this book series with this topic. Data quality assessment is the cornerstone of any data quality program. Below is a short list of main applications of data quality assessment results.

- It helps to describe the state of the data, understand how well it supports various processes, and estimate the cost of data problems to the business.

- It helps to plan and prioritize data cleansing initiatives and evaluate the potential ROI of data cleansing. It also provides immediate input to data cleansing in the form of the errors that must be corrected.

- It greatly simplifies data conversion and consolidation by providing information about the data quality in the source system, invaluable in the design of the target database and data transformation and consolidation algorithms.

- It helps to understand sources of existing data problems and investigate ways of improving data collection processes.

- It helps to understand implications of the data quality on newly planned data uses and data-driven processes before they are put in place. This reduces the number of unwelcome surprises when the new processes fail or at least do not perform as expected.

- It assists in testing system upgrades and mass updates since test cases can be selected among records with errors. This helps understand how well the changes will work with real imperfect data.

Also, recurrent assessment allows us to monitor ongoing data quality, identify new problems that manage to find the way into the databases, observe and manage data decay. As you can see, the importance of data quality assessment is hard to overstate.

2.2. DATA CLEANSING

It has been widely accepted that most databases are riddled with errors. Data cleansing is the process of correcting the erroneous data elements. Unfortunately, while data errors are spread throughout all parts of databases, the data cleansing efforts in practice mostly focus on customer data standardization, de-duplication, and matching. Cleansing the rest of the data is relegated to manual work.

The manual data cleansing work is rarely completed, as it usually takes great lengths of time, and the projects run out of patience before any measurable success can be shown. The problem is similar to that of manual data quality assessment. Even though the volume of work is far smaller (we are only concentrating on the erroneous data elements found through assessment), it also requires more skill and time. Indeed, only a highly competent data expert experienced with the specific data can be trusted to make mass data corrections. Such experts are rare and usually already overloaded in every organization. As a result, data cleansing gets stretched over very long periods of time.

The good news is that a better solution exists. It relies on the fact that most data errors are not arbitrary but are caused by some systematic processes, such as mistakes in data interfaces or flawed data collection procedures. If many errors were introduced by the same process, then they will follow a pattern. With some effort and analytical acumen, this pattern can be discovered, understood, and then used to make corrections to all similar errors by a single data-cleansing algorithm. This idea is the cornerstone of the rule-driven approach to data cleansing. I have successfully applied it in practice on numerous occasions. It allowed me to complete data cleansing projects in months rather than years and with very limited resources.

I must admit, however, that the approach is very challenging in practice, and it took me some years to fully understand the origin of its difficulties and ways to overcome them. In fact, looking back on some of my early projects, I am often puzzled how lucky I was to succeed in some of those data cleansing projects despite the long odds. I did not know where the hidden underwater currents were, and there was no place to look for advice.

Probably the greatest challenge of rule-driven data cleansing is that data quality rules are interdependent. Correction to a data element failing one rule may often result in violation of other rules. Failure to recognize this jeopardizes the data cleansing process, potentially introducing many new errors while attempting to fix the ones that were originally found.

To be done right, data cleansing must start with comprehensive data quality assessment. Such assessment must be rerun regularly during data cleansing (and after it is completed) to identify new data problems and ultimately ensure that the data quality was improved.

Also, it is absolutely critical to have an automated mechanism tracking the hierarchy of the data quality rules and their dependencies. This hierarchy could be used to track the implications of applying any corrective algorithm to the data. We would use it to proactively select only the records that need and are allowed to be processed by each data correction rule, and execute all rules in the proper order. Once a data change is made, the hierarchy could be further used to reevaluate all data quality rules that might be impacted by the correction.

Another major challenge is that automated data cleansing relies on computer programs to make corrections *en masse*. Therefore, there is always risk to miss some exceptions in the logic or simply to have bugs in the computer code. Debugging the programs takes much time and resources. Software development industry has long ago recognized this problem and addresses it through various quality assurance techniques. But how do we assure quality of data correction algorithms?

The easiest method is to execute the algorithm and verify the results by simply checking that the data corrections it made are as expected. This seems easy enough; however, with the large number of errors of different types, it is often necessary to design many interdependent correction algorithms. A flaw in the logic in one algorithm may not become obvious until another one is applied later on in the process. At this point, however, many other corrections have been made.

To deal with this situation, it is necessary to create a sophisticated audit trail mechanism. This mechanism would permit to electronically track all changes made to the data, easily rollback data corrections to any point if necessary, then perfect and rerun the algorithms with as many iterations as needed to achieve acceptable results. The audit trail mechanism is also extremely valuable beyond the completion of data cleansing as it provides reliable data lineage for all corrected data.

Of course, other challenges abound along the way. How do we identify error patterns? How do we devise best correction techniques? How do we use additional data sources? How do we report the results? When does automated data cleansing become inefficient and manual validation becomes preferable? These and many other questions will be answered in the "Data Cleansing" volume of this book series.

2.3. MONITORING DATA INTEGRATION INTERFACES

Most data comes into the database through various real-time, near real-time, or batch interfaces. These interfaces are the source of many data errors. The objective of interface monitoring is to prevent these errors from getting into the database, or at least to identify new problems as early as possible to minimize the damage they inflict. The solution to interface monitoring is to design programs operating between the source and target databases, which are entrusted with the task of analyzing the interface data before it is loaded and processed.

Monitoring real-time interfaces starts with the setup of various screens validating incoming data transactions. These screens check internal reasonability of the data transactions as well as their consistency with some existing data. It might be beneficial at times to put the questionable transactions into a holding area. However, in that case later transactions for the same object must also be held. Indeed, if we choose to temporarily hold a new order transaction due to lack of some attributes, then a following order cancellation transaction must also be held or it will inevitably fail in processing. Thus, managing a temporary holding area is quite a difficult undertaking.

Screens for real-time interfaces will miss many errors because there is simply not enough data or window of opportunity to use sophisticated data quality rules. The next step is to minimize the length of time the bad data stays in the database unnoticed. New data can be flagged and data quality rules can then be applied to the flagged records after they are loaded, but still before much damage is done. Until the flagged records are tested, they should be used with caution. Recurring data quality assessment is also critical for the databases, which receive much data through real-time interfaces. Detailed comparison of error reports allows us to identify new data problems, investigate their root causes, and hopefully improve the interfaces.

For batch interface, a far more sophisticated monitoring solution can be implemented, consisting of many different interdependent interface monitors. In general, these monitors fall into two categories: individual data monitors and aggregate monitors.

Individual data monitors use data quality rules to test data accuracy and integrity. Their objective is to identify all potential data errors. An individual data monitor can be viewed as performing recurrent data quality assessment on each batch feed. Such monitors vary dramatically in complexity. Simple screens validate the data inside a single batch and are trivial to implement, but they find few errors. Advanced monitors that compare data across batches or against target database identify more problems, but they require extensive development and processing.

Aggregate monitors search for unexpected changes in batch interfaces. They compare various aggregate attribute characteristics (such as counts of attribute values) from batch to batch, relying on the fact that such aggregate characteristics change little from batch to batch or follow predictable patterns. A value outside of the reasonably expected range indicates a potential problem. Aggregate monitors are easy to implement, though they require some special knowledge in data profiling and statistical time series analysis. They can be largely automated and will catch all unexpected changes in the batch interfaces.

The structure of data monitors depends on the batch interface architecture. It is relatively simple for snapshot batch files commonly used to feed data warehouses, but can be very complex for transaction batches often exchanged between operational transaction processing systems. In the latter case, the solution might involve a persistent staging area – a physical database where batch files are stored indefinitely along with necessary data lineage information and data quality findings.

If several databases all exchange information through various interfaces, the result is often a dangerous spider-web of data flows. Monitoring data quality through all of these interrelated interfaces is a huge challenge. It may warrant implementation of an information integration hub – a system designed specifically for centralized processing of multiple interfaces between multiple databases. Of course, an information integration hub has a persistent staging area as a backbone. This solution affords the most flexible and comprehensive data quality monitoring. It allows maintaining detailed data lineage and data quality meta data for future reference. It is a great answer to the information integration challenge.

Monitoring data quality of data integration interfaces is a broad and difficult subject. I expect to address it in the "Data Integration" volume of this book series.

2.4. ENSURING DATA QUALITY IN DATA CONVERSION AND CONSOLIDATION

Data conversion and consolidation projects are the worst data quality offenders. While other projects may cause more data errors overall, nothing can inflict as much damage in one shot as data conversion and consolidation. This is especially true for the projects involving "legacy" databases. If you think of data integration interfaces as artillery fire, and data decay as slowly debilitating starvation, then an average data conversion project is a megaton bomb while legacy data consolidation is a life-exterminating meteor.

The objective of any data quality program is to ensure that data quality does not deteriorate during conversion and consolidation projects. Ideally, we would like to do even more and use the opportunity to improve data quality since data cleansing is much easier to perform before conversion than afterwards.

The greatest challenge in data conversion is that actual content and structure of the source data is rarely understood. More often data transformation algorithms rely on the theoretical data definitions and data models. Since this information is usually incomplete, outdated, and incorrect, the converted data look nothing like what is expected. Thus, data quality plummets. The solution is to precede conversion with extensive data profiling and analysis. In fact, data quality after conversion is in direct (or even exponential) relation with the amount of knowledge about actual data you possess. Lack of in-depth analysis will guarantee significant loss of data quality.

Another problem is that straightforward data movement and transformation from source to target database rarely works. This is because every system is made of several layers, with data at the bottom, business rules in the middle, and various presentation layers at the top (see Figure 2-2). Information that comes out of the top layer is greatly affected by the business rules. When data is converted from one database to another, the business rule layers of the old and new system are usually quite different. This is especially true for conversion from "legacy" systems, which are notorious for elaborate hidden business rules. In fact, many of the old system rules may be designed specifically to hide and handle poor data quality. As a result, even if the data is converted with utmost accuracy, the information that comes out of the new system may become totally incorrect. The solution here is to investigate the business-rule layer of the source system. It is also critical to perform comprehensive data profiling and data quality assessment of the source data before mapping specifications are created.

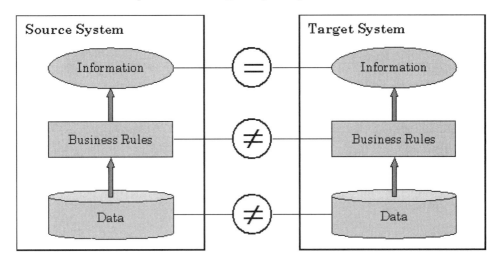

Figure 2-2: Data Conversion Challenge

Equally critical is to include data quality definition and acceptable quality benchmarks into the conversion specifications. No product design skips quality specifications, including quality metrics and benchmarks. Yet rare data conversion follows suit. As a result, nobody knows how successful the conversion project was until data errors get exposed in the subsequent months and years. The solution is to perform comprehensive data quality assessment of the target data upon conversion and compare the results with pre-defined benchmarks.

Finally, no matter how hard we try, the data will still have many errors. A data cleansing initiative is typically warranted. It is much easier to perform data cleansing before conversion because transformation tends to "mutate" the erroneous records to the point where the nature of the problem is much more difficult to recognize. Also, some bad data is inevitably and irrevocably lost in translation. Unfortunately data cleansing is rarely done during conversion in practice. The common wishful thinking is that since the new system is better it will automatically solve existing data problems. The truth is exactly opposite.

Another problem is inadequate allocation of time and resources to the effort. The data conversion usually requires much more time than anticipated. As a result it is rushed, and the problems are discovered after the conversion is over and the data quality greatly suffered. In reality, it is virtually impossible to create a proper timeline and list of expectations for the conversion without preliminary data profiling and data quality assessment.

Data consolidation is even more difficult than basic conversion because data from consolidates sources often overlap and conflict. Say we must consolidate a data attribute present in three systems – A, B, and C. The common approach is to build winner-losers matrix, which assumes precedence of one source over another. Since in reality no data is perfect (especially legacy data) such assumption inevitably fails.

What is even more troublesome is that data consolidation specifications are usually built without deep understanding of the actual structure, content, and quality of the data in each source. Comprehensive data profiling and quality assessment is key here, even more so than for simple data conversion. A priori understanding of overlaps and conflicts between the databases allows navigating a safe route rather than marching into the oncoming traffic lane head-on.

The correct approach to data consolidation is to view it in a similar light as data cleansing! We start with a comprehensive set of tests, comparing the data between all sources. We now have a full list of discrepancies. These data inconsistencies are conceptually very similar to the error found by the data quality rules. While some of these discrepancies may be legitimate, without proper care they will most likely turn into true data errors after consolidation. The next step is to analyze the discrepancies and look for patterns. Say we conclude that where any time values of a certain attribute in Systems A and B coincide, they can be trusted (regardless of the values in database C). Then we can mark those values as "trusted" and eliminate those discrepancies from the list. In theory, we can also make corrections to the mismatching values on C, which is why data consolidation can be viewed as very similar to data cleansing.

For each group of discrepancies, we can make an individual conclusion using various conditions. Every time a decision is made, good data must be marked as trusted and bad data can be corrected. With this technique, we decompose the list of all discrepancies into a set of simple groups and derive a simple solution for each group. With every step, we move closer to the ultimate data quality objective. The approach is certainly not simple, especially for more complex state-dependent and time-dependent data. It requires us to create and manage a rule hierarchy, the same as we discussed for data cleansing solution. However, it guarantees the success.

This is it in a nutshell, but clearly the topic deserves a comprehensive treatment, which I will do in the "Data Conversion and Consolidation" volume of this series.

2.5. BUILDING DATA QUALITY META DATA WAREHOUSE

The first items to be called meta data were data models. Over time the concept has taken a much broader form. We now apply term *meta data* to all data that provide information about other data. Meta data play a critical role in the information age. They tell us what the data really means, where it can be found, in which format it is stored, where it came from, and what it is used for. Meta data are the encyclopedia of knowledge about the data. They are the key without which the data is like a message written in a secret code.

Data quality initiatives produce enormous volumes of valuable meta data. Data quality assessment tells us about existing data problems and their impact on various business processes. When done recurrently, it also shows data quality trends. Data cleansing determines causes of errors and possible treatments. It also creates an audit trail of corrections so that, at a later point, we could tell how a particular data element came to look the way it does. Interface monitoring identifies ongoing data problems. It also tells about data lineage as does data conversion and consolidation.

On the other hand, data quality initiatives are a great consumer of meta data. They require detailed understanding of data catalogues, data models, and actual data content. As I said many times before, the success in data quality management is largely dependent on our knowledge and understanding of the data.

Data quality meta data warehouse is the collection of tools for organization and analysis of all meta data relevant to or produced by the data quality initiatives. In its most general form, it is a very complex solution, combining elements of object-oriented meta data repository with analytical functionality of a data warehouse. I must admit that while I have completed dozens of data quality initiatives of every possible kind, I have never seen or implemented a comprehensive data quality meta data warehouse. But I have a dream! The day will come when I entice my good friend, colleague, and great data warehousing expert, Dave Wells, to collaborate with me on the architecture of a comprehensive data quality meta data warehouse. Then together we will write the final volume of this book series.

SUMMARY

We have discussed the objectives, basic methods, and challenges of five key components of a comprehensive data quality program:

- Data Quality Assessment

- Data Cleansing

- Monitoring Data Integration Interfaces

- Ensuring Data Quality in Data Conversion and Consolidation

- Building Data Quality Meta Data Warehouse

The remainder of this book is dedicated to data quality assessment. I hope to address the other components in the future volumes of this book series.

CHAPTER 3
DATA QUALITY ASSESSMENT OVERVIEW

Imagine we could travel back in time some 20,000 years. We would find ourselves in the middle of a Stone Age landscape. The reason we call it "stone age" is because the early humans made tools and weapons from stone. In other words, stone was the most important resource. If we could walk into a typical hunter's hut (or a typical caveman's cave), we would certainly find spears with sharpened stone points. These spears were used by our early ancestors to hunt many large animals, including mammoths. Every time the food supplies dwindled, men would grab their spears and go hunting. Of course, hunting mammoths was a dangerous business, and in many cases the spear would not penetrate mammoth's skin. Most likely the widow of the poor hunter would make sure that her next husband used a different and better spear.

Over time, though, a different breed of hunters developed. These hunters would stretch and hang the skin of a previously killed mammoth on the wall and engage in strange cabalistic rituals. They would dance around, chant incantations, and throw the spears at the wall. All the time they observed which spear, thrown from which angle and distance, and accompanied by which dance and incantation, penetrated the mammoth's skin the best. What they learned was incredibly useful to make better spears; it also helped develop hunting strategies that best accommodated deficiencies of the existing weapons. These rituals were the earliest examples of quality assessment, and I tend to believe that it was those hunters who eventually became my ancestors.

Now let's come back to our time. We now live in an information age – the term intended to emphasize that information is our most important resource. Modern humans and companies alike fight their battles and hunt their proverbial mammoths with information. The success of corporations and government institutions largely depends on the efficiency with which they can collect, organize, and utilize data about their products, customers, competitors, and employees.

As was the case with early stone spear points, our data is far from perfect. In fact, most organizations are aware of the problems with their data and of the importance of data quality. But they have no idea of the extent of the problems. Typically, data quality is either grossly underestimated or grossly overestimated. The impact of data quality level is also rarely understood. This causes failure of many data-driven projects (such as new system implementations). Data quality improvement initiatives, when put in place, also often fail because no method of measuring data quality improvements is provided. So we waste enormous amounts of time and money every day.

To solve the problem we must start by assessing data quality. And while dancing and incantations at numerous meetings are of some value, the problem requires a more drastic solution – systematic evaluation of data in search for all errors and deficiencies. This is the objective of data quality assessment. In this chapter, we will provide a high-level overview of the data quality assessment process, including main steps, project timeline, and project team makeup. We then will proceed to discuss the process in detail in the remainder of this book.

3.1. PROJECT TEAM

The question, "Who shall be responsible for data quality assessment?" is the most frequently asked. Part of the reason for the uncertainty is that the data quality profession is still in its infancy, and so there is no clearly defined group with the appropriate expertise and responsibility. Even companies that form Data Quality departments often have them staffed by handpicked employees with general IT and data expertise but no specific data quality knowledge.

I recently received an e-mail from one of my conference class attendees, an employee of a household name corporation, who wrote: "I am new to the data quality management world and have found myself in charge of Enterprise-Wide Data Quality here at …" This single sentence explains the major challenge to our profession – most people in charge of data quality initiatives lack data quality experience. As a result, the projects tend to follow one of two polar scenarios.

In the first scenario, projects fall into the laps of technical people within the IT group. Another attendee of one of my classes – a database administrator – was asked by her boss to outline a data quality assessment strategy. Why her? Because, according to her boss, data quality assessment involves writing queries, manipulating data, and understanding databases – all parts of her resume. This, of course, makes as much sense as asking me to be a reporter for the sports section of the Chicago Tribune because I can type, published some articles, and watch sports a lot from the comfort of my living room couch.

In the second scenario, data quality assessment is performed inside business units by the data users. This appears to make some sense, as the data users can tell good data from bad and are mostly in need of quality data. So business departments sometimes initiate their own data quality assessment projects. Of course, the problem then is that business users lack technical expertise, which is why I keep getting this question at almost every class: "Is there a tool that can do data quality assessment without any custom coding or querying?" My answer does not make those who ask this question happy. Data quality assessment is an IT discipline and requires IT expertise.

In reality, it takes two to tango, so a data quality assessment team must include both IT specialists and business users, ideally at least two of each kind. In addition, it needs data quality experts – those who have read my book or attended my classes and who have firsthand experience in designing, implementing, and fine-tuning data quality rules.

3.2. PROJECT PLAN OVERVIEW

Data quality assessment projects consist of four phases:

- During the *planning* phase, project scope and objectives are defined.

- During the *preparation* phase, data and meta data are gathered.

- During the *implementation* phase, data quality rules are designed.

- During the *fine-tuning* phase, the error reports are validated by data experts, and data quality rules are enhanced to achieve maximum accuracy in error identification.

The recommended project team for an average size data quality assessment project (e.g. assessment of an HR database) consists of two data quality experts, one or two IT professionals, and at least two business users (data experts).

Figure 3-1 depicts the project plan for a five-month data quality assessment project. It illustrates the timeline and required resources during each phase. Of course, this timeline is quite arbitrary because all projects are different. I have been involved in small projects that were completed in four weeks and seen large ones that took over a year, but a five-month timeline is rather typical for data quality assessment of an average size database.

	IT Group	DQ Group	Business Group	
Planning	100%	100%	100%	2 weeks
Preparation	100%	25%	0%	2 weeks
Implementation	50%	100%	25%	10 weeks
Fine-Tuning	10%	100%	100%	10 weeks
				Time

Figure 3-1: Typical Project Plan

Each project phase is shown as a horizontal block in Figure 3-1. The planning phase is usually the shortest, except when data quality assessment is planned as an enterprise-wide initiative. The preparation phase also usually does not take more than a couple of weeks unless, of course, we are dealing with a legacy database. In that case, the length can easily double. The implementation and fine-tuning phases take the bulk of the time, about 50% each. Usually the implementation phase has a more predictable timeline, while fine-tuning can stretch and must be better controlled.

Vertical silos in Figure 3-1 correspond to each of the three groups involved in the project – IT on the left, data quality in the middle, and business users on the right. The numbers inside sections indicate how busy each group is during each phase. Overall, data quality experts will be busy throughout the project, while IT and business groups will only be involved about half of the time. Also, the IT group's services are mostly required during the preparation and implementation phases, while the business users are heavily taxed during fine-tuning. This is actually why I prefer to have multiple members in each group, even if the work can be performed by a single person.

3.3. PLANNING PHASE

Defining project scope is a crucial first step in the project. It drives budget, timeline, and priorities. The main issue here is to specify the set of data elements on which data quality assessment will operate. There are three fundamentally different choices.

The first option is to use data quality assessment in support of a specific data-driven initiative. A typical task is to determine quality of the data used in support of a particular business process. This creates a very narrow and focused scope of the project because we know exactly which data tables, records, and fields are relevant and can provide clear data quality definitions. For instance, HR database may be used, among other things, to calculate retirement pension benefits. A data quality assessment project can be initiated to determine quality of the data used in this process and estimate cost of the bad data.

This option is a great way to jump-start a data quality program in an organization that has none. Indeed, it is often easier to start with a small project that can produce tangible results in a short timeframe. I find this to be the easiest way to "sell" a data quality initiative to the management that is unaware of the full magnitude of the data quality challenge. Also, it is a good way to start gaining experience in data quality management. Frankly, the first data quality assessment project is always very hard (as is true for any discipline). The chance of success is exponentially higher on a small, well-defined project.

The main drawback of this option is that the amount of work necessary to assess data quality does not grow proportionally to the volume of the target data. To validate one data element we usually compare it against many other data elements. This automatically means that we are partially assessing quality of those other data elements as well, even if they are out of scope of the project. Similarly, a data quality rule validating a certain data element can be applied to all records, or just a subset, with almost the same amount of effort. Thus, narrowing down the recordset does not significantly decrease the workload.

My wife and partner in crime, Olga, was recently consulting on a project that started out as quality assessment and cleansing of compensation data for a small group of 800 employees. It was driven by a specific corporate initiative that absolutely needed to have these data in perfect condition. The project took some two months which sounds like a lot of work. But it took only one extra month to apply the same data quality rules (with some slight modifications) to the data for the remaining 80,000+ employees. Obviously ROI on this second step was much higher.

The second option is to perform data quality assessment of an entire database. This, of course, is a much bigger undertaking. It requires a broader look at the data and design of a much greater number of data quality rules. However, it is also far more efficient and produces more valuable results. At the end of the project, we can build a data quality scorecard that shows data fitness for a variety of individual objectives and projects. The results can also be reused later for data cleansing and other initiatives.

The final option is to take an enterprise-wide view of data quality assessment. This, of course, is a monster of a project, and it requires some prioritization. But it has one great advantage. Data across different databases is often related or even redundant. Many data quality rules can be designed comparing such data, and the resultant error reports are often far more comprehensive than what could be obtained if data in each database was validated separately. However, when the project objective is limited to assessment of data quality inside one database, it is often not justifiable to bring other databases into the equation. After all, it adds quite a bit of time and cost to the project. On the other hand, when data quality assessment is planned as an enterprise-wide exercise, we can assess data quality in several databases simultaneously and achieve superior results.

To summarize, the first option requires the smallest possible effort and offers clearly defined ROI. The second option provides the most efficient result-to-effort ratio. The third option is the most complex but will likely produce the most accurate and comprehensive results. The choice is yours. Of course, it is possible to start from option one and proceed gradually to options two and three.

Some other questions need to be answered to define project scope. The most significant is whether or not the assessment is intended as a one-time deal or as a recurring initiative. There is definitely a difference in the degree of planning and resources needed for these two types of projects.

Also, it is important to know if any data cleansing, mass data update, or database restructuring initiatives are planned during the course of the assessment project.

Any such concurrent projects will greatly impact data quality assessment. It is preferable not to have considerable changes to the data structure in the course of the data quality assessment, but if it is inevitable at least we must be prepared for it.

3.4. PREPARATION PHASE

The objective of this phase is to get ready for data quality rule design. This involves loading data to a staging area, gathering data models and data catalogues, and setting up a data quality meta data repository.

3.4.1. Loading Data to Staging Area

Implementation of data quality rules will take time and put a strain on the database. It is, therefore, recommended to load data into a staging area instead of doing assessment on "live" databases. A staging area minimizes interference with actual production database. There will be no performance slowdown due to additional development, debugging and execution of data quality programs.

Loading data to a staging area also allows for manipulation of the data whenever necessary or convenient for quality assessment. For instance, we could add surrogate keys for easier record referencing and normalize or de-normalize some tables. However, keep in mind that it is easier to review error reports and provide results to the users when the data in the staging area look largely like the data in the actual database. Therefore, certain restraint must be exercised in data restructuring, and it should be loaded to the staging area with minimal changes. I especially advise against changing field names and attribute values even if it is convenient.

Using a staging area affords a variety of other advantages. For instance, data quality rules sometimes must compare data from multiple heterogeneous sources, including relational databases, spreadsheets, and even legacy systems. Direct access and querying of the data in such situations are an implementation nightmare. A staging area brings all of the data into a homogeneous environment.

Also, inside a staging area we can make temporary changes to the data, add calculated fields and meta data tracking attributes to the tables, and perform many other convenient manipulations. In other words, a staging area offers a playground for data analysis and data quality rule implementation. Within a production database, such frivolity would be inconceivable.

Loading data to a staging area is a strictly technical task and must be done by the IT group. In theory it should not take much time, while in practice it often stretches over weeks. This usually does not depend much on the actual effort, but rather on how much stake the IT group holds in the project. The more an IT group buys into the project, the easier it is to get the data loaded to the staging area. Otherwise, database managers will feel "threatened" by the loss of control over the data and might stall the project.

3.4.2. Gathering General Meta Data

Data catalogues and data models are the source of numerous data quality rules and a good starting point for the data quality assessment. Data catalogue are collections of basic meta data about data attributes. They include basic attribute listings, detailed descriptions and usage patterns, as well as reference information, including valid values, their meanings, and default values. Data catalogues are key to understanding the cast of characters in the data quality assessment play.

Data models describe the structure of the data. They fall into four broad categories. Relational data models depict logical relationships between various entities and attributes. Subject area models define main data subjects – categories of high-level business objects whose data is stored in the database. State-transition models describe the life cycle of complex state-dependent objects. Temporal models describe the chronological structure of time-dependent data and event histories. Understanding these data models is key to designing data quality rules.

While data models are readily available, they might be inaccurate or obsolete. It is a good idea to find out who keeps these models up-to-date and how before relying on them in data quality rule design. When the models are unavailable (or incomplete), they can usually be reconstructed through a combination of reverse engineering, model building, and data profiling techniques.

3.4.3. Designing Data Quality Meta Data Warehouse

Data quality assessment uses meta data (e.g. data catalogues, data models, and data profiles) to design data quality rules. It also produces numerous error reports and large volumes of other data quality meta data. Data quality meta data warehouse is a collection of tools for organization and analysis of all these meta data.

Without a well-planned meta data repository, data quality assessment cannot be successfully completed. Hundreds of data quality rules and error reports with tens of thousands of errors are impossible to manage and easily overwhelm the project. On the other hand, a well-designed data quality meta data warehouse in itself is a valuable product with long shelf life. It presents the assessment project results in an interactive dimensional data quality scorecard, which offers a high-level view of data quality along with drill-downs to detailed error reports. It integrates data quality meta data with the data itself, and provides easy access to data quality meta data by both technical and non-technical users.

It is important to design the data quality meta data warehouse at the onset of the project so that all collected and produced meta data neatly falls into place. It is a strictly technical task, though non-technical team members must participate in the design of the meta data reports to make sure that they are easy to understand and analyze. In theory, it can get quite complex and take a fair amount of time. The good news is that data quality meta data warehouse architecture can be reused from project to project.

3.5. IMPLEMENTATION PHASE

The implementation phase is the meat of the data quality assessment project. This is when all data quality rules are identified, designed, and programmed. I often see project teams rushing to start writing queries and implementing data quality rules based on the data models. This is too hasty. The first step in the implementation phase is data profiling, and you must take your time with it.

3.5.1. Data Profiling

The term "data profiling" originated from attribute profiling techniques, which produce basic attribute statistics as well as value frequencies and distribution charts. Nowadays its meaning has greatly expanded and is used to describe various experimental techniques aimed at examining the data and understanding its actual structure and dependencies. Occasionally I have even seen it used to describe data quality assessment, but I draw the line between the two. Data profiling tells us what the data looks like; data quality assessment describes how good it is.

The reason data profiling is so important is that actual data is often very different from what is theoretically expected. Over time, data models and dictionaries become inaccurate. Data profiling is like an X-ray showing the hidden truth. It is the key to building correct data quality rules. As a rule of thumb, the more in-depth analysis and profiling we conduct the easier it is to design a comprehensive set of data quality rules and achieve greater success in data quality assessment.

There are many data profiling techniques. The following four groups are most useful in data quality assessment.

1. Attribute profiling examines the values of individual data attributes and yields information about basic aggregate statistics, frequent values, and value distribution for each attribute.

2. Relationship profiling is an exercise in identifying entity keys and relationships as well as counting occurrences for each relationship in the data model.

3. State-transition model profiling is a collection of techniques for analysis of the lifecycle of state-dependent objects and provision of actual information about the order and duration of states and actions.

4. Dependency profiling uses computer programs to look for hidden relationships between attribute values.

Data profiling is a valuable exercise in itself and produces meta data useful for many purposes. In fact, data profiling can produce enough valuable information to seriously question data quality and justify a data quality assessment project, if one has not been approved already.

Data profiling can take as much time as you afford it. Of course, it is faster with better tools, and the amount of time is proportional to the number of data elements in the database. Experienced analysts armed with good tools can profile an average-size database and organize all findings in a month with minimal support from the IT group. It is important to have business users available for regular consultations, as data profiling findings must be verified. Usually business users do not need to spend much time, just be available for a few hours a week to look at and explain the strange data phenomena.

3.5.2. Designing Data Quality Rules

Data quality rules are the main tool of the data quality assessment. They are constraints that validate data relationships and can be implemented in computer programs. It is rather trivial to identify scores of data quality rules; the challenge is in designing all or most of them. This requires a systematic approach. It is important to consider all rule types, rule sources, and rule design strategies. The more rules are initially designed, the better the final outcome of the data quality assessment project. Data quality rules fall into five broad categories.

1. Attribute domain constraints restrict allowed values of individual data attributes. They are the most basic of all data quality rules since they apply to the most atomic data elements.

2. Relational integrity rules are derived from the relational data models. They are more complex, apply to multiple records at a time, and enforce identity and referential integrity of the data.

3. Rules for historical data include timeline constraints and value patterns for time-dependent value stacks and event histories. Since time-dependent data are the most common database citizens (and since they are also most error-prone), these rules typically are a key part of data quality assessment.

4. Rules for state-dependent objects place constraint on the lifecycle of objects described by so-called state-transition models (e.g. insurance claims or job applications). Data for such objects is most important and can only be validated by a special class of data quality rules.

5. General dependency rules describe complex attribute relationships, including constraints on redundant, derived, partially dependent, and correlated attributes.

The entire Part II of this book is dedicated to the investigation of various data quality rules and methods for their identification and design.

Designing data quality rules is definitely the job for the data quality professionals, though business users must also contribute through interviews. This step overlaps with the data profiling. With experience, it does not take much time, even though the number of rules in an average data quality assessment project will reach several hundreds.

All identified data quality rules must then be coded in computer programs. Some rules can be implemented using tools or with simple queries, while others will require stored procedures or more complex programming. Unless performance considerations are critical, all rules should be implemented as separate units.

Furthermore, rules need to be designed in such a way as to make any rule re-execution possible at any point of time.

Rule coding is the most technical part of the project and definitely the responsibility of the IT group. Even though the number of rules is great, coding them is not too difficult. In my experience, it takes far less time to implement the rules than to design them. Thus, coding never slows down the project.

The only serious challenge in rule implementation is how to organize a comprehensive error catalogue. While on the surface it seems trivial to just produce various error reports, the task proves quite challenging. A good error catalogue must support the following functionality:

- Aggregate, filter, and sort errors across various dimensions.

- Identify overlaps and correlations between errors for different rules.

- Identify data records affected by a particular error or a group of errors.

- Identify all errors for a particular data record or set of records.

It is better to create a separate program responsible for logging and managing errors than to catalogue errors directly from the rule programs. The design of such a program takes some expertise and software development skill.

3.6. FINE-TUNING PHASE

Data quality assessment relies on our ability to use data quality rules to accurately identify all data errors. However, it is very difficult to design perfect data quality rules. The ones we come up with will often fail to spot some erroneous records and falsely accuse others. They may not tell you which data element is erroneous even when the error is identified, or they may identify the same error in many different ways. Error reports produced by such rules will be inaccurate and of limited value.

In order to guarantee the accuracy of error reports, we go through extensive manual data verification by the data experts. This is the step when the greatest time commitment is required from the business users, who must review and manually validate numerous data samples. Without such commitment, the project cannot succeed, and this must be adequately planned for in advance. Since this is a lot of work, it is preferable to buy time of several business users with data expertise. With such setup, this step can be completed in about a month.

Manual verification always yields holes and gaps in error identification by the data quality rules. The next step is fixing these problems. Several solutions are possible:

- Design of additional data quality rules ensures assessment completeness.

- Correction, improvement, or elimination of existing data quality rules improves assessment accuracy.

- Categorization of errors identified by a single data quality rule into multiple groups helps distinguish errors of different types.

This approach ensures that the data quality rules were implemented correctly, detected all errors, have no false-positives, and clearly indicate the location and nature of each error.

Rule fine-tuning involves much analysis and some additional programming. It usually takes several iterations to make error reports identified by the data quality rules match findings of data experts to an acceptable level.

Eventually we get to the point where the results of our data quality assessment can be trusted. Now comes the time to organize our results. Indeed, error reports produced by data quality rules are overwhelming in volume and complexity and, thus, are hard to use. To maximize their value, we must aggregate the reports into meaningful summaries and create a data quality scorecard.

Aggregate scores provide high-level measures of the data quality. Each score aggregates errors identified by the data quality rules into a single number – a percentage of good data records among all target data records. By selecting different groups of target data records, we can create many aggregate scores for a single database. Well-designed scores are goal driven and allow us to make better decisions and take action. They can measure data fitness for various purposes and indicate quality of various data collection processes. From the perspective of understanding the data quality and its impact on the business, aggregate scores are the key piece of data quality meta data.

A data quality scorecard is the central product of the data quality assessment project. It provides comprehensive information about data quality and allows both aggregated analysis and detailed drill-downs. At the top level of the scorecard are aggregate quality scores. At the bottom level is information about data quality of individual data records. In the middle are various score decompositions and error reports allowing us to analyze and summarize data quality across various dimensions and for different objectives.

A data quality scorecard is the key to understanding how well the data supports various data-driven projects. It is also critical for making good decisions about data quality initiatives. Building a comprehensive data quality scorecard is the final step of data quality assessment.

3.7. ONGOING DATA QUALITY MONITORING

It is critical to monitor data quality in "live" databases on an ongoing basis in order to see data quality trends, identify new data problems, and check the progress of data quality improvements initiatives. Well-designed data quality assessment solution creates a blueprint for recurrent data quality re-evaluation.

The idea seems rather trivial on the surface – all we need is to re-run data quality rules periodically against the most current data and compare the results. However, it presents several practical challenges. First, it requires adding time dimension to the data quality meta data warehouse. Secondly, we must use a consistent method for referencing erroneous data records so that we can identify which of the errors found by the assessments are the same and which are different. However, both of these challenges can be met rather easily.

The true test of our skill arises when data quality assessment must be performed with high frequency or against very large databases. In this case, we cannot afford to replicate the entire database to the staging area every time and must execute data quality rules against production data. Performance considerations become an issue, building data quality scorecard is far more difficult, and data quality meta data warehouses require more sophistication.

We will address various problems and solutions involved in recurrent data quality assessment in Chapter 14 of this book.

SUMMARY

Data quality assessment project consists of four phases:

- During the planning phase, project scope and objectives are defined. The main issue here is to specify the set of data elements on which data quality assessment will operate. This decision drives budget, timeline, and priorities. The planning phase is usually the shortest, except when data quality assessment is planned as an enterprise-wide initiative.

- During the preparation phase, data and meta data are gathered. The preparation phase also usually does not take more than a couple of weeks unless, of course, we are dealing with a legacy database. In that case, the length can easily double.

- During the implementation phase, data quality rules are designed. This phase can take up to half of the project timeline.

- During the fine-tuning phase, the error reports are validated by data experts, and data quality rules are enhanced to achieve maximum accuracy in error identification. This last phase takes many iterations and can stretch over a long period of time if not managed properly.

The data quality assessment team must include data quality experts, IT specialists, and business users, ideally at least two of each kind. Overall, data quality experts will be busy throughout the project, while IT and business groups will only be involved about half of the time. Also, the IT group's services are mostly required during preparation and implementation phases, while the business users are heavily taxed during fine-tuning.

It is often desirable to monitor data quality in "live" databases on the ongoing basis. A well-designed data quality assessment solution creates a blueprint for recurrent data quality re-evaluation.

Chapter 3 – Data Quality Assessment Overview

PART II – DATA QUALITY RULES

Data quality rules are constraints that validate data relationships and can be checked using computer programs. They form the cornerstone of data quality assessment. When properly designed, data quality rules allow identification and precise classification of the majority of data problems.

The key is to discover <u>all</u> data quality rules and ensure that the rules are <u>correctly</u> understood. When some rules are missing or misrepresented, the results of the data quality assessment can be completely jeopardized.

Imagine that you are appointed to be a home-plate umpire in a major league baseball game. Of course, you cannot do it without knowing the rules. The official rulebook of major league baseball contains 124 rules, many with numerous sub-rules. If you miss just a couple of rules, you may inadvertently influence the outcome of the game – the one play that you call erroneously could be decisive. If you do not know 10% of the rules, you can easily cause a riot. Also, complicated rules are no less important than easy ones, so learning all but 10% of the most complex rules still leave you 10% short of the target.

Data quality rules play the same role in data quality assessment as the rules of baseball in refereeing a major league game. They determine the outcome!

Unfortunately, identifying data quality rules is more difficult than learning rules of baseball because there is no official rulebook that is the same for all databases. In every project, we have to discover the rules anew. Also, some rules are easy to find, while others require lots of digging; some rules are easy to understand and implement, while others necessitate writing rather complex programs. But, as with baseball, all rules are equally important. Omitting a few complex and obscure data quality rules can (and most of the time will!) jeopardize the entire effort.

This part of the book is the closest I could come to the official data quality rulebook. It systematically discusses data quality rules of all kinds and places a special emphasis on the process and strategies for rule discovery. Speaking from personal experience in over 100 data quality assessment projects, I guarantee that if you stay the course and systematically apply what you learn in the next five chapters, you will get a comprehensive and accurate rule set.

In Chapter 4 we take the simplest view of the data as consisting of individual values of various attributes. This perspective yields the first category of data quality rules – attribute domain constraints. We discuss all kinds of these constraints and show how to discover them and ensure their correctness through analysis of meta data and especially through data profiling.

Chapter 5 takes a more advanced view of data structure – that consisting of interrelated entities and described by relational data models. This approach leads us to the discovery of various relational integrity rules.

Attribute domain constraints and relational integrity rules are quite easy to identify and implement. They are usually the first to be designed in any project. However, we are still way short of the mark – the majority of important data quality rules are more complex. In order to design those rules, we need to take the subject level view of the data. In other words, we have to remember that data represent attributes of real world objects, such as people, whose characteristics are interrelated and whose behavior is complex and restricted by logical constraints. These constraints can be translated into the data quality rules. In Chapters 6 through 8 we will discuss these subject-level data quality rules.

In Chapter 6 we investigate the time dimension of the data and discuss the rules arising from the dynamic relationships in the data. We start with simple currency, retention, and continuity rules; proceed to more complex timeline and value patterns; and finally graduate to advanced rules for event histories.

In Chapter 7 we look at the lifecycles of state-dependent objects and the rules governing the state-transition data. These rules are of utmost significance because state-dependent objects are often the most important database citizens, yet their data are most error-prone.

Finally, Chapter 8 discusses all other subject-level data quality rules. It describes various types of data dependencies and outlines the strategies and techniques that can help identify the rules.

CHAPTER 4
ATTRIBUTE DOMAIN CONSTRAINTS

At the most atomic level, the data in any database consists of individual values of various attributes. Those values generally represent measurements of the characteristics of real world people, things, places, or events. For instance, height and weight are characteristics of people; latitude and longitude are characteristics of geographical locations on Earth; and room number and duration are characteristics of a "business meeting" event.

Now, real world objects cannot take any shape and form. We do not expect people to be 12 feet tall, or meetings to be held on the 215th floor. What this means is that attribute values of these objects cannot take any values but only certain reasonable ones. For any attribute we can usually immediately tell whether or not a certain value is valid. Since databases consist of numerous atomic values of various attributes, this logic can be applied to validate the data and find the outliers.

The data quality rules used to validate individual attribute values are commonly referred to as attribute domain constraints. They are the simplest and most common of all data quality rules. Rare attributes have no restrictions on the permitted values. Despite apparent triviality, attribute domain constraints are rarely designed properly because they are usually based on incorrect or incomplete documentation.

This chapter offers full treatment of the topic with the main focus on practical challenges in identifying and designing various constraint types.

- Section 4.1 introduces attribute domain constraints.

- Section 4.2 discusses attribute-profiling techniques, which are critical for identification of the true attribute domain constraints.

- Section 4.3 presents optionality constraints.

- Section 4.4 discusses attribute format constraints.

- Section 4.5 describes valid value constraints.

- Section 4.6 presents precision and granularity constraints.

4.1. INTRODUCTION TO ATTRIBUTE DOMAIN CONSTRAINTS

Attribute domain constraints restrict allowed values of the individual data attributes. The simplest domain constraint is optionality, which prevents an attribute from taking Null, or missing, values. For instance, FirstName, and LastName are typically required attributes – a valid value must be present for each person. On the other hand MiddleInitial is optional.

Attribute domain is most often defined as a list of valid values, e.g. $\{M, F\}$ for the attribute representing gender. Domains of numeric attributes usually consist of a large or even infinite number of values. Such domains usually have constraints in the form of a range of permitted values. For instance, attribute representing hourly pay rate must have values no less than the minimum wage: $\{\text{Value} \geq \$5.75\}$.

Values of some text attributes must be made of only certain characters. For example, an address cannot have special characters. Individuals' names can only have alpha characters, as do city names. Such attributes are said to have domain constraint on the allowed set of characters. Another type of domain constraints typical for text attributes is a pattern mask. It applies to such attributes as social security numbers, phone numbers, or credit card numbers. For example, social security number has the mask *999-99-9999* where each *9* is a placeholder for any numeric character.

Attribute domain constraints can be deduced from analysis of the meta data, such as data models, data dictionaries, lookup tables, and actual attribute profiles. Data models usually explicitly indicate attributes with optionality constraints and sometimes even list valid values (or value ranges for numeric attributes). A data dictionary, when available, will provide lists of valid values along with a detailed value description for most attributes. Lookup tables offer another source of valid values.

However, all these meta data should be used with caution since they may be incorrect or incomplete. Data models typically reflect the data structure at the time of database design. Over time data models are rarely updated and quickly become obsolete, especially in the volatile area of attribute domains. Data dictionaries and lookup tables are also seldom up-to-date.

The cure to this common meta data malady is data profiling – a combination of techniques aimed at examining the data and understanding its <u>actual</u> content, rather than that described theoretically in the data models and data dictionaries.

4.2. ATTRIBUTE PROFILING

Attribute profiling examines the values of individual data attributes and produces three categories of meta data for each attribute: basic aggregate statistics, frequent values, and value distribution. Analysis of this information helps identify allowed values for an attribute (expressed by domain constraints). Many commercial tools are available that provide built-in functionality to collect comprehensive attribute profiles in a single pass. In absence of a commercial tool, attribute profiles can still be gathered (though somewhat less efficiently) with rather straightforward queries. Figure 4-1 illustrates attribute profile for attribute HireDate in entity E_EMPLOYEE_INFO.

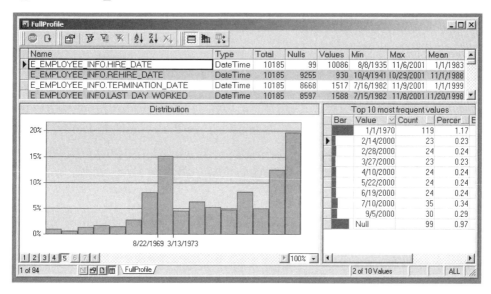

Figure 4-1: Attribute Profile Example

The top section in Figure 4-1 contains *basic attribute statistics*. It shows prevailing value type; number of Null values; minimum, maximum, and average values; and other aggregate statistics. Attribute HireDate has values ranging from 8/8/1935 to 11/6/2001 with the mean value of 1/1/1983. Out of 10,185 records, 99 have Null value.

The table on the bottom right shows the most *frequently occurring values* along with their counts and percentages. The frequent value chart is the key component of any attribute profile and offers best insight into the attribute domain. The chart indicates that the most frequent value of the attribute HireDate is 1/1/1970, found in 119 (1.17%) of all records. Null value is found in 99 records. Eight values occur over 20 times each (all in the year 2000). No other Not-Null value is found in that many records.

The graph on the bottom left contains overall *distribution of values*. The entire attribute domain is split into sections of equal size. A vertical bar shows a concentration of records within each section. In our example, the domain is split in 16 sections, each covering roughly a 3.5-year interval. The highlighted section indicates that roughly 15% of all records have HireDate between 8/22/1969 and 3/13/1973. Overall, the distribution is quite smooth except for an unusually high incidence of records in the two middle bars (between years 1965 and 1973). Graphical representation helps analyze the distribution. Ideally you should be able to "zoom-in" to and "zoom-out" of the chart to examine the distribution closer.

4.3. OPTIONALITY CONSTRAINTS

Optionality constraints prevent attributes from taking Null, or missing, values. On the surface, optionality constraints appear to be the easiest to identify. Most relational data models and data dictionaries specify attributes for which Null values are permitted. Also, common sense will often tell you which attributes must have a value.

The optionality assumptions are easy to test by looking at the results of attribute profiling. You simply check the count of Null values in the attribute profile. If the count is small compared to the total count of values, then the attribute value is likely required. Otherwise, it is likely optional.

For example, attribute HireDate in Figure 4-1 has 99 Null values out of the total of 10,185 records. This signals that HireDate values are required, and the 99 missing values are erroneous. Of course, a business user would tell that this value is required simply because she knows how the data is used.

It would be safe to conclude that if 3,000 out of 10,000 records had Null value, the attribute was likely optional. Examples of such attributes in Figure 4-1 are RehireDate and TerminationDate, each with over 8,000 Null values. Obviously, these attributes are optional because most employees in the HR database have never been terminated and rehired.

This topic seems too trivial to warrant much discussion. In fact, Non-Null constraints are often enforced for some attributes by relational databases. So what is the point to validate such constraints? The devil, as usual, is in the details.

First, Not-Null constraints are often turned off in the databases to allow for situations when attribute value is not available (though required!) but the record must be created. For the same reason, optionality is not always represented correctly in the meta data. Routinely, data models and data dictionaries reflect actual database configuration (i.e. Null value allowed), rather than the true data quality requirement. This is a wrong but unfortunately commonplace practice.

More importantly, default values are often entered to circumvent the Not-Null constraints. Attribute is populated with such a default when actual value is not available. Database designers are often unaware of such default values, and data dictionaries rarely list them. Even business users who enter them might forget all default values they use or used in the past. Yet, default values are no different from missing values for all practical purposes. They must be identified and eliminated from the valid attribute domain definition.

Figure 4-2 shows frequent value charts for attributes LastName, BirthDate, and PayRate. Each is a required attribute with no actual Null values. However, each has hidden default values:

- Attribute LastName has *NAME NOT DEFINED* as a frequent value occurring over 2,000 times. These are clearly defaults for missing names.

- Attribute BirthDate takes value 1/1/1922 on 209 occasions (1.54% of all records). Two other values are suspicious. These are definitely Null substitutes. It is highly unlikely for so high a fraction of company employees to share the same birth date. The next highest frequency is five (out of 13,000+) and is quite logical.

- Attribute PayRate has zero value in 661 cases. Since volunteers are usually not tracked by HR systems, a person cannot have a pay rate of $0. This is definitely another substitute for missing values.

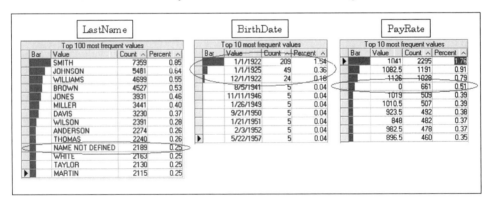

Figure 4-2: Examples of Default Values

How do we identify the default values? This is done by analysis of frequent values in the attribute profile. The default values are usually "strikingly inappropriate." Frequent values that do not look "real" are likely candidates.

The examples of common default values for text attributes are *None*, *Unknown*, *Undefined*, and *Not Available*. For date/time attributes, we look for values like *1/1/1900*, *11/11/1911*, and other dates that are out of the normal expected range. Most often such defaults are distant future or past dates, usually falling on the first or the last day of the year. For numeric attributes, the most typical default value is 0; though, I have seen many other choices, especially in the "legacy" systems.

In general, any value that appears more often than the others should be questioned as a candidate for a default value. For many attributes it is simply unlikely that the same value is shared by many entity occurrences.

4.4. ATTRIBUTE FORMAT CONSTRAINTS

Most values can be represented in a variety of ways. For example, date *11/15/06* can also be displayed as *15-Nov-06* or *11152006*, or in many other ways. The amount *$5000.00* can be also presented as *5,000* with implicit currency type or as *5.0E+3* in scientific format. My name *Arkady* can also be written as *arkady* without capitalization or as *__Arkady__* with leading and trailing spaces.

In theory, all of these forms of presentation can be considered irrelevant as they represent the same values. Human eye would typically have no problem recognizing the value. However, the computer programs accessing the data may have difficulties reading different formats properly. Further, even when the data is accessed correctly, lack of standardization may cause problems in reading and using the reports.

Format constraints define the expected form in which the attribute values are stored in the database field. Format constraints are most important when dealing with "legacy" databases. Modern databases usually hide the format of all but text attributes. However, even modern databases are full of surprises. From time to time, numeric and date/time attributes are still stored in text fields.

Format constraints for numeric, date/time, and currency attributes are usually represented as a value mask, a la *MMDDYYYY* standing for 2-digit month followed by 2-digit day and 4-digit year for the date. Hundreds of basic formats are possible for such attributes. Legacy databases are especially prolific in using numerous creative packed formats to store the data in the minimum amount of space. Discussion of these formats would easily take a chapter by itself and belongs more to the topic of legacy data conversion (I am planning to include it in the "Data Conversion and Consolidation" volume of this book series).

Format constraints are usually easy to identify. Data dictionaries typically show attribute format. In absence of a reliable data dictionary, data profiling tools can be used to collect frequencies of various formats. Analysis of frequency charts helps identify format constraints. Tools are also available on the market that can recognize complex legacy field formats and identify the disobedient values.

The format constraints are especially important for text attributes. Text attributes are most often made of a single word that has restriction on length, allowed set of characters, and mask. For example, first name must be made of alpha characters and dashes and start with a capital letter. Social security number must have the format *999-99-9999*. A more complex attribute, such as invoice number, may be defined as follows:

- The first character is a capital letter – the first letter of the client's name.

- The next three characters contain the designated numeric client identifier.

- The fifth character must be *A*, *B*, *C*, or *D* depending on the job type, followed by a dash.

- The next two characters are last two digits of the invoice year.

- The last three characters are numeric and indicate invoice order number for this specific job in this calendar year.

Such format constraint, while long and rather convoluted on paper, is easy to implement in a data quality rule. In fact, text attributes with a strict mask are the best from the data quality perspective.

Some text attributes are made of more than one word with little restriction on the individual characters. They are often referred to as free-flow text attributes. True free-flow values are very hard to validate. Fortunately, many supposedly free-flow text attributes have a strict word pattern in actuality.

In order to determine which value patterns are valid, we must first identify all present patterns. This task requires sophisticated text-parsing algorithms that may be only available in advanced profiling or standardization tools. The next step is to examine and explain each pattern. Values with strange patterns may be totally incorrect or simply require standardization.

Consider attribute FullName, which contains full name for all employees. Applying the parsing algorithm produced the following results:

- Over 95% of all values have a pattern *{LastName, FirstName}*.

- Of the remaining values, about 200 (or 3%) consist of one word, most of them records with only the Last Name. Such values are incomplete.

- The other 128 values consist of two words without any separators, most likely in the format *{FirstName LastName}*. These values need to be standardized.

The format constraint for this attribute is a complex pattern mask, requiring all values to have pattern *{LastName, FirstName}*.

4.5. VALID VALUE CONSTRAINTS

Many attributes have a finite set of valid values. ***Valid value constraints*** limit permitted attribute values to such a prescribed list. Unfortunately, valid value lists are often unavailable, incomplete, or incorrect. To identify valid values, we first need to collect counts of all actual values (note that here we need <u>all</u> values rather than just frequently occurring values). These counts can then be analyzed, and actual values can be cross-referenced against the valid value list, if available.

Values that are found in many records are probably valid, even if they are missing from the data dictionary. This typically happens when new values are added after the original database design and are not added to the documentation. Values that have low frequency are suspect. The conclusions need to be confirmed by business users.

Figure 4-3 shows frequency charts for the attributes FullTimeHours and EmployeeType and illustrates how frequency charts can be used to identify attribute domain constraints.

Let's first assume that there are no documented constraints on values of attribute FullTimeHours, which lists a weekly work schedule for full-time employees. Analysis of the attribute profile clearly shows that the domain consists of four values: *40*, *37.5*, *35*, and *0* hours per week. These values account for 99.95% of all records. The first three are legitimate full-time schedules, while zero is used as a

Null substitute for part-time employees. The remaining 12 values appear a total of 34 times and are invalid.

Now, suppose that attribute EmployeeType is defined in the data dictionary as a 2-letter code. The first letter must be *R* ("regular") or *T* ("temporary"), and the second letter must be *P* ("part-time") or *F* ("full-time"). An attribute profile identifies several non-conforming codes. Further research shows that value *O* is actually valid (standing for "occasional" employment). The other four values are invalid. They were sporadically used by the data entry personnel to store some additional information in the third, unused, character of the attribute storage.

	FullTime Hours					EmployeeType		
	All values					All values		
Bar	Value	Count ∧	Percent ∧		Bar	Value	Count ∧	Percent ∧
	40	44744	59.47			RF	12895	94.91
	37.5	21903	29.11			TF	399	2.94
	35	5899	7.84			O	146	1.07
	0	2657	3.53			RP	85	0.63
	24	9	0.01			RFT	34	0.25
	25	7	0.01			TP	23	0.17
	18.7	5	0.01			TFN	3	0.02
	1	3	0.00			TFR	1	0.01
	20	2	0.00			TF5	1	0.01
	36.5	2	0.00					
	28	1	0.00					
	27	1	0.00					
	17.5	1	0.00					
	37	1	0.00					
	10	1	0.00					
	21	1	0.00					

Figure 4-3: Examples of Valid Value Lists

For numeric and date/time attributes, the number of valid values is typically infinite (or at least too large to be enumerated in practice). The examples of such attributes are date of birth and annual compensation. However, even for these attributes certain values are not valid. For instance, annual compensation cannot be negative. Further, an employee date of birth can be neither too far in the past nor too close to present day. In these situations, the attribute domain constraints take form of a valid value range rather than a list.

In some cases, the valid value range can be simply deduced theoretically. For instance, annual compensation cannot be negative but can be very small. A poor soul hired on the afternoon of December 31st can legitimately receive annual compensation of $10. Thus domain constraint for this attribute naturally takes form

$$Value \geq \$0$$

In other cases valid range boundaries are difficult to define. For instance, consider employee age attribute. It is safe to say that no employee in a large U.S. corporation is over 100 years old or is younger than 10, but what about someone who is 78 or 15.5? Where do we set the boundary?

The answer is that for many attributes there is no definite line separating good values from bad. The domain constraint must be set using heuristic logic. We can say that it is highly unlikely for an employee to be over 75 or under 16 years old. Any data outside of this range is suspect, though some still might be correct. Narrowing the valid range down has the effect of potentially catching more errors at the cost of raising more false alarms. On the other hand, a wider range will miss more errors.

Analysis of the value distribution from the attribute profile also helps identify valid range boundaries. Figure 4-4 shows the left half of the distribution for employee's age. The density of values drops around age 16. This is a good cutoff for the valid value range. A similar approach yields a right boundary of 78 years of age. The final domain constraint for employee age attribute takes the form:

$$16 \leq Age \leq 78$$

Some numeric and especially date/time attributes have very complex domain constraints. Instead of a single range, the domain is defined as a set of ranges following a certain pattern. For example, year-end bonus payment date may only fall in December and January. Extensive analysis of value distributions is the only way to identify such domain constraints. Any pattern in the distribution must be studied.

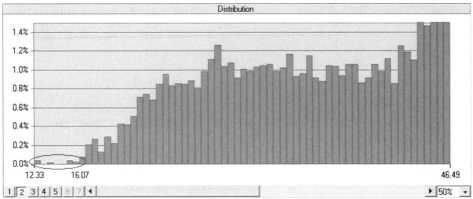

Figure 4-4: Distribution of Employee Age Values

Also, for date/time attributes, it is very useful to calculate frequencies of values falling in each calendar month, day of the month, and day of the week. Profiling the HireDate attribute from an HR database may show that 70% of all employees were hired on Monday, and additional 27% were hired between Tuesday and Friday. This certainly makes sense – employee date of hire normally is required to fall on a weekday, except business holidays. In theory, we could hypothesize this domain constraint from business analysis of the attributes. However, in practice it is easier to find patterns in attribute profiles and than to explain them theoretically.

4.6. PRECISION CONSTRAINTS

For some attributes, value precision is restricted. Such domain constraints are rarely (if ever) defined in data dictionaries. Yet data with incorrect precision can be as bad for business use as any other bad data.

Precision constraints require all values of an attribute to have the same precision, granularity, and unit of measurement. The required precision for numeric attributes typically takes the form of the number of decimals or the rounding rules. For instance, length of employment is often required to be calculated to three decimals for the purposes of employee benefit calculations. On the other hand, annual salary for the same calculation must be rounded to the nearest hundred.

Data profiling can be used to calculate distribution of values for each precision level. Fluctuation of the distribution from random is a sign of a prevailing precision. Data profiling tools can usually compute precision frequency charts directly or at least can be coaxed to do it using relatively simple formulas.

Figure 4-5 illustrates the use of data profiling in defining precision constraints. The frequency chart on the left shows distribution of value precision for attribute AnnualPayRate. The observed precision is to the nearest hundred of dollars in roughly 75% of records. Another 12% of records are expressed in $1,000's, and almost 1.8% of values are rounded to the nearest $10,000. These findings are consistent with the prevailing attribute precision level of "hundreds of dollars." Now the question is whether or not other precision levels are acceptable or erroneous.

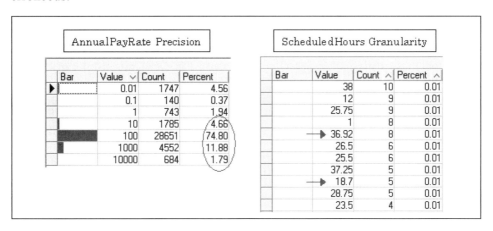

Figure 4-5: Examples of Precision and Granularity Constraints

Lower precision frequency (12% and 2%) is consistent with random occurrences. For example, values $45,000 and $50,000 are valid as values with precision in $100's and in $1,000's. With prevailing precision in $100's, we generally expect 10% of records to be rounded to $1,000's and 1% of records to $10,000's for this reason. In practice, the numbers usually are slightly higher due to the higher human appeal of round numbers.

On the other hand, higher precision values could be erroneous or represent legitimate exceptions. For instance, precision to nearest $10's and even $1s may be valid, as annual compensation rate of $36,550 and even $29,355 is plausible. If the percentage of such values on the chart decreased dramatically (say, was less than 1%), I would vote for the values being erroneous. As it is, both explanations are possible, and only a business user can tell the required and valid precision. In this example, precision of $10's and lower was deemed valid, while the remaining records were considered erroneous. This example shows that in data practice, too much precision can be equally wrong as too little.

Precision constraints can apply to both numeric and date/time attributes. For numeric values, they define the desired number of decimals. For the date/time attributes, precision can be defined as calendar month, day, hour, minute, or second. Profiling precision of date/time attributes is somewhat tricky. The values falling on the first or last day of the month would be considered to have the precision level of a month. Similarly, we treat value 5.50 as having one decimal for profiling purposes, even though it can possibly be truly measured to two decimals but have the exact value of 5.50.

Granularity constraints are similar to precision constraints. Consider attribute ScheduledHours listing weekly scheduled hours for part-time employees. The value frequency chart for this attribute is shown on the right side of Figure 4-5. Profiling indicates that all but a few values are measured in increments of 0.25 hour. Further analysis proves that actual data collection processes drive this granularity. Only such values are valid. The values 18.7 or 36.92 are erroneous.

Another similar constraint is the unit of measurement. Weight can be measure in pounds, kilograms, or tons. Price can be represented in dollars, euros, or francs. The appropriate data quality rules will require all values of an attribute to have the same unit of measurement. When different values of the same attribute are measured in different units it may turn into a costly data quality issue. A classical example of the problem is an expensive satellite whose orbit decayed quickly at the cost of millions of dollars because a piece of data was entered in a wrong unit of measurement.

SUMMARY

In this chapter, we have discussed various types of attribute domain constraints.

- Optionality constraints prevent attributes from taking Null values or any defaults used as substitutes for missing values.

- Format constraints define the form in which attribute values must be stored in the database field. Format constraints for numeric and date/time attributes usually take the form of a value mask. Text attributes may have restriction on length, allowed set of characters, mask, or word patterns.

- Valid value constraints limit permitted attribute values to a prescribed list. Constraints for numeric and date/time attributes usually take the form of valid value ranges.

- Precision constraints require all values of an attribute to have the same precision, granularity, and unit of measurement.

There are many practical challenges in identifying true attribute domains. Comprehensive attribute profiling is the key. Without detailed understanding of attribute profiles, domain constraints will always be incomplete and incorrect.

Chapter 4 – Attribute Domain Constraints

CHAPTER 5
RELATIONAL INTEGRITY RULES

Of all revolutions in information technology, the introduction of relational data models arguably had the greatest impact. It gave database designers a recipe for systematic and efficient organization of data. Now some 30+ years since their introduction, relational databases are the cornerstone of the information universe.

The idea behind relational data modeling is surprisingly simple. All individual data elements stored in a database can be classified into attributes of structurally similar persons, things, places, or events. By creating separate listings of such similar objects and organizing their attributes into columns, we form a tabular data structure. This part was understood from the early days of database design and led to the proliferation of "legacy" databases with all attributes listed, column after column, in never-ending rows. For instance, an HR database would list all employees in separate records with hundreds of attributes, such as name, address, compensation rates at different dates, and position history.

Relation data modeling took this idea a giant step forward. It suggested decomposing complex objects with repeating simpler parts, and storing information about such parts in separate listings. For instance, employee data in a relational structure are broken down into a table with basic indicative data, table with paycheck data, table with position history data, and many other tables. Various tables are then glued together by the relationships that tie parts of the same object, e.g. data for the same person is related by a common employee identifier used throughout all tables.

In the previous chapter, we took the most simplistic view of the data as made up of individual unrelated attributes. Relational data models offer a higher-level notion of the data structure. In doing so, they also place many constraints on the data. This chapter offers comprehensive treatment of the data quality rules that can be derived from the relational data models:

- Section 5.1 introduces key relational data modeling concepts. The reader can find detailed explanation for these concepts in numerous textbooks.

- Section 5.2 presents identity rules.

- Section 5.3 discusses reference rules.

- Section 5.4 describes cardinal rules.

- Section 5.5 presents inheritance rules.

5.1. RELATIONAL DATA MODEL BASICS

Relational data models describe high-level logical data structure using several central data modeling concepts.

- *Entity* is a class of structurally similar persons, things, places, concepts, or events about which the data is recorded. Each representative of an entity is called entity occurrence.

- *Attribute* is a most primitive atomic characteristic of an entity.

- *Relationship* is an association between occurrences of two entities.

- *Relationship cardinality* indicates how many occurrences of each entity can participate in the relationship.

- *Primary key* is a nominated set of attributes that uniquely identifies each entity occurrence.

- *Foreign key* ties an attribute or a collection of attributes of one entity with the primary key of another entity.

Figure 5-1 shows two entities tied by a simple relationship in a data model diagram. EMPLOYEE is an entity describing all employees for an organization; POSITION is an entity describing all available positions. Entity EMPLOYEE has six attributes: EmployeeID, FirstName, LastName, Gender, BirthDate, and CurrentPositionID. The underlined attribute EmpID is nominated as the primary key and thus each EMPLOYEE entity occurrence must have a unique value of EmpID.

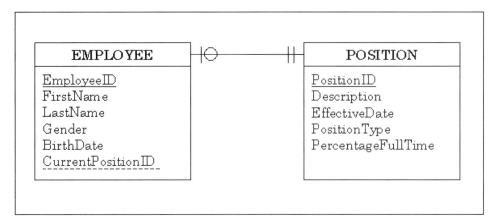

Figure 5-1: Simple Data Model Diagram

Entities EMPLOYEE and POSITION in Figure 5-1 are tied by the following relationship:

Each employee must occupy <u>exactly one</u> position.

Each position may be occupied by <u>zero or one</u> employees.

The relationship is depicted using standard information engineering (IE) notation. The relationship cardinality on the right side of the relationship equals 1, while cardinality on the left side of the relationship is *{0 or 1}*. The relationship uses foreign key, which ties values of attribute CurrentPositionID in EMPLOYEE entity to the values of the primary key attribute PositionID in POSITION entity. Thus for each employee, we can look up the value of CurrentPositionID attribute in POSITION entity and find the details about his position.

Entities, entity occurrences, and attributes are concepts used in logical data models. However, many readers are probably more familiar with tables, records, and fields. While it is not always a one-to-one correspondence, entities are usually associated with relational database tables; entity occurrences correspond to individual records; and individual fields typically represent attributes.

In all examples in this book, physical tables match logical entities. This allows us to use the terms interchangeably, which helps simplify the reading. In reality, a physical database table will often store data for several distinct logical entities, if the entities have identical or at least similar attributes. Alternatively, occurrences or attributes of a single entity may be divided among multiple tables. Finally, a data field may store values of several attributes. Such adjustments are made for performance optimization or convenience.

We refer to the data quality rules that are derived from the analysis of relational data models as ***relational integrity rules***. These rules are relatively easy to identify and implement, which makes a relational data model a starting point in any data quality assessment project.

It is important to remember that relational integrity rules (and actually most other data quality rules) <u>must</u> be defined in terms of logical data models, rather than physical database design. In other words, it is entities and attributes that are governed by identity, reference, cardinal, and inheritance rules. The properly defined rules can then be translated into the language of tables, records, and fields used by the rule validation algorithms.

5.2. IDENTITY RULES

Identity Keys ensure that every real world entity (person, thing, place, concept, or event) represented in the data is uniquely identifiable and can be distinguished from all other entities of the same type. They provide a fundamental link between the data and real world objects.

Imagine the pirates dividing the stolen loot according to the personnel table. Mad Dog is engaged in a fight till death with recently recruited Mad Doug whose name was accidentally misspelled by the spelling-challenged captain. Wild Billy who changed his name to One-Eyed Billy after the last battle is trying to sneak in and collect two shares in accordance with the register. The share for still listed but drowned Wooden-Peg Jim is up for grabs. Life would be tough for pirates in the information age. But it is equally tough for employees, customers, and other objects whose data is maintained in the modern databases.

An ***identity rule*** is a data quality rule, which validates that every record in a database table corresponds to one and only one real world entity and that no two records reference the same entity. Identity rules usually must be enforced for all entities in a relational data model. Therefore, the number of identity rules in a typical data quality assessment project will be close to the number of entities.

A reader familiar with database design will naturally ask, "Aren't identity rules always enforced in relational databases through primary keys?" Indeed, according to sound data modeling principles every entity must have a ***primary key*** – a nominated set of attributes that uniquely identifies each entity occurrence. In addition to the uniqueness requirement, primary keys impose not-Null constraints on all nominated attributes.

While primary keys are usually enforced in relational databases, this does not guarantee proper entity identity. One of the reasons is that surrogate keys are often created and nominated as primary keys. ***Surrogate keys*** use computer generated unique values to identify each record in a table, but their uniqueness is meaningless for data quality.

Figure 5-2 shows several records from the E_EMPLOYEE_PROFILE table, which lists all employees along with their basic indicative data. The table has surrogate key attribute EmpID declared as a primary key and enforced by the database. Of course uniqueness of EmpID for all records is guaranteed by design; yet it does not mean that each employee is properly identified in the data. Employee *Millard Abraham* has two records with distinct values of EmpID but identical social security number (stored in the SSN attribute). This is clearly an error – the two records are duplicates referencing the same real person.

EmpID	SSN	LastName	FirstName	BirthDate	Gender	CompanyCode
141857	834-51-2788	ACCARDI	LAURENE	9/30/1954	F	B8
235572	770-27-1938	CADY	CONRAD	11/19/1950	M	B3
275356	770-27-1938	BURR	LINCOLN	1/17/1958	M	N4
186860	851-57-8703	BUBB	CHARLES E	8/4/1942	M	B6
346981	988-65-1411	ABRAHAM	MILLARD	7/19/1943	M	N2
155107	988-65-1411	ABRAHAM	MILLARD	7/19/1943	M	N2
247826	989-85-2689	CHIU	HARLAN	1/1/1922	M	N2
39159	991-96-8738	ABRUZZO	DIEGO	1/1/1922	M	N2
39160	996-96-8738	ABRUZZO	DIEGO	1/1/1922	M	N2
145944	997-77-5120	BART	MANFRED	1/11/1931	M	NC

E_EMPLOYEE_PROFILE

10 of 10 — Figure41 — FLTR SRT ALL

Figure 5-2: Examples of Identity Rule Violations

The example suggests that the database primary key does not necessarily represent the true identity key. In this case, the SSN attribute is a more appropriate candidate for the identity key. Indeed, all people are expected to have unique values of social security number. The good news is that the logical data models will often list the true identity key as an alternate key, even when a surrogate key is created and used as a primary key. When such a key is not listed in the data model, we shall analyze various attributes and attribute combinations to see which of them hold candidacy for the true identity key.

Now we can implement the identity rule to compare values of the true identity key for all records. Any duplicate values are erroneous. The problem is usually created by one of two processes. In some cases multiple records are created for the same real world entity as in the example of *Millard Abraham* in Figure 5-2. In other cases, the error can be caused by an erroneous value entered in the key attribute. For instance, records for *Conrad Cady* and *Lincoln Barr* have identical values of SSN attribute, thus violating the identity rule. The records clearly represent distinct individuals and are not duplicates of the same entity. This can be determined by looking at their names, birth dates, and other attributes. One of the records has an incorrect SSN value.

Even validating uniqueness of the correct identity key may not be enough to find all identity violations. Consider again data in Figure 5-2. Employee *Diego Abruzzo* is listed twice with different SSN values. Further analysis shows that these values have only one distinct digit (compare *996-96-8738* with *991-96-8738*). Identical values of BirthDate (*1/1/1922*), Gender (*M*), and CompanyCode (*N2*) also support the theory of two records belonging to the same person. This is a case of duplicate records, which do not violate the identity key constraint but still break the identity rule.

Finding these cases of hidden mistaken identity require sophisticated de-duplication software. Fortunately, various tools are available on the market for de-duplication of records for persons or businesses.

5.3. REFERENCE RULES

Reference rules ensure that every reference made from one entity occurrence to another entity occurrence can be successfully resolved. Each reference rule is represented in relational data models by a ***foreign key*** that ties an attribute or a collection of attributes of one entity with the primary key of another entity. Foreign keys guarantee that navigation of a reference across entities does not result in a "dead end."

Foreign keys are the glue holding the database together. Without foreign keys, the data is like leaves covering the ground in the fall – you know that each leaf fell from one of the trees, but it is impossible to say from which one.

Almost every entity in a relational data model will have one or several foreign keys. The usual exceptions are tables with basic subject data and reference tables. Therefore, the number of reference rules in a typical data quality assessment project will slightly exceed the number of entities.

Foreign keys are always present in data models but are often not enforced in actual databases. This is done primarily to accommodate real data that may be erroneous! Solid database design precludes entering such records, but in practice it is often considered a lesser evil to allow an unresolved link in the database than to possibly lose valuable data by not entering it at all. The problem is intended to be fixed later, but "later" often never comes. Foreign key violations are especially typical for data loaded during data conversions from "legacy" non-relational systems, or as a result of incomplete record purging.

Figure 5-3 illustrates a reference rule for entity E_STATUS_HISTORY containing the history of employment events. The data model includes a foreign key that links E_STATUS_HISTORY with strong entity E_EMPLOYEE_PROFILE, which stores employee basic indicative data. The data quality rule requires each record in E_STATUS_HISTORY table to reference a record with same value of EmpID attribute in E_EMPLOYEE_PROFILE. The two selected records in E_STATUS_HISTORY table violate this rule – both reference employee #114603, but no record of such employee is found in the parent table.

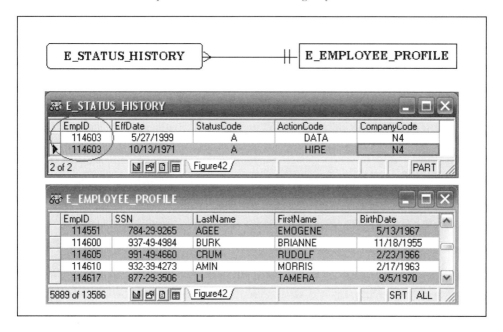

Figure 5-3: Example of Reference Rule Violations

The problem may have been caused by various reasons. The value 114603 in EmpID field may be erroneous, and the records actually belong to another employee. Alternatively, the record for employee 114603 may be missing from E_EMPLOYEE_PROFILE table, e.g. it may have existed in the past but erroneously purged. This second alternative will often result in numerous violations of reference rules for various tables. Assuming that the record for employee 114603 is missing from E_EMPLOYEE_PROFILE, each dependent entity with various employee data for this employee will have one or more orphan records.

5.4. CARDINAL RULES

Cardinal rules define the constraints on relationship cardinality. Cardinal rules are not to be confused with reference rules. Whereas reference rules are concerned with the identity of the occurrences in referenced entities, cardinal rules define the allowed number of such occurrences.

Probably the most famous example of a practical application of cardinal rules is Noah's ark. Noah had to take into his vessel two animals of each species – male and female. Assuming that he had tracked his progress using a relational database,

Noah would need at least two entities – SPECIES and ANIMAL – tied by a relationship with a cardinality of exactly one on the left side and two on the right side. In fact, Noah's task was even more complex as he needed to ensure that the two selected species were of different gender – an inheritance rule that we will discuss in the next section. And, of course, he needed to ensure the proper identity of each animal. I imagine that had Noah used modern technology and had the data quality been consistent with a common level of that in modern databases, we would remember the story of Noah's ark in the same context as the mass extinction of the dinosaurs.

Cardinal rules can be initially identified by analysis of the relationships shown in the relational data models. Almost every relationship in the data model will yield two cardinal rules (limiting the number of occurrences for each entity participating in the relationship). Therefore, the number of cardinal rules in a typical data quality assessment project will be close to twice the number of relationships.

Figure 5-4 illustrates a relationship between entities EMPLOYEE and POSITION. The crow's feet notation is used to describe the relationship and is translated as follows:

Each employee must fill <u>exactly one</u> position.

Each position must be filled by <u>zero or one</u> employees.

The underlined portion of the relationship defines the cardinal rules for this relationship. The highlighted records violate the rules. The record for employee #44932 violates the first rule (he fills zero positions). Records for position #7717 violate the second rule (it is filled by three different employees).

Relationship cardinality is often represented incorrectly in relational data models. For example, optionality is sometimes built into the entity-relationship diagrams simply because real data is imperfect. Strong entities are routinely allowed to have no corresponding weak entity records simply because database designers expect bad and missing data. This is the very problem we are trying to address by the data quality initiative. The situation often occurs when data models are reverse-engineered from actual databases in which constraints have been relaxed to accommodate data imperfection.

Another problem is that commonly used data modeling notations do not distinguish cardinality beyond *zero*, *one*, and *many*. Thus, cardinality "many" is used as a proxy for "more than one." Consider the situation from Figure 5-4 where each position is allowed to be filled by two part-time employees. The allowed relationship cardinality is then {0,1,2}. However, many data models will not put any restrictions on the cardinality of such a relationship.

Figure 5-4: Example of Cardinal Rule Violations

In order to identify true cardinal rules, we use *relationship cardinality profiling* – an exercise in counting actual occurrences for each relationship in the data model. Once counted, the results are presented in a cardinality chart showing how many of the parent records have 0, 1, 2, and so on corresponding dependent records.

I have not seen a tool that offered built-in functionality for relationship cardinality profiling. However, with the rapid development of data profiling software, we can hope that such functionality will be soon available. In the absence of a tool, data for cardinality charts can be gathered with nested queries.

Figure 5-5 illustrates the cardinality chart for the relationship between EMPLOYEE and POSITION entities from the example above. Profiling shows that out of 13,515 listed positions:

- 573 positions are open

- 10,214 positions are filled by 1 employee each

- 2,619 positions are occupied by 2 employees each

- 95 positions are filled by 3 employees each

- 14 positions are occupied by 4 or more employees each

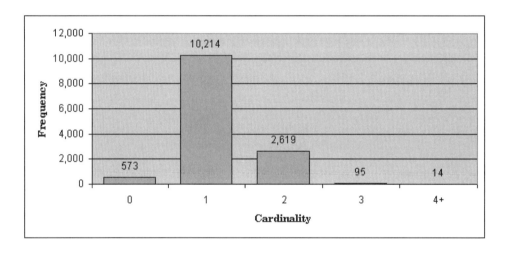

Figure 5-5: Cardinality Chart for the POSITION– EMPLOYEE Relationship

Large frequency is usually indicative of legitimate cardinalities, while rare occurrences are suspicious and require further investigation. Analysis of the sample data would show that {0,1,2} are legitimate cardinalities. The cardinality of 3 or more is erroneous. Now we can implement the cardinal rule as follows:

Each position must be filled by <u>no more than two</u> employees.

The records for 109 positions violating this rule will be caught along with the records for employees occupying these positions.

5.5. INHERITANCE RULES

Inheritance rules express integrity constraints on entities that are associated through generalization and specialization, or more technically through sub-typing. Consider entities EMPLOYEE and APPLICANT representing company employees and job applicants respectively. These entities overlap as some of the applicants are eventually hired and become employees. More importantly, they share many attributes, such as name and date of birth. In order to minimize redundancy an additional entity, PERSON can be created. It houses common basic indicative data for all employees and applicants, and frees up the original entities to store only those attributes unique to employees and applicants. These three entities are said to have a sub-typing relationship.

Data models distinguish *complete* (or exhaustive) and *incomplete* (or non-exhaustive) sub-typing relationships. The former require that each occurrence of the super-type entity participates in at least one of the sub-types. The latter allow some super-type occurrences to belong to neither of the sub-types. In the example above, if each person is an employee and/or applicant, then the relationship is complete. If other classes of persons (such as next of kin) are stored in the PERSON table, the relationship is incomplete.

Further data models distinguish *conjoint* (or overlapping) and *disjoint* (or non-overlapping) sub-typing relationships. The former allow an occurrence of the super-type to belong to more than one sub-type, while the latter require the occurrences of the sub-types to be mutually exclusive. The relationship in our example is conjoint because some employees can also be applicants and vice versa. On the other hand, a relationship between a super-type PERSON and sub-types PERSON_MALE and PERSON_FEMALE is disjoint.

Sub-typing relationships and their forms are usually clearly shown in the data models. However, sometimes they are erroneously represented by a combination of several independent foreign key relationships, so you must be vigilant. An indication of a possible hidden sub-typing relationship is when three entities have the same primary key, and two of them have foreign keys that link them with the third entity. Of course, the number of sub-types can be greater than two.

Inheritance rules enforce validity of the data governed by the sub-typing relationships. For instance, the rule based on the complete conjoint relationship between entities PERSON, EMPLOYEE and APPLICANT has the form:

Every person is an employee, an applicant, or both.

Any PERSON occurrence not found in either EMPLOYEE or APPLICANT entity is erroneous (or more likely points to a missing employee or applicant record).

SUMMARY

Relational data models are a gold mine for data quality rules. In this chapter, we have discussed four types of such relational integrity rules:

- Identity rules make sure that every record in a database table corresponds to one and only one real world entity and that no two records reference the same entity.

- Reference rules ensure that every reference made from one entity occurrence to another entity occurrence can be successfully resolved.

- Cardinal rules define constraints on the allowed number of related occurrences between entities.

- Inheritance rules express integrity constraints on entities that are associated through generalization and specialization.

Unlike attribute domain constraints discussed in the previous chapter, relational integrity rules affect several records at a time. Also, in case of a rule violation, it is not immediately obvious which of the records are incorrect. This makes implementation and usage of relational integrity rules somewhat more complex.

CHAPTER 6
RULES FOR HISTORICAL DATA

Most real world objects change over time. Newborn babies grow into playful toddlers, love-stricken teenagers, somewhat depressed adults, and finally wise matriarchs and patriarchs. Employee positions change over time, their skills increase, and so hopefully do their salaries. Stock markets fluctuate, product sales ebb and flow, corporate profits vary, empires rise and fall, and even celestial bodies move about in an infinite dance of time.

For any real world object, all but a few attributes are dynamic in nature. The databases charged with the task of tracking various object attributes inevitably have to contend with this time-dependency of the data. Occasionally, only the current values of attributes are of interest. For instance, we can choose to only track the current address of our customers, however more often at least some part of the history is stored.

Historical data comprise the majority of data in both operational systems and data warehouses. They are also most error-prone. There is always a chance to miss parts of the history during data collection, or incorrectly timestamp the collected records. Also, historical data often spend years inside databases and undergo many transformations, providing plenty of opportunity for data corruption and decay. This combination of abundance, critical importance, and error-affinity of the historical data makes them the primary target in any data quality assessment project.

The good news is that historical data also offer great opportunities for validation. Both the timestamps and attribute values usually follow predictable patterns that can be checked using data quality rules. This chapter offers comprehensive treatment of the data quality rules for historical data:

- Section 6.1 introduces historical data.

- Section 6.2 describes basic data quality rules for historical data.

- Section 6.3 discusses advanced data quality rules for historical data.

- Section 6.4 presents event histories – the more sophisticated sibling in the family of time-dependent data – and data quality rules specific for them.

6.1. INTRODUCTION TO HISTORICAL DATA

We use the term *time-dependent attribute* to designate an object characteristic that changes over time. Any value of such an attribute is only meaningful when it is accompanied by the date or time of measurement. For instance, it is meaningless to say that my weight is 165 pounds unless I just got off the scales in the doctor's office. We can only say that at a certain time, e.g. at noon on November 29, 2006, my weight was 165 pounds. Combining measurements at various points in time yields my weight history. We refer to any such series of time-stamped attribute measurements as *value history*.

A simple value history is usually stored in an entity containing three attributes: object identifier (my name in the above example), timestamp indicating the measurement date, and the time-dependent attribute itself. We refer to any database entity with time-dependent attributes as a *time-dependent entity*. Several time-dependent attributes can coexist within a single entity. Consider, for instance, periodic customer surveys. The answers would be likely stored in a single entity with the number of time-dependent attributes equal to the number of survey questions.

Occasionally value histories are stored in repeating groups of attributes within a single record. This de-normalized form is common in "legacy" databases but sometimes occurs in relational databases when the number of measurements is fixed or small.

Value histories are most common in data warehousing. The typical data warehouse or data mart will consist of snapshots of attribute values taken from various operational systems. Thus for each attribute, it contains the value history with the measurements taken every time a new snapshot is brought to the data warehouse.

The table and accompanying chart in Figure 6-1 show my height history since the early childhood. It was initially collected in the form of entries into my "Baby

Book," and later combined with measurements reflected by pencil marks on the door to my bedroom. It is clearly an example of historical data. My records could be combined with the data for a million of other people and stored in a time-dependent entity PERSON_HEIGHT with attributes Name, MeasurementDate, and Height.

The key feature differentiating value histories from other time-dependent data is that attribute values are <u>only</u> known at the times of measurement. Nothing can be directly deduced about the values between measurements. For instance it is known with certainly that I was about 64 inches tall (5'4") in May 1984 and grew to 69 inches tall (5'9") by October 1985. It is possible that I gained all five inches in the first week after the first measurement, or alternatively that I had a growth spurt the week before the second measurement. However, neither conclusion can be drawn from the data itself.

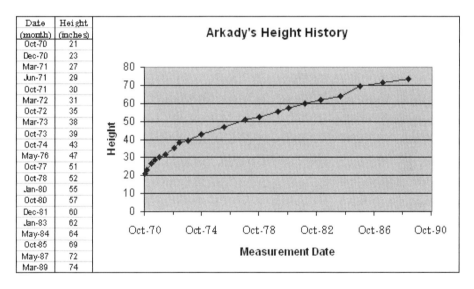

Date (month)	Height (inches)
Oct-70	21
Dec-70	23
Mar-71	27
Jun-71	29
Oct-71	30
Mar-72	31
Oct-72	35
Mar-73	38
Oct-73	39
Oct-74	43
May-76	47
Oct-77	51
Oct-78	52
Jan-80	55
Oct-80	57
Dec-81	60
Jan-83	62
May-84	64
Oct-85	69
May-87	72
Mar-89	74

Figure 6-1: My Height History Data and Chart

Let's take a more in-depth look at the data in Figure 6-1. The measurements have been taken at periodic but rather random dates. Yet, these dates are not truly arbitrary. For instance, the first measurement coincides with my date of birth. This would be true for all people – the earliest record for any person could not precede the date of birth. In fact we may reasonably expect the first measurement to be taken exactly on the day of birth. This type of constraint is common for historical data and is usually called the retention rule. In general retention rules enforce the desired depth of the historical data. They are usually expressed in the form of constraints on the overall duration or the number of records in the history.

Further, my height measurements ceased in 1989 when I was 18.5. There was no point to take further measurements – to my great disappointment I finally stopped growing, just two inches short of my older brother. Again this would be similar for most people, as they stop growing in late teens or early twenties. The constraints on the date of the most recent historical record are usually called currency rules.

The values of my height measurements also follow certain predictable patterns. For instance, the values never decrease and change by no more than five inches in one year (except in the first year). This would hold true for all people, as we generally do not get shorter and our rate of growth stays within a reasonable limit, such as six inches per year. This simple example illustrates how many constraints apply to even the simplest of historical data. These constraints can be translated into data quality rules.

Values of some attributes are more meaningful when accumulated over a period of time. Even for the same attribute, atomic historical data may be useful for one purpose, while cumulative numbers may be more helpful for another. For example, individual product sales must be tracked for order procurement but are useless in analysis of consumer demand patterns. For the latter purpose, it is more pertinent to collect weekly, monthly, or quarterly cumulative sales volumes. We refer to any such series of cumulative time-period measurements as *accumulator history*.

Accumulator histories are very common in data warehousing but are also found in many other databases. For example, payroll databases store annual taxable compensation histories of employees. Insurance databases track total amounts of claims per policy period for the insured.

Accumulator histories are usually stored in time-dependent entities containing at least four attributes:

- Object identifier (product identifier in the product sales example above)

- Time interval beginning date

- Time interval ending date

- Attribute(s) for which the values are accumulated

The key feature differentiating accumulator history is that attribute values are not measured at certain points in time, but rather are accumulated over time intervals. The table in Figure 6-2 shows an example of employee compensation history.

EmployeeID	BegDate	EndDate	WageAmt
338	1/1/1999	12/31/1999	51400
338	1/1/2000	12/31/2000	54000
338	1/1/2001	12/31/2001	56200
338	1/1/2002	12/31/2002	55400
338	1/1/2003	12/31/2003	57100
338	1/1/2004	12/31/2004	62400
338	1/1/2005	12/31/2005	65000
338	1/1/2006	12/31/2006	66500

W2_WAGE — 1 of 8

Figure 6-2: Employee Compensation History Example

Accumulator histories are typically governed by an even greater number of constraints than basic value histories. Consider the example in Figure 6-2. The time periods must have no gaps and overlaps and all have the same granularity of one calendar year. The most recent record must show compensation for the most recent calendar year. Compensation values also follow patterns, e.g. they must be consistent with the annual pay rate and length of employment. In practice, accumulator histories are even more suitable for comprehensive data quality assessment than value histories.

6.2. BASIC DATA QUALITY RULES FOR HISTORICAL DATA

We will start with the discussion of data quality rules for historical data from basic *timeline constraints*, which validate that all required, desired, or expected measurements are recorded and that all timestamps are accurate. These rules can be broken down into categories of currency, retention, continuity, and granularity.

6.2.1. Currency Rules

Currency rules enforce the desired "freshness" of the historical data. They usually are expressed in the form of constraints on the effective date of the most recent record in the history. Currency testing identifies the youngest record in the historical data and compares its timestamp to a pre-defined threshold.

Figure 6-3 illustrates the currency rule for a sample of annual employee compensation history. The rule requires the most recent record for each employee to match the last complete calendar year, 2006 in our example. Data for employee #338 meet the criteria, while the history for employee #339 only goes up to 2004 and thus violates the rule.

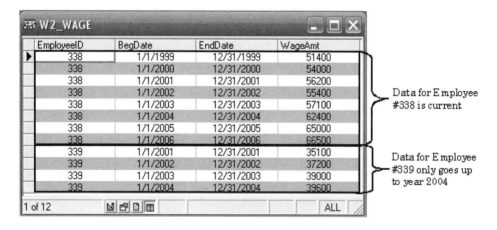

Figure 6-3: Example of Currency Rule

The rule in this example fixes the timestamp of the most recent record as a function of today's date. Such form is common for historical data with timestamps falling on fixed dates. In some "legacy" value histories, the last measurement

98

might even be required to fall on a constant pre-defined date. For instance, if a survey was conducted regularly in the past but then discontinued, then the currency rule for the history will require the most recent record for all participants to fall on the exact date of the last survey.

An alternative form of the currency rules restricts maximum age of the most recent record. The term "age," while technically incorrect, is commonly used to describe length of time since the record's birth (represented by its effective date). For example, patients may be expected to visit the dentist at least every six months for regular checkups. While the time of the last visit will differ for all patients, it has to be no earlier than six months before the today's date. Thus, the age of the record from the last visit must be less than six months.

In some types of historical data, currency will be defined differently for different objects. For instance, if the compensation history table W2_WAGE in Figure 6-3 includes data for both active and terminated employees, then the currency rule cannot require each person to have records up to 2006. This will only be true for active workers. For the terminated employees, the most recent record must be for the year of termination. Thus, if employee #339 resigned on December 15, 2004, his latest compensation history record must be for the year 2004; and his data in the example would be correct.

6.2.2. Retention Rules

Retention rules enforce the desired depth of the historical data. They are usually expressed in the form of constraints on the overall duration or the number of records in the history.

Retention rules often reflect common retention policies and regulations requiring data to be stored for a certain period of time before it can be discarded. For instance, all tax-related information may need to be stored for seven years pending possibility of an audit. Further, a bank may be required to keep data of all customer transactions for several years. All of these retention rules take the form of constraints on the age of the oldest record in the historical data.

In some cases the required age of the oldest record will vary from object to object. Figure 6-4 shows an example of a retention rule for annual employee compensation history. Payroll data retention policies often require five years of history to be present. The data for employee #338 meets this criteria, while the data for employee #339 seems to violate the rule. However, what if employee #339 was hired on January 22, 2001? In that case no compensation data beyond 2001 can possibly exist. Thus, the proper retention rule will require the compensation history to go back at least five calendar years or up to the year of hire.

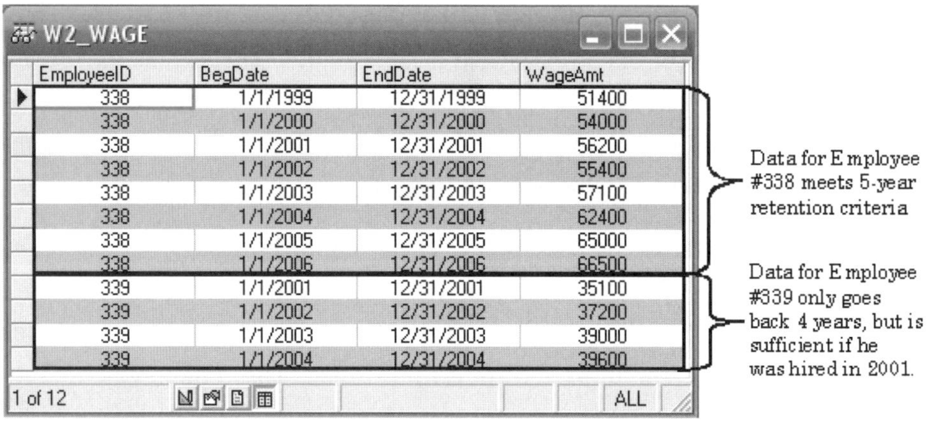

EmployeeID	BegDate	EndDate	WageAmt
338	1/1/1999	12/31/1999	51400
338	1/1/2000	12/31/2000	54000
338	1/1/2001	12/31/2001	56200
338	1/1/2002	12/31/2002	55400
338	1/1/2003	12/31/2003	57100
338	1/1/2004	12/31/2004	62400
338	1/1/2005	12/31/2005	65000
338	1/1/2006	12/31/2006	66500
339	1/1/2001	12/31/2001	35100
339	1/1/2002	12/31/2002	37200
339	1/1/2003	12/31/2003	39000
339	1/1/2004	12/31/2004	39600

Figure 6-4: Example of Retention Rule

In the examples above, the minimum age of the oldest record was restricted. Occasionally maximum age is also constrained, when the presence of older records is considered undesirable. For example, payroll database may store employee compensation data by paycheck for the current year in entity WAGE_CURR_YEAR, and cumulative annual compensation data for previous years in another entity WAGE_PREV_ANNUAL. Any overlap in the data is undesirable and is eliminated during the year-end data rollup when values from WAGE_CURR_YEAR entity are aggregated and moved to WAGE_PREV_ANNUAL. The presence of any records in WAGE_CURR_YEAR with effective dates in prior years is likely a data entry error. Such errors would be caught by the retention rule requiring the timestamps of all records in WAGE_CURR_YEAR table to fall in the current year.

In some cases, retention rules demand the minimum number of records in the data history rather than its duration. For instance, a golfer's handicap is determined as a function of scores in the last 20 rounds of play. These last 20 rounds may all be in the last month, as they are for some of my more fortunate friends; but they go back all the way to the last year for me. The retention rule here requires score history to include no less than 20 rounds regardless of their temporal distribution.

6.2.3. Continuity and Granularity Rules

Typical accumulator history is made of a sequence of measurements aggregated over continuous identical time periods. For instance, product sales history might be a collection of the last 20 quarterly sales totals. Employee compensation history may be required to include annual compensation for the last five calendar years. These constraints can be represented by a combination of two data quality rules:

- ***Granularity rules*** require all measurement periods in accumulator histories to have the same size. In the product sales example, it is a calendar quarter; for the employee compensation example, it is a year.
- ***Continuity rules*** prohibit gaps and overlaps in accumulator histories. They require that the beginning date of each measurement period immediately follows the end date of the previous period.

Granularity and continuity rules do not apply to value histories where measurements are taken at points in time rather than accumulated over longer time periods.

Figure 6-5 illustrates the employee compensation history example. The earliest history record violates granularity rule – its duration is less than a year. There is a timeline gap between the records for years 2003 and 2005 – the record for year 2004 is missing. Finally, the two most recent records overlap. The last record is most likely redundant and must be removed.

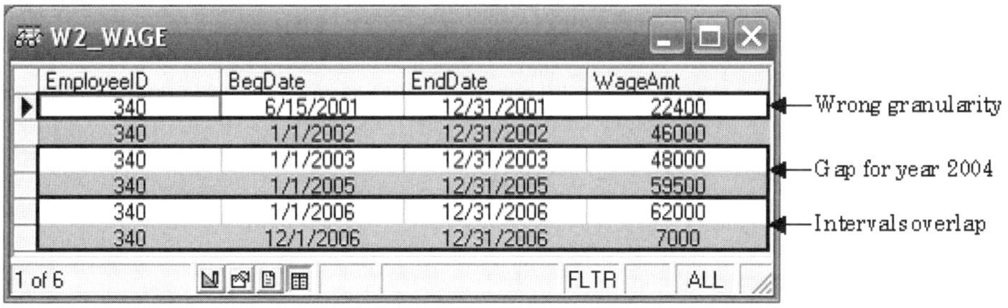

W2_WAGE

EmployeeID	BegDate	EndDate	WageAmt
340	6/15/2001	12/31/2001	22400
340	1/1/2002	12/31/2002	46000
340	1/1/2003	12/31/2003	48000
340	1/1/2005	12/31/2005	59500
340	1/1/2006	12/31/2006	62000
340	12/1/2006	12/31/2006	7000

Figure 6-5: Example of Continuity and Granularity Rules

6.3. ADVANCED DATA QUALITY RULES FOR HISTORICAL DATA

Basic rules enforce that historical data cover the entire desired space of time. However, this does not yet guarantee that the data is complete and accurate. More advanced rules are necessary to identify possibly missing historical records or to find records with incorrect timestamps or values of time-dependent attributes. All such rules are based on validation of more complex patterns in historical data. They generally fall into categories of timeline patterns and value patterns, which will be discussed next.

6.3.1. Timeline Patterns

Value history timestamps usually do not fall on random dates but follow some patterns. My height measurements shown in Figure 6-1 were mostly dated in October because I usually checked my height on my birthday. If this was true for all people, we could set a data quality rule requiring records to be present with dates falling in the month of birth for each person and every year between the year of birth and age 20. This would be an example of a *timeline pattern rule*.

Timeline pattern rules usually require all timestamps to fall into a certain repeating date interval, such as every March or every other Wednesday or between the first and fifth of each month. Occasionally the pattern takes the form of minimum or maximum length of time between measurements. For example, participants in a medical study may be required to take blood pressure readings at least once a week. While the length of time between particular measurements will differ, it has to be no longer than seven days.

Timeline patterns are common to many historical data. However, finding the pattern can be a challenge. One useful technique is to collect counts of records by calendar year, month, day, or any other regular time interval. For example, frequencies of records for each calendar month (year and day of the record does not matter) will tell if the records have effective dates spread randomly over the year or if they follow some pattern.

The chart on the left of Figure 6-6 shows a frequency chart for the calendar month of fiscal year-end bonus payments from a corporate payroll database. Here we aggregated data over the last 15 years. Almost 93% of all records are dated in March with additional 6.3% in February. Further research proved that bonuses in that company were always paid between the last week of February and the first week of April. All other dates are invalid.

The table on the right of Figure 6-6 shows bonus history for employee #78172. All records with the exception of the highlighted one are dated in mid-March. The record dated 1/2/1992 does not fit the timeline pattern and is erroneous. Additional analysis shows that the record was actually for the holiday pay mistakenly classified as year-end bonus.

All values				E_PAY_SPECIAL_HISTORY		
Bar	Value	Count	Percent	EmpID	EffDate	Bonus
1	5	0.01		78172	3/15/2001	6400
2	2404	6.30		78172	3/15/2000	5900
3	35403	92.82		78172	3/12/1999	5792
4	239	0.63		78172	3/13/1998	4000
5	10	0.03		78172	3/15/1993	2500
6	5	0.01		78172	3/13/1992	3350
7	11	0.03		78172	1/2/1992	650
8	14	0.04		78172	3/15/1991	3475
9	4	0.01		78172	3/15/1990	3620
10	2	0.01		1 of 9		FLTR
11	8	0.02				
12	37	0.10				

Figure 6-6: Bonus Timestamp Profile and Timeline Pattern Rule

6.3.2. Value Patterns

Value histories for time-dependent attributes usually follow systematic patterns. *Value pattern rules* utilize these patterns to predict reasonable ranges of values for each measurement and identify likely outliers.

The simplest value pattern rules restrict <u>direction</u> in value changes from measurement to measurement. In my height history example, measurements were not allowed to decrease. This is by far the most common rule type. Electric meter measurements, total number of copies of this book sold to-date and many other common attributes always grow or at least remain the same.

A slightly more complex form of the rule restricts the <u>magnitude</u> of value changes. It is usually expressed in maximum (and occasionally minimum) allowed change per unit of time. For instance, height changes might be restricted to six inches per year. This does not mean that values from measurement to measurement may not change by more than six inches, but rather that the change cannot exceed six inches times the length of the interval in years. Also, this type of constraints work well for measurement made farther apart.

The value change constraints work well for attributes whose values are rather stationary. This does not apply to many real world attributes. For instance, regular pay raises rarely exceed 10-15%, but raises for employees promoted to a new position routinely reach 20-30% or even more. Since (hopefully) the majority of employees experience a promotion at least once in their career, we could not use value change constraint for pay rate histories. However, pay rates still do not change arbitrarily.

Figure 6-7 illustrates this point. The table on the left contains pay rate data for two employees, while the chart on the right illustrates the data visually. Observe the data for each employee. Pay rate for employee #8052 is growing steadily, and he even experiences a big raise once in the year 2004. Data for employee #2121 has a similar pattern, except the raise in 2003 is followed by an immediate drop in the following year. Normal behavior of pay rate history for an employee of most companies is a steady increase over the years (of course I came up with this example a few years ago!). Sudden increase in pay rate followed by a drop signals an error in the data (or the end to the dot-com bubble). In our example the highlighted pay rate of $734.50 in 2003 is erroneous. It was caused by a typo and true pay rate was $634.50 – consistent with previous and later values.

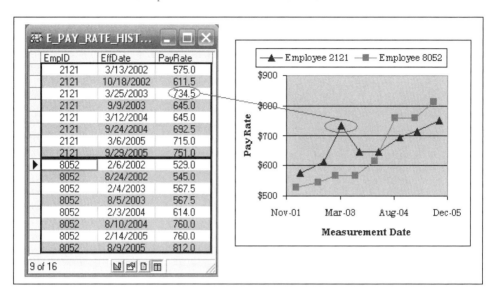

Figure 6-7: Value Pattern for Pay Rate History

The value pattern rule that can identify such errors must look for spikes and drops in consecutive values. Here we do not restrict individual value change, but rather do not permit an increase to be followed by a decrease and vice versa. In other words, the rule restricts <u>volatility</u> of value changes. Rules of this type are applicable to many data histories.

The rules restricting direction, magnitude, and volatility in historical data are easy to recognize and implement. However, they only catch obvious offenders. Many unreasonable values slip through the cracks because true value patterns can be rather complex. If the historical data is suspect, and identifying the majority of erroneous values is important, we can use more sophisticated time series models.

The idea behind these models is to view historical data as a sequence of measurements, each mathematically comprised of two parts – systemic component and a random "shock." The systemic component can then be expressed using a strict mathematical equation, such as the regression line. The random shock can be described using methods of mathematical statistics. Then, the reasonable range of values for each measurement can be predicted and used to validate the actual data.

The great advantage of time series analysis, and especially the more advanced statistical models, is that they provide probability estimates for the likelihood of the particular actual values fluctuations. In other words, rather than making rules based on common sense (such as no changes of over 25% from value to value) we can say that a chance of a specific observed value being observed under normal conditions is, say, 0.01. This approach provides much more accurate error listings with fewer false positives. However, it is important to recognize that unexpected value fluctuations, while unlikely, are possible. Therefore, advanced value pattern rules must be used with great care so as not to produce long listings of "errors" which turn out to be not errors at all.

The reader interested in the topic of time series analysis and modeling can find it studied in many textbooks, so we will not discuss it more in depth here. Also, implementing rules using time series models will require statistical analysis software. Fortunately, numerous statistical packages are available on the market.

6.4. DATA QUALITY RULES FOR EVENT HISTORIES

Time is arguably the most important aspect of our life. We are surrounded by calendars and watches, and rare is the activity that does not involve time. Ever since my son entered elementary school, his life became a collection of timestamps and time intervals: school schedule, soccer schedule, play date, time to do homework, TV time, time to play video games, time to go to bed, number of days till Christmas and to the next vacation, and even the number of years left to accumulate college funds. And it stays that way for an entire life, except rare Hawaii vacations. I fully realized our dependence on time when I once estimated that we reference time at least once every five minutes in our conversations. This phenomenon stays true in the databases we build. Much of the data is time-stamped, and absolute majority of the database entities contain histories.

So far in this chapter we discussed data quality rules for attribute value histories, i.e. histories of measurements of various characteristics of people, businesses, things, and other objects. The next most common content in information systems is the data about events. Car accidents, doctor appointments, employee reviews and pay raises are all examples of events. Since events naturally occur at a point in time and event timing is usually of importance, the event data is automatically historical.

We refer to any listing of events as **event history**. Event histories are more complex than value and accumulator histories. First, events often apply to several objects. For instance, a doctor's appointment involves two individuals – the doctor and the patient. Secondly, events sometimes occupy a period rather than a point in time. Thus, recording a doctor's appointment requires appointment scheduled time and duration (or alternatively scheduled start and stop times). Finally, events are often described with several event-specific attributes. For example, the doctor's appointment can be prophylactic, scheduled, or due to an emergency. It can further be an initial or a follow-up visit, and it will often result in diagnosis.

As a result, time-dependent entities tracking event histories often contain many attributes, including:

- Event identifier;

- Object(s) impacted by or involved in the event;

- Event effective date/time and duration (or end date/time);

- Event-specific attributes.

When the number and types of involved objects and event-specific attributes varies from event to event, the event history is often stored in a collection of interrelated entities. For example, car accident data can be divided among parent ACCIDENT entity with event identifier, accident type, and accident time attributes; dependent ACCIDENT_AUTO entity with references to involved automobiles; and dependent ACCIDENT_PARTY entity with references to involved drivers and passengers.

As the complexity of events grows, so does the number of constraints governing the event histories. Consider again the doctor appointments history. For each appointment the duration should be reasonable – we do not expect to spend six hours in the dentist's office for simple filling, unless the waiting time is included. Here the appointment duration is not just constrained by common sense (as in no less than 30 minutes) but is also related to the diagnosis. Further, a doctor cannot see several patients at the same time (again, of course, common sense does not always apply to the medical profession).

The list of constraints will go on and on. All of these constraints translate into data quality rules that can be used to validate the event histories. In the practice of data quality assessment, rules for event histories often occupy the bulk of the project and find numerous errors.

Data quality rules discussed in this chapter apply to event histories as well. However, event histories are more complex than value histories. Naturally, the data quality rules for the event histories are also more diverse and complex. Rules that are specific to event histories can be classified into event dependencies, event pre-condition and post-conditions, and event-specific attribute constraints.

6.4.1. Event Dependencies

Various events in the event histories often affect the same objects. Because of this, different events may be interdependent. Data quality rules can use these dependencies to validate the event histories.

The simplest event rule of this kind restricts frequency of the events. For example, patients may be expected to visit the dentist at least every six months for regular checkups. While the length of time between particular visits will differ, it has to be no longer than six months.

Sometimes event frequency can be defined as a function of other data. For example, an airplane is required to undergo extensive maintenance after a certain number of flights. Here frequency of maintenance events is not a function of time but of another data attribute. Assuming good safety procedures, a greater than required number of flights between maintenance events is a likely indication of a missing record in the event history.

A constraint can also be placed on the number of events per unit of time. For example, a doctor may not be able to see more than 15 patients in a normal workday. Higher number of doctor visits will likely indicate that some of the records in the event history show erroneous name of the doctor or date of the visit.

The most complex type of rules applies to situations when events are tied by a cause-and-effect relation. For example, mounting a dental crown will involve several visits to the dentist. The nature, spacing, and duration of the visits are related. Relationships of this kind can get quite complex with the timing and nature of the next event being a function of the outcome of the previous event. For instance, a diagnosis made during the first appointment will influence following appointments.

In most cases event dependencies can only be found by extensive analysis of the nature of events. Business users will provide key input here. On the flip side, event dependencies and other complex data quality rules for event histories are typically the source of finding numerous hidden data errors.

6.4.2. Event Conditions

Events of many kinds do not occur at random but rather only happen under certain unique circumstances. Event conditions verify these circumstances.

Consider a typical new car maintenance program. It includes several visits to the dealership for scheduled maintenance activities. These activities may include engine oil change, wheel alignment, tire rotation, and break pad replacement. For each activity, there is a desired frequency. In fact, my new car has a great gadget that reminds me when each of the activities is due. It does it in a beautiful voice, but in no uncertain terms. A typical message will be "Your tires are due for rotation. Driving the car may be VERY unsafe. Please, make a legal U-turn and proceed to the nearest dealership at a speed of no more than 15 miles an hour."

Since I do not appreciate this kind of life-threatening circumstance, the next time I decided to visit the dealership before maintenance was due. Unfortunately, for obvious business reasons, the dealership would not do the maintenance before it is due. As it was, my only option was to wait for the next announcement and find my way to the nearest dealership at the speed of 15 miles an hour.

On a more serious note, this constraint is an example of *event condition* – a condition that must be satisfied for an event to take place. Each specific car maintenance event has pre-conditions based on the car make and model, the age of the car, car mileage, and the time since the last event of same type. All of these conditions can be implemented in a data quality rule (or rules) and used to validate car maintenance event histories in an auto dealership database.

In a more formal mathematical literature, event conditions are commonly divided into three groups:

- Pre-conditions must be satisfied before an event can take place.

- Post-conditions must be met for the event to be successfully completed.

- Coincidental conditions simply are always true when an event occurs.

This classification is based on the cause-and-effect approach. Certain things cause or precede the event; some other things are caused by or follow the event. Yet more things simply happen simultaneously with the event itself because both are caused by the same reason. I find that these gradations, while theoretically valid, often bring confusion to the design of data quality rules. It is important to remember that from the perspective of rule design, it typically does not matter what is the cause and what is the effect. Event condition rules usually just verify that when events are recorded, appropriate conditions are met and/or vice versa. Still it sometimes helps to identify event conditions by thinking about causes and effects of the events.

Event conditions are common to most event histories, yet rarely fully understood. As was the case with event dependencies, in order to identify these constraints we must analyze the events from the business perspective and interview business users.

6.4.3. Event-Specific Attribute Constraints

Events themselves are often complex entities, each with numerous attributes. In the example of recording automobile accident information, each event must be accompanied by much data – involved cars and their post-accident condition, involved drivers and their accident accounts, police officers and their observations, witnesses and their view of events. The list of data elements can be quite long, and the data may be stored simply in extra attributes of the event table or in additional dependent entities.

Event-specific attribute constraints enforce that all attributes relevant to the event are present. The exact form of these constraints may depend on the nature of the event and its specific characteristics. For instance, a collision must involve two or more cars with two or more drivers (each driver matched to one and only one car).

This condition will typically translate into a relatively complex combination of conditional relational integrity and attribute optionality constraints.

It gets even more exciting when different events may have different attributes. For instance, collision events have somewhat different attributes than hit-and-run events. The former embroil two or more cars, each with a driver; the latter usually involve a single car with no identified driver. Thus the name "event-specific attribute constraints" has two connotations – both the attributes and the constraints are event-specific.

The good news is that these constraints only seem complex when you try them first time. With some experience, event-specific attribute constraints become easier to design. At the same time, these constraints are rarely enforced by databases, and erroneous data in this area proliferate.

SUMMARY

Historical data comprise the majority of data in both operational systems and data warehouses. They are also the most error-prone. In this chapter we discussed various types of data quality rules for historical data, specifically:

- Basic timeline constraints validate that all required, desired, or expected measurements are recorded and that all timestamps are accurate. These rules can be broken down into categories of currency, retention, continuity, and granularity.

- More advanced rules are necessary to identify possibly missing historical records or to find records with incorrect timestamps or values of time-dependent attributes. All such rules are based on the validation of patterns in historical data. They generally fall into categories of timeline patterns and value patterns.

- Event histories are more complex than value histories. As the complexity of events grows, so does the number and sophistication of constraints governing the event histories. Rules that are specific to event histories can be classified into event dependencies, event pre-condition and post-conditions, and event-specific attribute constraints.

The combination of abundance, critical importance, and error-affinity of the historical data makes them the primary target in any data quality assessment project. While the data quality rules for historical data are rather complex to design and implement, they are crucial to data quality assessment since they usually identify numerous critical data errors.

CHAPTER 7
RULES FOR STATE-DEPENDENT OBJECTS

In the previous chapter, we discussed data quality rules for historical data, with the crescendo on event histories. If event histories were not complex enough, things can sometimes get even more exciting. Most complex objects can go through a sequence of states in the course of their life cycle as a result of various events. Job application is an example of such objects. Its life cycle is a progression from submission, through pre-screening, to applicant interviews, to possible job offers, and up to an eventual hiring or rejection decision. Such objects are called state-dependent.

While data describing the lifecycle for state-dependent objects can be viewed as an event history, it is more complex than that. We are not dealing here with just a series of unfortunate events and event-specific attributes, but also with sequences of object states and state-specific attributes. The bottom line is that state-dependent objects add another dimension of complexity to event histories. Yet, these objects are often the most important database citizens, and their data are most error-prone.

Adequate descriptions of the lifecycle of state-dependent objects use a special apparatus of state-transition modeling. State-transition models provide a wealth of important data quality rules, which are relatively easy to identify and implement. The first three sections of this chapter introduce state-transition models. The remaining three sections present various types of data quality rules governing the lifecycle of state-dependent objects.

- Section 7.1 introduces key concepts of state-transition models.

- Section 7.2 describes how state-dependent objects can be identified among the relational entities.

- Section 7.3 discusses state-transition model profiling – a collection of techniques used to analyze the lifecycle of state-dependent objects.

- Section 7.4 presents data quality rules that can be derived directly from the analysis of state-transition diagrams.

- Section 7.5 discusses timeline constraints on the lifecycle of the state-dependent objects.

- Section 7.6 describes advanced rules governing the lifecycle of the state-dependent objects.

7.1. INTRODUCTION TO STATE-DEPENDENT OBJECTS

Consider a career of a loyal Bad Data Corporation employee, Jane Gooding. She was originally hired in 1959 at the age of 26. During the next 19 years, she remained with the company with the exception of two maternity leaves in 1964 and 1967, respectively. In 1978 she quit her job but returned four years later. After 13 more years of hard work, Jane finally retired at the age of 62.

Jane's employment history can be described as a sequence of chronological events, each bringing about a change in her employment status. For instance, a new hire event on 3/13/1959 starts Jane's career as an active employee (status *Active*). Jane's resignation on 5/15/1978 changed her employment status from *Active* to *Terminated*. Figure 7-1 illustrates the timeline of Jane's career.

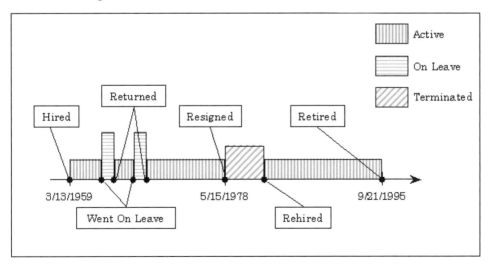

Figure 7-1: Employment Timeline for Jane Gooding

The objects that go through a sequence of states in the course of their life cycle as a result of various events are referred to as ***state-dependent objects***. Employees, job applications, insurance claims, and product orders are all examples of state-dependent objects.

Different employees have different careers. Some take one or more leaves of absence, while others do not. Some are terminated and later rehired; others resign and never come back. Thus, their careers consist of a varying number, sequence, and duration of events and employment statuses. However, not just any combination is allowed. For instance, no employee can be terminated twice in a row without being rehired in between. In order to design data quality rules for state-dependent objects, we need a model distinguishing valid from invalid life cycles.

State-transition models describe constraints on the life cycle of state-dependent objects through two key concepts: state and action.

- ***State*** is a unique set of circumstances in which an object may exist. At any point in its life, the object must be in one and only one state. The states that identify possible beginning and ending points of the object's life cycle are called ***terminators***.

- ***Action*** is a unique event that results in a change of state. An action may have conditions that must be satisfied before it can take place (action pre-conditions) or after it is completed successfully (action post-conditions).

State-transition models are usually presented by state-transition diagrams. Figure 7-2 depicts such a diagram for state-dependent object EMPLOYEE. The five shaded ovals represent valid object states: *Active* (*A*), *Terminated* (*T*), *On Leave* (*L*), *Retired* (*R*), and *Deceased* (*D*). At any point in time, each object must be in exactly one of these states. Further, each object must begin the life cycle in terminator state *Active* as illustrated by the white circle on the top of the diagram.

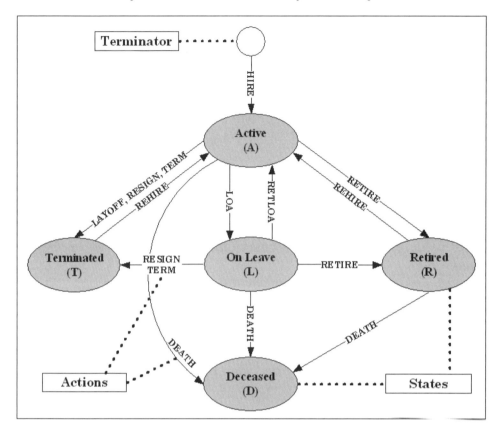

Figure 7-2: State-Transition Diagram for Object Employee

Valid actions are shown as arrows connecting various states. For example, action *DEATH* applies to objects in *Active* state and changes their state to *Deceased*. Note that some actions can apply to objects in different states (e.g. action *DEATH* can also apply to employees in states *On Leave* or *Retired*). Also, sometimes multiple actions can apply to the same object yielding similar state transitions. For instance, two distinct actions can apply to employees *On Leave* and change their state to *Terminated*.

We will use this model throughout this chapter in many examples of the data quality rules and data errors.

7.2. IDENTIFYING STATE-DEPENDENT ENTITIES

The first step towards using state-transition models in data quality assessment is to identify state-dependent entities in the relational data models. There are two approaches.

You can start with the analysis of high-level business objects, whose data is maintained in the database. Then try to identify conceptually what kind of states they can be in and what kind of actions apply to them. For instance, insurance claims get filed, screened, and finally denied or approved. Now it is a simple matter of finding the entities in the database that track the desired data.

Alternatively, you can examine each entity and identify the ones tracking state-dependent data based on attributes. Presence of timestamp attributes (such as EffDate) is a good starting point because state-dependent data is typically chronological. Occasionally, simple sequencing of actions and states is used instead of timestamps. Thus, entities with attributes like SeqNum are also state-dependency candidates.

The presence of chronological order is not enough to classify an entity as state-dependent. For example, interest rate history and pay rate history are time-dependent but not state-dependent. The next clue is existence of action and/or state attributes with names such as ActionCode, StateCode, or StatusCode. In fact a combination of timestamp with any coded attribute (that is any attribute taking a discrete set of values) makes the entity a good candidate for state-dependency.

Figure 7-3 shows the entity E_STATUS_HISTORY storing employment status history. Attribute EmpID defines the employee identity. There are one or more records in the table for every employee. Each record corresponds to a period between employment events. The effective date of each record (attribute EffDate) is the event date and is exactly one day after the end of the previous period (attribute EndDate). The attributes ActionCode and StateCode reference the employment event and the state of the employee after the event, respectively.

The table in Figure 7-3 shows the data for previously discussed employee Jane Gooding. For example, the first record shows that Jane was hired on 3/13/1959, and her state became *Active* (*A*). She stayed in that state until 1/17/1964 when she went on the maternity leave as indicated by the following record. The number of records describing Jane's life cycle equals the number of events in her employment history. The last record has Null value in EndDate attribute, indicating that *Retiree* (*R*) is her current state.

E_STATUS_HISTORY

EmpID	- Defines employee identity
EffDate	- Shows effective date of the action
EndDate	- Shows last day in current state
ActionCode	- Indicates employment action
StateCode	- Indicates new employment state

E_STATUS_HISTORY

EmpID	EffDate	EndDate	ActionCode	StateCode
229516	3/13/1959	1/17/1964	HIRE	A
229516	1/18/1964	6/23/1964	LOA	L
229516	6/24/1964	2/21/1967	RETLOA	A
229516	2/22/1967	6/4/1967	LOA	L
229516	6/5/1967	5/14/1978	RETLOA	A
229516	5/15/1978	5/21/1982	RESIGN	T
229516	5/22/1982	9/20/1995	REHIRE	A
229516	9/21/1995	Null	RETIRE	R

1 of 8   Figure53   SRT PART

Figure 7-3: Example of a State-Dependent Entity

The five shown attributes contain full information about the lifecycle of a state-dependent object EMPLOYEE. Some of the attributes may often be missing in practice. The EndDate can be omitted without any loss of information – its value can always be deduced as one day before the EffDate of the next chronological record. Attributes ActionCode and StateCode are not always present together. Sometimes only states are tracked when it is deemed not significant to know which of the actions caused the change in state. In other cases, only actions are tracked if each action uniquely identifies the new state to which the object is transitioned.

When any of the attributes are missing, it is often beneficial to complete the data before applying data quality rules to it. End dates, actions, and states can be deduced from the available data. This, of course, assumes that we have brought the data to a staging area first and can manipulate it freely. Having a complete set of attributes makes implementing data quality rules easier and more efficient.

7.3. PROFILING STATE-TRANSITION MODELS

State-transition models provide a wealth of important data quality rules. Unfortunately, they are often unavailable or unreliable. This problem can be easily mitigated, as state-transition models can be built quite easily from the data and available meta data through analysis and profiling.

Understanding the nature of the object from the business perspective is a good starting point. A business user will quickly tell you what states the object can take, which of the states are valid terminators, what actions can apply to the object in each state, and what is the impact of each action on the object state. This information can be used to build a state-transition diagram.

However, data does not always follow common sense. As is the case with most other types of models and meta data, the only way to get them right is to use data profiling.

State-transition model profiling is a collection of techniques for analysis of the lifecycle of state-dependent objects that provides <u>actual</u> information about the order and duration of states and actions. Combining the results of the data profiling with the information obtained from business users will yield the correct state-transition model.

7.3.1. State and Terminator Profiling

The first step in building state-transition models is to identify all object states and select terminator states from among them. Valid states are derived from the frequency diagram of the StateCode attribute obtained through attribute profiling. Selecting terminators is a bit more complex. Understanding the nature of the object from the business perspective is a good starting point. For instance, it is clear that employees should always start their lifecycle from state *Active* upon being hired. However, data does not always follow common sense.

I was involved in several HR data consolidation projects following corporate acquisitions. When the data for employees from the acquired company is merged into the acquirer's HR database, it is often deemed unnecessary to bring all the data. For instance, past employment history for the retirees may be considered useless – all that is required is to store the retirement date and the information about post-retirement employee benefits. Thus, if the data for Jane Gooding from Figure 7-3 was integrated into the acquirer's HR database, only the most recent record would be brought. Her employment history would then seem to start in *Retiree* state. The situation would be the same for thousands of other retirees.

Starting your employee career with retirement seems like a dream unless you happen to have a very rich uncle. But it is commonplace in employment state-transition models – *Retiree* state is often a valid terminator. This example suggests that state-transition models for real world data may defy logic. The only way to get them right is to use data profiling.

Terminator profiling is the easiest technique. It involves collecting terminator frequencies and analyzing their logical validity. A ***terminator profile*** shows how often each state actually appears as the first (terminator) record in the object lifecycles. States with high frequency are likely to be valid terminators. If the count is small compared to the total count of values, the data must be questioned.

Table 7-1 shows terminator frequencies in the table E_STATUS_HISTORY from our case study. State *Active* is clearly the only valid terminator (occurring over 98% of times).

Terminator	Frequency	Percentage
Active	13,310	98.20%
Terminated	209	1.54%
On Leave	33	0.24%
Retiree	2	0.02%
Deceased	0	0.00%
TOTAL	**13,554**	**100.00%**

Table 7-1: Terminator Profile for EMPLOYEE Object

7.3.2. State-Transition Profiling

The next step in building state-transition models is to identify all valid state transitions. This is equivalent to drawing arrows between state shapes in the state-transition diagram.

As was the case with terminators, state transitions often defy logic. For instance, it seems mildly strange to find any employment states following *Deceased* state. Yet it is frequently considered legitimate in real world data. HR systems often restrict retroactive editing. Imagine *DEATH* event erroneously entered into the data. If the employee is later found in the good health, the correction may take form of entering the *REHIRE* action on the following day. The system is then programmed to recognize such a sequence of events and ignore the *DEATH* record. While this seems illogical, it is a solution I have seen in practice often. In one case an additional state *Pending Death* was introduced into the model. It was recorded every time to indicate pending confirmation of the employee death. The inside joke in the IT department was to code the system to popup a "Call 911 immediately" message window upon *Pending Death* event.

Data profiling as usual comes to the rescue. The technique here is to collect frequencies of all state transitions in actual data. Analysis of their logical validity is then used to build proper state-transition models and implement data quality rules. A ***state-transition profile*** shows how often each state transition occurs. High frequencies indicate valid transition; low frequencies point to possibly erroneous ones.

Table 7-2 shows a portion of the state-transition profile for table E_STATUS_HISTORY from our case study. Included are frequencies of transitions from various states to state *Deceased*. Transitions from state *Active* or *Retiree* to state *Deceased* are clearly valid, while the transition from *Terminated* to *Deceased* is infrequent. While it seems that terminated former employees are as likely to die as the retirees, additional analysis of the business processes shows that such information will never be collected. The state transition is invalid, and observed transition occurrences are erroneous.

From State	To State	Frequency	Percentage
Active	*Deceased*	58	71.60%
Retiree	*Deceased*	21	25.93%
Terminated	*Deceased*	2	2.47%
On Leave	*Deceased*	0	0.00%
Deceased	*Deceased*	0	0.00%
TOTAL		**81**	**100.00%**

Table 7-2: Profile of State Transitions to *Deceased* State

7.3.3. Action Profiling

The last step in building state-transition models is to identify the actions responsible for valid state transitions. This is equivalent to specifying valid actions along all arrows on the state-transition diagram.

Again we will use data profiling to collect frequencies of all actions accompanying each state transition in actual data. Analysis of their logical validity is then used to build a proper state-transition model and implement data quality rules. An ***action profile*** shows how often each action yields a specific state transition. High frequencies indicate valid actions; low frequencies point to possibly erroneous ones.

Tables 7-3 and 7-4 show portions of the action profile for the table E_STATUS_HISTORY from our case study. Table 7-3 lists frequencies of all terminator actions leading to the initial *Active* state. It is clear that *HIRE* action is the only legitimate terminator action here, accounting for over 97% of all cases. The other two actions are either erroneous or are cases of partially missing employment history.

Terminator	Action	Frequency	Percentage
Active	HIRE	12,943	97.25%
Active	REHIRE	335	2.52%
Active	RETLOA	31	0.03%
TOTAL		**13,309**	**100.00%**

Table 7-3: Profile of Terminator Actions Leading to *Active* State

Table 7-4 lists all actions resulting in state transition from *On Leave* to *Terminated*. Two distinct actions are valid here: *RESIGN* and *TERM*. The other two actions (*RETIRE* and *LOA*) are out of place.

Action	Frequency	Percentage
RESIGN	83	76.85%
TERM	21	19.45%
RETIRE	2	1.85%
LOA	2	1.85%
TOTAL	**108**	**100.00%**

Table 7-4: Profile of Actions Leading from *On Leave* State to *Terminated* State

7.3.4. Conclusion

We have discussed various techniques for state-transition model profiling, including state profiling, terminator profiling, state-transition profiling, and action profiling. Using all of the information from these various data profiles, combined with conceptual analysis and information from the business users, allows us to reverse-engineer accurate state-transition models.

State-transition model profiling is generally more complex than regular attribute profiling. While I have not seen tools that specifically address this important area of data profiling, some existing tools can be cajoled into providing necessary information with little maneuvering. The profiling can also be done using some advanced queries and data manipulation techniques.

7.4. RULES DERIVED FROM STATE-TRANSITION DIAGRAMS

Reading state-transition diagrams is easy. An object's life cycle must start from a terminator and can generally follow any path through the arrows. This suggests a broad data quality rule that can be derived directly from the state-transition diagram and applies to a chronological sequence of records describing an object's life cycle:

- Each record must have a valid state and action;

- First record must have a valid terminator with a valid terminator action;

- Any two sequential records must have states connected with a valid arrow, and the action of the later record must be a valid action for that arrow.

The data quality rule defined in this broad form will identify all discrepancies between the model and actual data. It is also relatively easy to implement. We simply need to go through all records in chronological order and validate that they follow a valid life cycle path on the state-transition diagram. However, this generic data quality rule lumps together errors of many different types, making the results more difficult to analyze. An alternative approach is to validate a state-transition model through a series of more atomic data quality rules as described below.

7.4.1. Domain Constraints

Three distinct rules can be designed to check the validity of states, actions, and terminators in accordance with the state-transition model.

A *state domain constraint* limits the set of allowed <u>states</u> to only those shown in the state-transition model. The number of allowed states equals the number of state shapes in the state-transition diagram. Invalid states are usually typos inside otherwise valid records. The true state can often be deduced based on the action value.

An *action domain constraint* limits the set of allowed <u>actions</u> to only those shown in the state-transition model. The actions are shown near the arrows connecting state shapes. Sometimes the same action appears near several arrows. Invalid actions are usually typos inside otherwise valid records. The true action can often be deduced based on the state value.

A ***terminator domain constraint*** limits the set of allowed <u>terminators</u>, specifically states in which an object can start and end its life cycle. The terminator domain value set is always a subset of the state domain. Invalid terminators often are a symptom of missing records at the beginning of the life cycle.

For the employee state-transition model discussed in this chapter, the domain constraints take the following form:

- State domain consists of five values: *Active* (*A*), *Deceased* (*D*), *On Leave* (*L*), *Retired* (*R*), and *Terminated* (*T*).

- Action domain consists of nine values: *DEATH*, *HIRE*, *LAYOFF*, *LOA*, *REHIRE*, *RESIGN*, *RETIRE*, *RETLOA*, *TERM*.

- Only *Active* (*A*) state is allowed as terminator.

Figure 7-4 shows employment history data that violates all three constraints:

- The record marked (1) has invalid state code *S*, likely a typo.

- The record marked (2) has invalid action code *RETHIRE*, also a typo.

- The record marked (3) is the terminator and must have state code *A*, but is *L* instead.

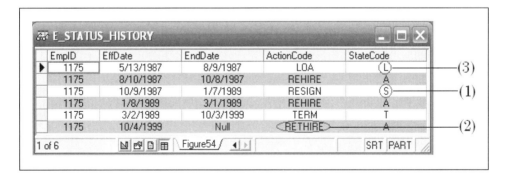

Figure 7-4: Employment History Data Violating Domain Constraints

State and action domain constraints are technically no different from the regular attribute domain constraints discussed in Chapter 4. It is simply a more appropriate place to design, or at least verify, them during the analysis of the state-transition model.

7.4.2. Transition Constraints

Two additional rules can be designed to check the validity of state transitions in accordance with the model.

State-transition constraints limit state changes to those allowed by the state-transition model. For example, a person who is already terminated cannot be terminated again without being rehired in between. The number of allowed state transitions equals the number of arrows connecting the shapes on the state-transition diagram. Invalid state-transitions often signify a missing action in between.

State-transition constraints are often represented by the state-transition matrix, with "from" states listed in rows and "to" states listed in columns. Invalid transitions are marked with "X" at the intersection. Table 7-5 shows a state-transition matrix for our employee state-transition model. The "X" at the intersection of *Active* row and *On Leave* column indicates that transition from state *Active* to state *On Leave* is allowed. On the other hand, transition from state *Active* to itself is not allowed, as is designated by the empty space at the intersection of *Active* row and column.

		To State				
		Active	On Leave	Terminated	Retired	Deceased
From State	Active		X	X	X	X
	On Leave	X		X	X	X
	Terminated	X				
	Retired	X				X
	Deceased					

Table 7-5: State-Transition Matrix For Employee Object

State-action constraints require that each action is consistent with the change in the object state. For instance, when the record with *Active* state is followed by the record with *On Leave* state, the action recorded with the second record must be *LOA*, which is the action listed near the arrow connecting the two states in Figure 7-2.

Figure 7-5 shows an example of employment history data that violate transition constraints:

- The transition marked (1) from state *Terminated* to state *On Leave* is not allowed by the state-transition matrix in Table 7-5 and is therefore invalid.

- The transition marked (2) from state *Active* to state *On Leave* is erroneously accompanied by *RESIGN* action. Only *LOA* action is allowed for this transition.

EmpID	EffDate	EndDate	ActionCode	StateCode
292	2/4/1980	10/20/1995	HIRE	A
292	10/21/1995	5/11/1996	RESIGN	L
292	5/12/1996	2/21/2003	REHIRE	A
292	2/22/2003	11/12/2003	TERM	T
292	11/13/2003	Null	LOA	L

Figure 7-5: Employment History Data Violating Transition Constraints

Let's consider the first error in more detail. We can clearly see that the data is incorrect. But do we know which record is erroneous? The rule itself does not tell us. It is possible that Jeff has never been terminated and in reality simply worked until 11/13/2003 when he went on the leave of absence. In that case, the first record is erroneous. Alternatively, he may have terminated as the data shows and the leave record is entered by mistake. It is also possible that both records are valid, but Jeff was rehired somewhere in between though the data is missing the rehire record.

In Part III of this book, we will deal more with such situations and discuss how to deal with the uncertainly of the errors. However, it is not critical for the project at hand. This is where data quality assessment is fundamentally different from data cleansing. For data quality assessment purposes, it is enough to know that there is an error. Data cleansing requires us to go the extra mile and figure out what is the nature of the error and how it can be fixed. This makes data cleansing much more complex and exciting. I am planning to dedicate one of the volumes of this book series to the topic of data cleansing.

7.5. TIMELINE CONSTRAINTS

Not all data quality rules for state-dependent objects can be derived directly from the state-transition diagram. Some constraints apply to the timeline and duration of the object lifecycle.

7.5.1. Continuity Rules

Continuity rules prohibit gaps and overlaps in state-transition history. In other words, they require that the effective date of each state record must immediately follow the end date of the previous state record. For example, the continuity rule for employment history in our example requires the effective date of each employment record to be exactly one day after the end date of the previous record. Continuity rules for state-dependent objects are similar to general continuity rules for historical data discussed in the previous chapter.

Figure 7-6 shows an example of employment status history that violates the continuity rule:

- The transition marked (1) has a timeline gap – the employee appears to be active from 3/15/1998 through 5/11/2001, but the following termination event has an effective date 6/12/2001 instead of expected 5/12/2001.

- The transition marked (2) has a timeline overlap – the employee appears to be terminated up until 8/21/2003, but the effective date of the following *REHIRE* event is 6/15/2003.

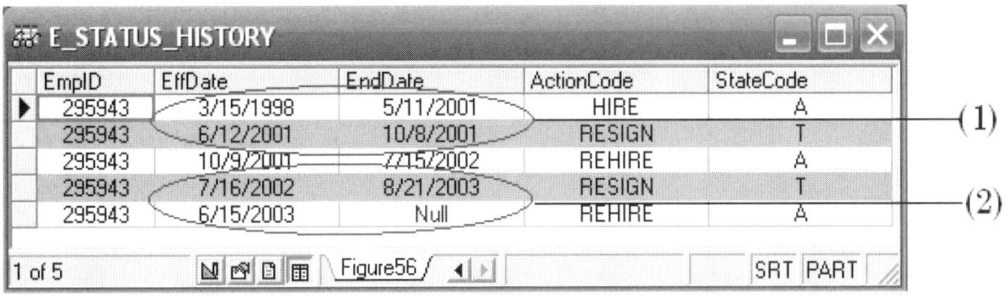

EmplD	EffDate	EndDate	ActionCode	StateCode
295943	3/15/1998	5/11/2001	HIRE	A
295943	6/12/2001	10/8/2001	RESIGN	T
295943	10/9/2001	7/15/2002	REHIRE	A
295943	7/16/2002	8/21/2003	RESIGN	T
295943	6/15/2003	Null	REHIRE	A

Figure 7-6: Employment History Data Violating Continuity Rules

Violation of a continuity rule is always an error. However, it is often not clear what the nature of the error is. For an overlap, one of the two dates is certainly incorrect, though it may not be clear which one – the end date of the previous record or the effective date of the next one. In case of a gap, it is also possible that another record is missing for the gap period.

The exact form of the continuity rule depends on the unit of time used in the lifecycle timeline. The unit of time for many real world objects is a calendar day, but for some state-dependent objects the timeline is more detailed. For example, order procurements can often go through states that only last hours or even minutes. Thus, the appropriate unit of measurement is minutes. The continuity rule will then require the effective date of each order procurement record to be exactly one minute after the end data of the previous record. Further, in particle physics the particle lifetime often is measured in milliseconds or less, and still a particle can go through a sequence of interactions and states. The state-transition history for such a particle will have continuity rules represented in very small time measurement units.

Occasionally, timing of state-transitions is considered immaterial, and only the order of states and actions is tracked. In such cases, the lifecycle is represented as a sequence of events that are simply numbered {1, 2, 3}. The continuity rule then requires the sequence of event numbers to be continuous without gaps. Sequences {1, 2, 3, 5} and {1, 2, 2, 3} will then be erroneous.

7.5.2. Duration Rules

An object can often stay in a particular state for only a limited amount of time. On the other hand, it can be required to stay in certain states for at least a certain minimum amount of time.

Duration rules put a constraint on the maximum and/or minimum length of time an object can stay in any specific state. The simplest form of the duration rule is the ***zero-length rule***, which requires the length of time spent in each state to be positive. In other words, the end date of any state record must be after the effective date. Violations of this rule create time warps common in science fiction and leading to well-known time travel paradoxes.

As a curious student of physics, I read many books about the nature of time. Beginning with Albert Einstein, physicists have been looking for possibilities of traveling back in time. According to modern physics theories, time travel can only be achieved inside the black holes or in other exotic places in the universe. I believe that (as usual) scientists are looking too far. In my experience, time travel is very common and is simply a secret that database administrators keep from physicists in hopes of getting the Nobel Prize.

While zero-length rule is common to all states and objects, some duration rules are more complex and vary by state. For example, the length of a hospital stay after a heart bypass surgery can be no less than a week. Thus, a patient must be in *Hospitalized* state after *BYPASS SURGERY* action for at least seven days (though some insurance companies would disagree). This is an example of a ***minimum duration rule***. Rules like that are very common and easy to implement.

Alternatively, an order shipped via overnight mail must be (hopefully) delivered within two business days, or one if it was shipped before 3pm. Thus, the order must be in state *Shipped* initiated by action *OVERNIGHT SHIPMENT* for no more than two business days. This is an example of a ***maximum duration rule***. Note that here the maximum duration for a state is also a function of the action applied to the object. For different actions, the maximum (or minimum) duration in a given state will vary.

7.5.3. State Duration Profiling

Identifying minimum and maximum duration rules is not simple. These constraints are rarely listed in documentation and must be deduced through analysis of the business processes underlying the state-transition models. Business users can usually help.

A useful profiling technique that helps identify probable duration rules is called *state duration profiling*. It involves obtaining attribute profiles for derived attribute State Duration with a condition on the value of state (and possibly action). The state duration profile can be gathered using standard data profiling tools or simple aggregate queries.

Figure 7-7 shows state duration distribution for *On Leave* state from our case study example. More formally it is the distribution of values of the calculated field {EndDate – EffDate} for all records meeting condition {StateCode = L}. The observed distribution shows a sharp drop-off after 366 days. This is not by chance. According to the business rule, any leave of absence of over one year must be coded as a termination. We can thus derive a maximum duration rule: an employee must not be in state *On Leave* for more than one year.

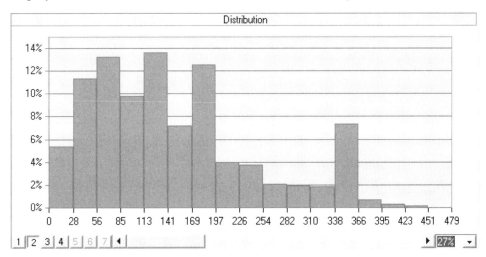

Figure 7-7: State Duration Profile For State *On Leave*

Figure 7-8 shows employment history that violates the duration rules:

- The record marked (1) violates the zero-length duration rule. This often happens when an erroneous action is entered and immediately corrected rather then deleted.

- The record marked (2) has a duration of over three years and violates the maximum duration rule for state *On Leave*.

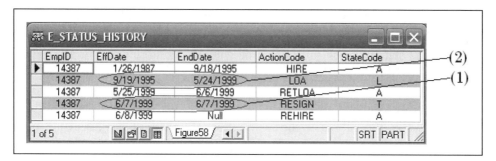

Figure 7-8: Employment History Data Violating Duration Rules

7.5.4. Cumulative Duration Rules

Occasionally, the duration rules will apply to the cumulative amount of time the object can spend in a particular state. When I teach the full-day data quality assessment class at conferences, I am usually required to present for about six hours with several breaks. The same rules apply to all other full-day class instructors. Consider a database tracking the time each instructor spends in class. The instructor is a state-dependent object going through a repeating sequence of states: {*In Class*, *On a Break*, *In Class*, *On a Break*, ...}. The duration rule will state that the cumulative amount of time in state *In Class* must be no less than 5hr 30min and no more than 6hr 30 min. This is an example of a ***cumulative duration rule***. Other duration rules will also apply. For instance, the duration of each individual *In Class* segment can be no more than two hours.

Cumulative duration rules can get rather complicated. A friend of mine, who lives and works in a beautiful European country, told me that according to their federal labor laws a person cannot work for more than 213 days in a given calendar year. In his company, once an employee reaches the magic number, his entry keycard no longer works. While I envy my friend's life, I do not envy the programmers of the keycard entry system who had to incorporate this cumulative duration rule into the software. Let's assume that the HR system tracks the employment history in a typical way – that is as a series of employment events discussed throughout this chapter. The cumulative duration rule then states that the <u>total</u> length of time an employee can spend in *Active* state during <u>each</u> calendar year is no more than 213 <u>business days</u>.

7.6. ADVANCED RULES

Sometimes actions are too complex to be adequately described by a simple action code. Rather, some additional action-specific attributes must be stored. Similarly, for some states more detailed information must be tracked besides just the state code. Finally, actions usually do not occur at random, but rather can only happen under certain unique circumstances. Advanced data quality rules verify these circumstances and validate action-specific and state-specific attributes.

Action-specific and state-specific attribute constraints are present in all but the simplest state-transition models and must be identified in the process of data quality assessment. They typically yield numerous errors.

7.6.1. Action-Specific Attribute Constraints

Action-specific attribute constraints enforce that action-specific attributes are populated consistently with the actions. Consider for example the lifecycle of the state-dependent object Order. When a product is shipped, the package tracking number must be recorded along with the action. The data quality rule for this event will require a valid tracking number to accompany *SHIPPED* action. Further, when a payment is received it might be necessary to store the form of payment (and the amount in case of a partial payment). The data quality rule will enforce that a valid payment code (and payment amount) accompanies *PAYMENT RECEIVED* action.

Sometimes action-specific attributes are stored along with the action in the main state-dependent entity. Since different attributes may apply to different actions, it is possible to have dozens of action-specific attributes in the entity. The data quality rules will then enforce that for each action: all but a few attributes relevant to that action must remain Null, while the relevant attributes must be populated with valid values.

Figure 7-9 shows a possible structure of the state-dependent entity ORDER_STATE along with applicable action-specific attribute constraints. In the entity you find all basic state-transition attributes and, additionally, three action-specific attributes: TrackingNumber, PaymentForm, and PaymentAmount. The appropriate action-specific attribute constraints take the form of conditional attribute optionality rules.

<table>
<tr><td colspan="2">

ORDER_STATE

OrderID
EffDate
EndDate
StateCode
ActionCode
TrackingNumber
PaymentForm
PaymentAmount

</td><td>

Rule 1. Conditional Attribute Optionality

If	ActionCode = 'SHIPPED'
Then	TrackingNumber Is Not Null
Else	TrackingNumber Is Null

Rule 2. Conditional Attribute Optionality

If	ActionCode = 'PAYMENT_RECEIVED'
Then	PaymentForm Is Not Null
And	PaymentAmount Is Not Null
Else	PaymentForm Is Null
And	PaymentAmount Is Null

</td></tr>
</table>

Figure 7-9: Action-Specific Attributes Stored Within State-Dependent Entity

Things get even more cumbersome when the same field is "overloaded" and stores action-specific data for all actions. This approach was very common in "legacy" systems and is still used a lot in practice. Then the data quality rule must verify that the value of the attribute is consistent with the action.

Another method to track action-specific attributes is to create additional dependent entities for different actions. In our example an additional entity ORDER_SHIPPED would be used to track action-specific attributes for *SHIPPED* action, while entity ORDER_PYMT_RCVD would be used to store action-specific attributes for *PAYMENT RECEIVED* action. Both new entities are the sub-types of the main state-dependent entity ORDER. In this case, the action-specific attribute constraint will require that for each action, an appropriate dependent record is created and populated with valid values.

Figure 7-10 shows the data model for this data structure along with the data quality rules that enforce the action-specific attribute constraints. The rules here take the form of standard relational integrity constraints – foreign keys and inheritance rules – and domain optionality constraints.

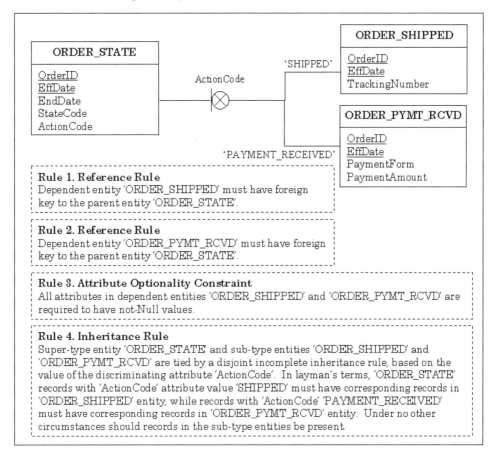

Figure 7-10: Action-Specific Attributes Stored in Additional Entities

7.6.2. State-Specific Attribute Constraints

For many state-dependent objects, it is necessary to track some state-specific data. For example, an active employee can be designated as full-time or part-time and regular or temporary. These attributes are not action-specific since they can change without any state-altering action, i.e. employees can freely change from part-time to full-time and vice versa but still remain in the same state *Active* from the perspective of the state-transition model. At the same time, these attributes are only applicable to objects in certain state(s). An employee can go from part-time to full-time employment while in states *Active* and (possibly) *On Leave*, but not in any other state.

State-specific attribute constraints enforce that state-specific attributes are populated consistently with the states. They fall into two general categories: existence rules and prohibition rules. ***Existence rules*** require that such attributes are populated with some valid values while the objects are in appropriate states. The opposite is enforced by ***prohibition rules***, which require that state-specific attributes are not populated (or at least their values do not change) while the objects are not in the appropriate state. In our example, the rules will take the form:

1. *Attributes FTPTCode and RegTempCode must be populated with valid values while the object is in state Active or On Leave*

2. *Attributes FTPTCode and RegTempCode must <u>not</u> be populated while the object is in any state other than Active or On Leave*

Occasionally the second rule is replaced with a weaker constraint:

2*. *Values of attributes FTPTCode and RegTempCode must <u>not</u> change while the object is in any state other than Active or On Leave*

Typically, state-specific attributes are stored in separate time-dependent entities. In our example, entity EMPLOYEE_TYPE could be created with attributes EmpID, EffDate, EndDate, FTPTCode, and RegTempCode. Rule 1 will then require that the intervals between EffDate and EndDate in the EMPLOYEE_TYPE entity envelop all the periods when the employee is in state *Active* or *On Leave*. Rule 2 requires that the intervals between EffDate and EndDate in the EMPLOYEE_TYPE entity do not overlap at all with the periods when the employee is in any state other than *Active* and *On Leave*. Rule 2* requires that the effective date of any EMPLOYEE_TYPE record does not fall inside the periods when the employee is in any states other than *Active* and *On Leave*.

Figure 7-11 illustrates the rules. The boxes at the bottom show the timeline for employment history of an employee. This particular employee was hired in 1959, resigned in 1981, was rehired in 1992 and finally retired in 1998. Above the boxes are three scenarios for the EMPLOYEE_TYPE data. The first (bottom) scenario meets all data quality rules. The second (middle) scenario violates rule 1 – state-specific data are missing between 1959 and 1974. It also violates rule 2 – the data cover the period between 1981 and 1992 when the person was not employed with the company. However, this scenario does not violate rule 2*. Finally, the third (top) scenario violates rule 2* – the employee changes from part-time to full-time employment, while in *Terminated* state.

Rule violations of this nature are very common for state-dependent objects and more often than not, point to data errors in the state-dependent entity itself. While these rules require rather advanced custom code to implement, they are very important and typically yield a feast of data problems.

Additional complications arise when state-specific attributes are stored within the state-dependent entity, rather than in separate dependent entities. For instance, employee type attributes can be simply added to the main state-dependent entity E_STATUS_HISTORY. The problem is that now attribute changes that are not accompanied by state-transitions must be tracked. Looking at the example in Figure 7-11, we find such an event in 1974 when the employee switched from full-time to part-time employment while remaining in *Active* state. How would this be tracked in the state-dependent entity?

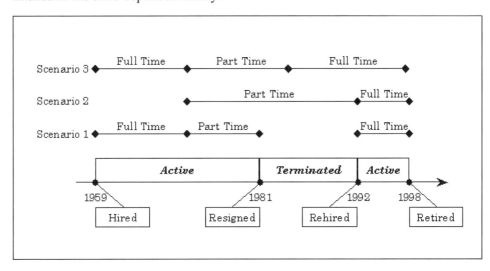

Figure 7-11: Examples of Violations for State-Specific Attribute Constraints

The most common solution in practice is to introduce a non-state-changing action, named something like *DATA*, and use it every time state-specific attributes change values but the state itself does not change. This new action is a legitimate element of the state-transition model – it applies to objects in one or more states (*Active* and *On Leave* in our example) and can be viewed as resulting in state transition from these states to themselves. It can be added to the state-transition diagram and validated through normal domain and transition constraints discussed above in Section 7.4.

The state-specific value constraints in this case are easier to validate. They simply require that state-specific attributes are populated in all state records to which the attributes apply and not in any other records. In our example, the rule demands that attributes FTPTCode and RegTempCode are not Null for all records with StateCode value *Active* (*A*) or *On Leave* (*L*), and are Null in the remaining records. Note that in more general cases, different attributes may be applicable to different states.

Figure 7-12 illustrates this data structure. The employee goes through a normal life cycle of been hired, resigning, been rehired, and retiring. In addition, the employee has several changes in state-specific attributes recorded by *DATA* actions within the periods of active employment.

The data in Figure 7-12 seems to be in accord with the state-specific attribute constraint (and all other data quality rules). Values of attributes FTPTCode and RegTempCode are present in all records with StateCode values *Active* (*A*) and are absent in all records with StateCode values *Terminated* (*T*) and *Retired* (*R*). However, the data is inaccurate. Records marked (2) and (3) are listed with action *DATA* suggesting a change in values of one or more of the state-specific attributes. However, a comparison of values between records (1), (2) and (3) shows no change! This malady is sometimes referred to as "virtual duplicates" – the records carry mostly identical information, but are not exact duplicates. Records (2) and (3) could be removed without any loss of information.

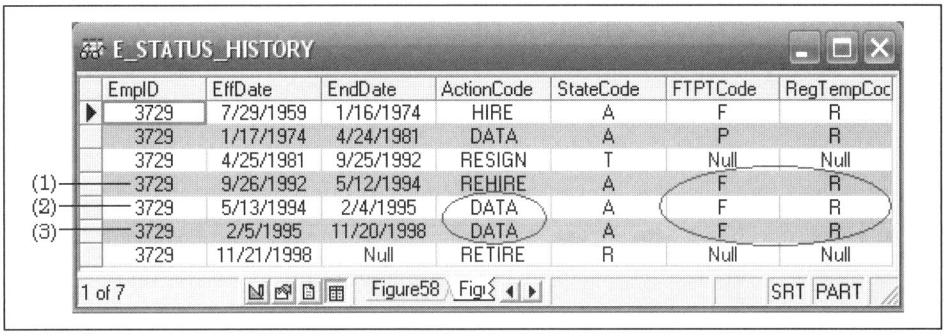

EmpID	EffDate	EndDate	ActionCode	StateCode	FTPTCode	RegTempCoc
3729	7/29/1959	1/16/1974	HIRE	A	F	R
3729	1/17/1974	4/24/1981	DATA	A	P	R
3729	4/25/1981	9/25/1992	RESIGN	T	Null	Null
3729	9/26/1992	5/12/1994	REHIRE	A	F	R
3729	5/13/1994	2/4/1995	DATA	A	F	R
3729	2/5/1995	11/20/1998	DATA	A	F	R
3729	11/21/1998	Null	RETIRE	R	Null	Null

1 of 7   Figure58 Fig   SRT PART

Figure 7-12: Example of "Virtual Duplicates"

"Virtual duplicates" are very common in state-dependent entities containing additional state-specific attributes. While many records serve no purpose, the error is often considered immaterial since it does not impact data use in any way other than performance. The root cause for the problem can be often traced to initial conversion or an interface that creates more records than necessary because the source system tracks data in more detail.

Alternatively, "virtual duplicates" can point to a mistake in a value in one of the state-specific attributes. For instance record marked (2) in Figure 7-10 might be erroneous in that the true value of attribute FTPTCode is *P* rather than listed value *F*. This correction would immediately eliminate both problems – now both records (2) and (3) would carry legitimate changes in a state-specific attribute. For this reason, a "virtual duplicate" should never be ignored in a data quality assessment project.

Occasionally, values of state-specific attributes are permitted to be present even when the object is in one of the states to which the attributes technically do not apply. It is done usually when it is desired to have easy access to the last values of such attributes from the most current record. For instance, it may be desired to be able to know whether a retiree was last full-time or part-time even while looking at his current record with state *Retired*. State-specific attribute rules apply mostly in the same fashion in that case, with one exception: While the attribute values are allowed for all states, the values can only change when the object is in one of the applicable states.

Consider the example in Figure 7-13. The attributes FTPTCode and RegTempCode are allowed to have values for all records. For instance, the most recent record – marked (1) – shows an employee in state *Retired*, but still lists him as a part-time temporary employee. Of course, we know that this person now has better things to do than come to work every morning, but we can also see that he was working part-time even before retiring. It is convenient to have access to this information without having to reference earlier records. The problem is with the record marked (2). It shows that the employee resigned and changed state to *Terminated*. It also lists him as part-time, yet the previous record while the person was still employed lists him as full-time! This cannot be true. State-specific attributes can never change values when the object is in one of the states to which the attributes do not apply. Catching the problems of this nature requires more sophisticated state-specific attribute constraints.

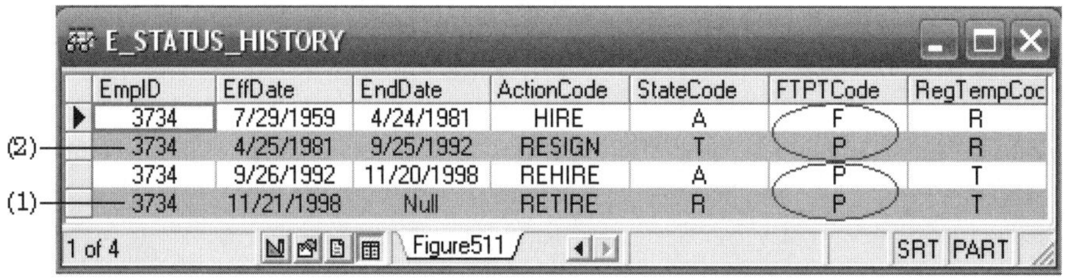

EmplD	EffDate	EndDate	ActionCode	StateCode	FTPTCode	RegTempCoc
3734	7/29/1959	4/24/1981	HIRE	A	F	R
3734	4/25/1981	9/25/1992	RESIGN	T	P	R
3734	9/26/1992	11/20/1998	REHIRE	A	P	T
3734	11/21/1998	Null	RETIRE	R	P	T

Figure 7-13: Example of Invalid Changes in Attribute Values

To summarize the discussion, state-specific and action-specific attribute constraints, while rather simple in concept, can take many different forms when applied to the real data. It is important to recognize that the form of this data quality rule will depend on the way the data for the state-dependent object is organized in the database.

7.6.3. Action Pre-Conditions and Post-Conditions

State-changing actions and events do not occur at random, but rather can only happen under certain unique circumstances. Action pre-conditions and action post-conditions verify these circumstances. They are very similar to the event conditions discussed in the previous chapter.

Action pre-conditions are the conditions that must be satisfied before an action can take place. For example, an employee may not be hired without her job application being previously considered and approved. Thus, a pre-condition for the *HIRE* action in the employment state-transition model is presence of a job application history record for the same person with state *Job Offer Accepted* and effective date shortly before the effective date of the *HIRE* event. Another example of a pre-condition is that a loan is defaulted when a payment is past due by at least 90 days. Thus an action *DEFAULTED* can only be applied to state-dependent object loan when payment history shows payment sufficiently in arrears. In reality the pre-condition in this case can be quite more complicated and involve written legal terms of the loan.

Action post-conditions are the conditions that must be satisfied after the action is successfully completed. For instance, upon retirement the employee must have post-retirement benefits calculated and entered in the appropriate tables of the HR system. Thus, a post-condition for the *RETIRE* event in the employment state-transition model is the presence of an employee benefits record for the same employee with all necessary attributes filled in and effective dated by the retirement date. An example for Loan object would be that a previously defaulted loan can be reinstated into a satisfactory status once all payments, along with interest and penalties, are brought up-to-date.

Action pre-conditions and post-conditions are very common in state-transition models, yet rarely fully understood. In order to identify these constraints, we must analyze the objects from the business perspective and interview business users. On the other hand, these more complex data quality rules will often find many otherwise hidden, but critical, data quality errors.

SUMMARY

State-dependent objects go through a sequence of states in the course of their life cycle as a result of various events. Data for the state-dependent objects is very common in real world databases and is also most error-prone. In this chapter we discussed various types of data quality rules for state-dependent objects, specifically:

- State domain constraints limit the set of allowed <u>states</u> to only those shown in the state-transition model.

- Action domain constraints limit the set of allowed <u>actions</u> to only those shown in the state-transition model.

- Terminator domain constraints limit the set of allowed <u>terminators,</u> that is, states in which an object can start and end its life cycle.

- State-transition constraints limit state changes to those allowed by the state-transition model.

- State-action constraints require that each action is consistent with the change in the object state.

- Continuity rules prohibit gaps and overlaps in state-transition history.

- Duration rules put a constraint on the maximum and/or minimum length of time an object can stay in any specific state.

- Action-specific attribute constraints enforce that action-specific attributes are populated consistently with the actions.

- State-specific attribute constraints enforce that state-specific attributes are populated consistently with the states.

- Action pre-conditions are the conditions that must be satisfied before an action can take place.

- Action post-conditions are the conditions that must be satisfied after the action is successfully completed.

Some of these rules are rather simple, while others can be quite complex and vary significantly depending on the data structure. In all cases, data quality rules for state-dependent objects are key to successful data quality assessment, since data for such objects is typically very important and yet contains numerous "hidden" errors.

CHAPTER 8
ATTRIBUTE DEPENDENCY RULES

It is important to remember that data represent attributes of real world objects, such as people, whose characteristics are interrelated and whose behavior is complex and restricted by logical constraints. These constraints can always be translated into data relationships and used to test the data quality.

In the last two chapters, we presented two specific views of the data for complex real world objects. In Chapter 6 we investigated the time dimension and discussed the data quality rules arising from the dynamic relationships in the data. In Chapter 7 we looked at the lifecycles of state-dependent objects and the rules governing the state-transition data. However, this still leaves numerous miscellaneous attribute dependencies in the data describing real world objects.

Finding such general attribute dependency rules is more difficult yet is key to the success of any data quality assessment project. In this chapter, we discuss various strategies and techniques that help us find success with this challenging task.

- Section 8.1 describes various types of attribute dependencies, including redundant attributes, derived attributes, partially dependent attributes, attributes with dependent optionality, and correlated attributes. Understanding these categories aids tremendously in the search for data quality rules.

- Section 8.2 discusses analytical methods and informal investigative techniques for finding attribute dependencies. Specifically, we address expert knowledge gathering, in-depth data model investigation, and data gazing.

- Section 8-3 presents more formal dependency profiling methods, which use data mining, statistical models, and pattern recognition techniques to discover hidden data relationships.

- Section 8-4 outlines the process of identifying data dependencies across different databases.

8.1. INTRODUCTION TO ATTRIBUTE DEPENDENCY RULES

We say that two attributes are dependent when the value of the first attribute influences possible values of the second attribute. Dependencies between two attributes (sometimes referred to as binary relationships) are the simplest to identify and use. However, often more than two attributes participate in the relationship. In the latter case, values of one of them (called the dependent attribute) are somehow affected by the values of the other attributes. Attribute dependencies generally fall into five broad categories: redundant attributes, derived attributes, partially dependent attributes, attributes with dependent optionality, and correlated attributes.

8.1.1. Redundant Attributes

Redundant attributes are data elements that represent the same attribute of a real world object. While attribute redundancy goes against basic data modeling principles, it is common in practice for several reasons. First, redundancy is widespread in "legacy" databases and certain systems that were converted from the "legacy" databases. Secondly, redundancy is often used even in modern relational databases to improve efficiency of data access, information presentation, and transaction processing. Finally, some data across different systems is invariably redundant.

Redundancy across databases is the most common reason for using redundancy data quality rules. Consider, for example, HR, payroll, and employee benefits administration systems. They all track data about company employees and inevitably have much overlap. At a minimum, all three databases will track employee name, address, and date of birth. Obviously, these data elements are redundant and must have identical values.

While many data integration techniques are put in place to keep the data in different systems consistent, it is a tremendous challenge. Considering that we struggle to keep the data inside a single database coherent, it is no surprise that the data across systems is often out of sync. However, this is a blessing in disguise for data quality initiatives. Comparison of redundant attributes across databases is a sure way to identify (and eventually correct) numerous data problems.

Attribute redundancy is also common within a single database. A common example is a situation where current values of some attributes are stored in a separate entity in addition to being present in the most recent record of a historical data stack.

Figure 8-1 illustrates a more complex situation. Original date of hire for an employee can be found as the effective date of the earliest record in state-dependent entity E_STATUS_HISTORY. Similarly, last termination date can be found as the effective date of the most recent termination event in the same entity. However, querying these data on the fly would be very inefficient. Many HR systems prefer to store these attributes along with other basic employee data in a separate entity (E_EMPLOYEE_INFO in Figure 8-1). This creates attribute redundancy.

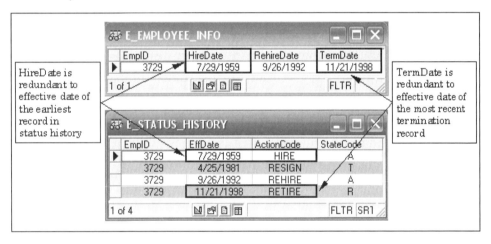

Figure 8-1: Example of Attribute Redundancy

Theoretically, the values of redundant attributes must always coincide. This requirement, when applied to redundant attributes Attribute1 and Attribute2, translates into a simple ***attribute redundancy rule*** expressed in mathematical form as:

$$Attribute1 = Attribute2$$

While redundant attributes are expected to have identical values for all entities, in practice they beg to differ. This happens because it is often extremely difficult to create a failsafe process for the data synchronization (which is, of course, the original reason behind the strong objections of the data-modeling discipline against attribute redundancy).

In many databases, no automatic mechanism exists to synchronize the values, and the task is relegated to the data entry personnel. This approach, of course, guarantees numerous discrepancies in the values of the redundant attributes. Sometimes recurring offline processes are used to synchronize the data, but the technique has a major flaw in that the data remains inconsistent between synchronization events.

The ideal technique is to set up automatic triggers that are tripped any time one of the redundant attributes is changed and fire events to change the other ones. However, even this technique is not failsafe. Triggers are often hard to implement. Consider the example of the employee's original date of hire in Figure 8-1. Capturing situations when HireDate attribute is changed in E_EMPLOYEE_INFO table is easy, but correctly propagating this change to the E_STATUS_HISTORY table is far from trivial. On the other hand, capturing all situations when the effective date of the earliest record in E_STATUS_HISTORY table is changed proves quite complex.

8.1.2. Derived Attributes

Values of *derived attributes* are calculated based on the values of some other attributes. This approach is very common when the calculation is rather complex and involves data stored in multiple records of possibly multiple entities. Performing the calculation on the fly is then very inefficient.

Consider, for instance, golf handicap index. It is a very important attribute for any golfer as it determines handicap that one player has over another in a competition to compensate for the possibly significant difference in skills. For instance, a player with handicap 10 must score at least five shots less than a player with handicap 15 to win. Without handicap the better player would virtually always win, making competing meaningless.

To make it fairly reflect players' skills, handicap formula has to be rather complex. It must account for play under different conditions on golf courses of varying difficulty. The actual formula is a weighted average of the best 10 out of the last 20 scores, with weights representing golf course difficulty. Calculating my golf handicap index would require accessing and processing many records, including the history of my scores and linked information about the difficulty of the golf courses I have played. In practice, doing it on the fly is highly inefficient. Instead the central database for all members of the Chicago District Golf Association stores pre-calculated values of handicap index. The index is recalculated for all members every two weeks and stored in a handicap history table. It is an example of a derived attribute.

While the golf handicap may not seem to be a mission critical example (unless you have just lost $20 on a round of golf to someone with an incorrect handicap), derived attributes permeate most databases. Business examples would be length of employment used for employee benefits eligibility and unused insurance deductible.

Obviously the values of derived attributes must be in sync with the attributes used in the calculation. This translates into a **derived attribute constraint** expressed in mathematical form as:

$$Attribute1 = Func\ (Attribute2,\ Attribute3,\ ...,\ AttributeN)$$

In this formula, Attribute1 is the derived attribute, while Attribute2 and others are used to calculate its value using routine designated as *Func*.

One of the most common special cases of derived attribute constraints is a **balancing rule**, which requires an aggregate attribute to equal the total of atomic level attribute values. For instance, annual compensation stored in W2_WAGE entity is aggregated for each employee and calendar year. On the other hand, entity E_PAYCHECK stores details of each paycheck for each employee by pay period and compensation type. Obviously, annual compensation is a derived attribute and must equal the sum of individual payments for that calendar year (and applicable pay types). This constraint is implemented by a balancing rule.

Derived attribute constraints often find numerous errors. The reasons are largely the same as those for the discrepancies in redundant attributes – it is very hard to create a failsafe yet practical mechanism to keep the data in sync. With derived data it is even more complex. The derived attribute is typically a function of many other attributes, so it is impractical to set up triggers on changes for all of them. Instead the calculation is usually either explicitly requested by users or performed systematically for all the data. In the former case, a recalculation may have been forgotten. In the latter case, some records may be missed due to a program bug. In both cases retroactive changes often throw the data of balance.

8.1.3. Partially Dependent Attributes

The values of redundant and derived attributes are prescribed exactly by the dependency. Oftentimes, the relationships between attributes are not so exact. The value of one attribute may restrict possible values of another attribute to a smaller subset, but not to a single value. We call such attributes *partially dependent*.

Consider the relationship between attributes HireDate and TerminationDate containing the original date of hire and the latest termination date (if any) for each employee. Clearly a person must be hired first and terminated later. This translates into a simple attribute dependency rule:

$$TerminationDate > HireDate$$

This relationship is bi-directional, i.e. both attributes affect one another. Without changing its meaning, we could rewrite the rule as:

$$TerminationDate - HireDate > 0$$

This form better reflects the fact that both attributes play equal roles in the constraint.

Sometimes the attributes participating in a relationship have a discrete set of values. For example, job titles of an employee and his or her boss are somewhat related. If I were a junior programmer, my supervisor would be likely to hold a title of senior software developer or project manager, but not that of sales coordinator or loan officer. This constraint would be implemented through a matrix with valid title combinations. Now, we could take the subordination table, which lists reporting relationships between company employees, look up title for each employee in the position table, and verify the value combination against the valid value matrix.

Regardless of the type of the attribute, the common theme here is that the rule restricts possible value combinations of two or more attributes to a subset of all values, but not down to a one-to-one relationship. Any database is full of attribute relationships, and it is simply a matter of patience and analysis to identify many of them. This work always pays off, as the data quality rules for partial attribute dependencies will find large pockets of errors.

8.1.4. Attributes with Conditional Optionality

Conditional optionality represents situations where values of one attribute determine whether or not the other attribute must take Null or not-Null value (that is to be prevented or required). Attributes with conditional optionality technically are a special case of partially dependent attributes discussed above. However, they deserve separate consideration due to their highly frequent occurrence in practice.

Consider attribute EmployeeType, which indicates whether or not an employee is working a full-time or part-time schedule. In the former case, attribute AnnualSalaryRate would be required, while ScheduledHours and HourlyPayRate would be prevented. In the latter case AnnualSalaryRate would have to be Null, while ScheduledHours and HourlyPayRate would take not-Null values.

A rather trivial special case of conditional optionality is the situation where two attributes are *mutually exclusive* (also called disjoint attributes), i.e. the mere presence of a value of one attribute precludes another attribute from taking a not-Null value and vice versa. This situation occurs mostly with event-specific and state-specific attributes, e.g. LastDayWorked and NextSalaryReviewDate. Since a person is either terminated or employed, only one of these attributes can be populated. Note that this example does not preclude values of both attributes to be absent at the same time. The situations where one or the other attribute must always be present are also common.

An opposite situation is when two attributes can either be both present or absent. For instance, LastDayWorked and TerminationDate are such attributes (sometimes referred to as conjoint attributes). For an active employee both must be Null, but upon termination both will take not-Null values. The dependency between these two attributes is mutual, i.e. values of both are either present or absent. Sometimes the dependency can have a direction. For instance, terminated employees will often continue to get severance payments for a while. Thus, attribute LastDayPaid may not have a value for some time after LastDayWorked is populated. However, the opposite is not true – any employee with a value of LastDayPaid must have a value in LastDayWorked.

8.1.5. Correlated Attributes

So far we have discussed situations where values of some attributes somehow restrict allowed values of other attributes. Occasionally the relationships can be subtler. Values of one attribute can change the likelihood of values of another one, though not firmly restricting any possibilities. We call such attributes *correlated*.

My golf score and my placement in the local club tournament are correlated – the better the score the higher the position. However, they are not truly dependent. With any given score I could theoretically place anywhere from first to last place. Let's say I posted an otherwise average handicap adjusted score of 72. It could be that the weather conditions were horrible, everybody shot poorly, and my score was by far the best. Alternatively, it is conceivable that the field in the tournament was small and everyone played extremely well on a nice sunny day, so that my score was dead last. Both scenarios are possible, but highly unlikely. That score most likely would land me in the middle of the pack.

More generally we can say that knowledge of the score influences our expectations for tournament placement and vice versa. This can be used to implement a data quality rule. We could build a chart of likely value pairs {score; placement} and treat the other value pairs as potentially erroneous. Of course, the rule is inexact and will yield some false positives, but it will also catch many errors.

An example from everyday business databases is the correlation between gender and first name. The majority of names are distinctly male or female. Thus there is a definite relationship between these attributes; however, it is not exact in nature.

Finding a female named Fred or male named Rachel is unexpected but not impossible. And in some cases the names are truly common to both genders, as in cases of Terry and Lee. Still the relationship can (and should) be used in a data quality rule. Unlikely pairs of values should be flagged as potentially erroneous.

I recently reviewed the results of a project where a database with nearly a million records was analyzed. In it were found almost 45,000 distinct first names. Of them over 2,600 were listed for both men and women. When unexpected name/gender pairs were identified by the data quality rule, some 20,000+ records were found. Of them, absolute majority (over 95%) proved to be erroneous.

8.2. IDENTIFYING DEPENDENCIES THROUGH ANALYSIS

Most of the data quality rules can be identified through rather formal procedures. Attribute domain constraints can be found in data dictionaries and through systematic attribute profiling. Relational integrity constraints are deduced from data models. Timeline constraints for historical data and various rules for event histories can be identified systematically. Rules for state-dependent objects can be inferred from state-transition models.

Still, as the rules get progressively more complex, the search for them becomes more of an art than a science. At the level of event conditions or value patterns for historical data, it takes a creative and inquisitive mind to find the rules. General attribute dependencies presented in this chapter fall in the same category. Yet, these more complex business rules are very important as they often find numerous less obvious data errors.

While there is no exact recipe to discover complex attribute dependencies, a few analytical techniques can be used. In this section, we will discuss informal investigative techniques. The next section is devoted to more formal profiling methods.

8.2.1. Gathering Expert Knowledge

Nobody knows the data better than the users. Unknown to the big bosses, the people in the trenches are measuring data quality every day. And while they rarely can give a comprehensive picture, each one of them has encountered certain data problems and developed standard routines to look for them.

Talking to the users never fails to yield otherwise unknown data quality rules with many data errors. And it is really simple. The only trick is not to ask the users about data quality rules. They often will not be able to offer any. The right questions to ask are:

"What data do you usually check manually before using?"

"What are some typical data problems you encounter?"

A useful technique is to ask business users to track all data quality findings during a week or two and make notes on all identified errors. Often it is simply useful to sit next to those data experts and watch them while they work.

8.2.2. Investigating Data Relationships

Review and analysis of the data model and other meta data are the keys to finding complex data quality rules. Redundant attributes can be usually identified through meta data review. Derived attributes can be identified by reading documentation and analyzing the meaning of each entity and attribute.

More complex attribute dependencies can be uncovered with a thorough investigation. The secret is to systematically consider each data element and inquire:

"If I knew the value of this attribute, what could I say about other data?"

Anytime value of one data element restricts acceptable values of another data element, we have an opportunity to design a data quality rule.

For instance, a data dictionary might say that attribute LastDayPaid is populated with the date of the last paycheck for terminated employees. We can find several useful facts in that statement:

- All employees with not-Null value of LastDayPaid are terminated. Thus, their current employment status found in attribute CurEmpStatus must be *Terminated* (*T*). The opposite would also be true.

- LastDayPaid is the date of the last paycheck, which is also found in attribute EffDate of the most recent record of entity E_PAYCHECK.

We can now implement three attribute dependency rules:

If LastDayPaid Is Null Then CurEmpStatus = 'T'

If LastDayPaid Is Not Null Then CurEmpStatus <> 'T'

LastDayPaid = Max([E_PAYCHECK].[EffDate]) or Null

Now, consider a more advanced example. Entity E_POSITION in the HR database of Bad Data Corporation contains a history of positions that each employee occupied in the company. Let's say there is a record in it indicating that Arkady Maydanchik has been an Assistant Manager since 1/1/2006. What can we deduce from that?

- First, that means that I was actively employed in 2006. Thus, employment status history table must show me in *Active* status during that period.

- The salary history table must show my salary through that period, too. Further, my salary should be consistent with the salary range for the Assistant Manager position.

- We can also conclude that an Assistant Manager position must exist in my department and be occupied by none other than me. This can be crosschecked against the department position table.

- Finally, I must have a manager and one or several subordinates. This can be verified against a table containing data on the reporting relationships.

It is often convenient to represent such logic in the form of a fact tree.

Figure 8-2 illustrates the fact tree for the last example. It can be used to design numerous attribute dependency rules.

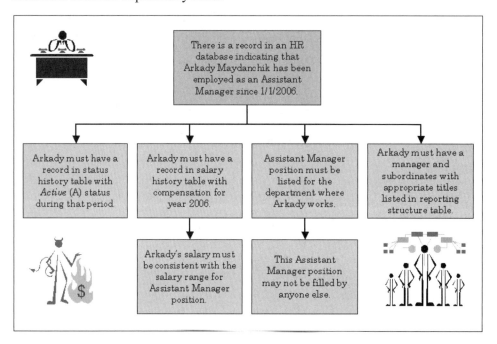

Figure 8-2: Fact Tree Example

8.2.3. Data Gazing

I know many people who enjoy staying out late on a beautiful night, stargazing and wondering in awe what strange and unimaginable things happen in the Universe. I often get the same emotion while browsing various databases, which is why I call it data gazing.

Data gazing is simply a process of looking at the data and trying to reconstruct the story behind these data. Following the real story helps identify parameters about what might or might not have happened. Once you find that the story behind certain data elements contradicts common sense, you can usually come up with data quality rules to catch the disobedient data.

I remember sitting with a client a few years ago in front of a computer and discussing the data quality of their HR database. As we talked, I was browsing through the data for various employees. One record caught my attention so much that I could not hold my excitement. "Wow!" – I said – "What an employee you have here! Her name is Maria. For 11 years Maria worked for your Philadelphia office until she moved to California. Knowing that you do not have an office on the West Coast and do not practice telecommuting, I can only imagine how difficult it was for Maria to come to work every morning after a four-hour flight. But she persevered. Not just that, but since your company was apparently in trouble, Maria worked the next two years without getting paid. Eventually I guess the stress from the travel wore her out and she resigned. But your company must have felt a great obligation to such a loyal employee, and so since then and till this day you keep Maria on the payroll. This is quite unique!" My colleagues looked at me in shock before bursting in laughter about the funny anecdote. But I did not make up the story. I just read it from the data, literally word-by-word.

The point is that data represent characteristics of real world objects, such as people, whose behavior is complex and restricted by logical constraints. And so, as my story made no sense, the underlying data was contemptuously wrong. It is just more difficult for our human mind to find the inconsistency in the data, compared to the inconsistencies in real world stories. But with some effort, it can be done.

Data gazing is also a useful means to find patterns in known data errors. These patterns can be used to devise an appropriate data quality rule. Here is a practical example. A few years ago I was involved in a payroll data quality assessment project. Looking at historical pay rate data, we kept finding strange records. Some were duplicates; others had clearly too high or too low amounts. Still others looked valid but proved incorrect when reviewed by payroll specialists or compared to paper records. We just could not put our fingers on the pulse and figure out what data quality rule(s) would help us identify all of these problems.

In the process of data gazing, we discovered that many of these strange pay rate records had a value of *5* in the field with a mysterious name ATI1. Most of the normal records had a value of *1* in this field. Interestingly, data users never used this field and most were not aware of its existence. In fact, this field was not even listed in the data dictionary! Such ghosts always pique my natural curiosity.

Additional research led me to a former company contractor who gamely remembered that ATI1, ATI2, and ATI3 fields were added to certain tables some six years ago in an attempt to implement an audit trailing mechanism. In fact, ATI1 was an acronym for AuditTrailInformation1, and value 5 in it stood for "deleted to correct a data entry mistake." That project was cancelled and extra audit trailing records and fields were cleared but apparently not without a trace. The remaining strange records were artifacts of that failed project. Now we were able to design a trivial data quality rule to identify several thousands of bad records. This would have been virtually impossible without data gazing.

8.3. IDENTIFYING DEPENDENCIES THROUGH DATA PROFILING

Dependency profiling uses computer programs to look for hidden relationships between attribute values. Some of the methods are relatively simple, while others use complex statistical models and pattern recognition techniques.

For modern databases, the return on investment from using more sophisticated pattern recognition techniques to identify data quality rules often quickly diminishes. On the other hand, for "legacy" databases with unknown schemas sophisticated dependency profiling is often the best way to identify data quality rules.

Dependency profiling is a very complex topic, and its complete analysis could fill an entire book. However, in practice advanced methods are very difficult to implement from scratch. For that reason, we will only discuss techniques that can be implemented without sophisticated software tools.

8.3.1. Value Affinity

We use the term *value affinity* to describe the pattern that occurs when certain combinations of values among two or more attributes are observed very often. The easiest way to identify value affinity patterns is by building a *value affinity matrix*. Each row in the matrix corresponds to the values of one attribute, and each column corresponds to the values of the other attribute. Each cell then shows the number of records with the appropriate combination of values.

Consider attributes PayPeriod and PayCycle in E_PAY_RATE_HISTORY entity of the payroll database. The first attribute describes employee pay rate and takes two values: *A* ("annual") for salaried employees and *W* ("weekly") for temporary and occasional employees. The second attribute specifies how frequently each employee gets paychecks. The domain of the second attribute includes four values: *W* ("weekly"), *B* ("bi-weekly"), *S* ("semi-monthly"), and *M* ("monthly"). Table 8-1 shows a value affinity matrix for these two attributes.

		PayPeriod		
		A	*W*	TOTAL
PayCycle	*W*	2,375	89,536	91,911
	B	2,777	1,510	4,287
	S	16,693	4*	16,697
	M	12,208	131**	12,339
	Null	4,249	1,187	5,436
	TOTAL	38,302	92,368	130,670

Table 8-1: Value Affinity Matrix for Attributes PayPeriod and PayCycle

Some value affinity patterns can be immediately observed. For example, 16,693 out of 16,697 records with PayCycle value *S* also have PayPeriod value *A*. That is, almost 99.98% of all employees paid semi-monthly have annual pay rate. This is suggestive of an actual attribute dependency. Further analysis of the business process would confirm the theory and yield this data quality rule:

If PayCycle = 'S' Then PayPeriod = 'A'

The four records (cell marked by *) with PayCycle value *S* and PayPeriod value *W* are erroneous.

Here is another pattern – almost 99% of all records with PayCycle value *M* also have PayPeriod value *A*. This is another true attribute dependency – only salaried employees with annual pay rates are paid monthly. We can add another data quality rule:

If PayCycle = 'M' Then PayPeriod = 'A'

The 131 records (cell marked by **) with PayCycle value *M* and PayPeriod value *W* are erroneous.

Not all value affinity patterns translate into data quality rules. For instance, 89,536 out of 91,911 records with PayCycle value *W* also have value *W* in PayPeriod. This is over 97% and suggests a value dependency. However, further analysis would indicate that both salaried and temporary employees can receive weekly paychecks. While it is far more common for temporary employees (those with PayPeriod value *W*), the records for salaried employees (those with PayPeriod value *A*) are totally legitimate.

The last examples shows that value affinity patterns cannot be translated into data quality rules without some investigation. Sometimes patterns are simply accidental. However, in many cases such patterns uncover true attribute dependencies and help design important data quality rules. In our example, the two data quality rules would identify 135 otherwise hidden errors (cells marked by asterisks in Table 8-1).

For many attributes it is not the values but rather their mere presence or absence that shows affinity. Conjoint attributes are either both present or absent at the same time. Disjoint, or mutually exclusive, attributes come one at a time, i.e. when values of one attribute are predominantly absent when values of another one are present.

This form of value affinity is easy to identify by looking at a simplified value affinity matrix. Here only Null and not-Null values are considered, and the matrix has only four cells, one for each value combination. Table 8-2 shows such a matrix for values of attributes NextSalaryReviewDate (rows) and LastDayWorked (columns).

		LastDayWorked		
		Not Null	*Null*	TOTAL
NextSalaryReviewDate	*Not Null*	13	10,104*	10,117
	Null	581**	2	583
	TOTAL	594	10,106	10,700

Table 8-2: Example of Value Affinity Matrix

We can see from the matrix that 10,117 records have a not-Null value of NextSalaryReviewDate. Some 10,104 of them contain Null in LastDayWorked (cell marked by *). This is a whopping 99.87%. Similarly, out of 594 records with not-Null values of LastDayWorked, 581 (or 97.81%) have Null in NextSalaryReviewDate (cell marked by **). These attributes are clearly mutually exclusive.

You can also combine the two affinity concepts and build a matrix that lists values of one attribute in rows and only Null/not-Null in the columns. This technique helps identify conditional optionality constraints.

With a large number of attributes, it may be impractical to perform all the analysis. Indeed for just 20 attributes the number of attribute pairs is 380. Even if each attribute can take only five values, we have potentially 9,500 value combinations to review, hardly a reasonable task. This is where attribute dependency profiling tools must come in. However, even in absence of such a tool you can write a rather simple program that will produce value affinity matrixes for various attribute pairs and identify cases with a high value affinity (say over 95%). Then you can go through a systematic review of this subset of potential attribute dependencies.

Of course, value affinity matrixes only help you find dependencies between values of two attributes. Sometimes the relationships involve more than two attributes. Finding value affinity for attribute triplets or groups of higher order is practically impossible without a "smart" pattern recognition tool. The good news is that complex relationships involving many attributes usually have serious business reasons. So these relationships are easier to find through analysis and investigation, discussed in the previous chapter, rather than through data profiling.

8.3.2. Value Correlation

A search for value affinity is the main dependency profiling technique for identifying conditional optionality constraints and for finding dependencies between attributes with discrete sets of values. Finding dependencies between numeric attributes is usually much more difficult.

One relatively easy technique it to search for highly correlated attributes. Attributes are correlated when their values move in unison. In general, the relationship can be quite complex, but typical attribute relationships are linear. This means that increase in values of one attribute is accompanied by a proportional increase (or decrease) in values of another attribute. We call the relationship linear because when depicted on a two-dimensional plot, values of such attributes tend to stay near a straight line.

To identify attributes with a linear relationship, we can use simple statistical correlation coefficient. Table 8-3 shows a correlation matrix for four attributes in entity E_EMPLOYEE_INFO. Values close to 1.00 or −1.00 indicate a strong attribute dependency. Values near 0 suggest a complete lack of linear dependency.

	HireDate	TerminationDate	LastDayWorked	PayRate
HireDate	1.00	0.41	0.47	− 0.01
TerminationDate	0.41	1.00	0.99*	− 0.02
LastDayWorked	0.47	0.99*	1.00	− 0.02
PayRate	− 0.01	− 0.02	− 0.02	1.00

Table 8-3: Correlation Matrix for Several Attributes

It is immediately clear from Table 8-3, that attribute PayRate is completely uncorrelated with the other attributes (as expected). The correlation between attribute HireDate and the other two attributes is less than 0.5 – noticeable but not significant. However, the correlation between attributes TerminationDate and LastDayWorked (marked by *) is 0.99, meaning that these two attributes are strongly dependent. Further analysis would show that one precedes the other by one day in the majority of cases, suggesting the data quality rule:

$$TerminationDate = LastDayWorked + 1\ day$$

Of course, this relationship is rather obvious and could be deduced theoretically. However, it is often difficult to remember all possible relationships in a large database with hundreds of attributes. Correlation profiling helps to make sure that no rules are forgotten.

In theory, attribute dependencies can get quite complex and so do the pattern recognition methods for their finding. However, since these techniques are outside of practical capabilities in mos1t projects, we will not discuss them in this book.

8.3.3. Value Clustering

Value clustering occurs when the distribution of attribute values falls into two or more clusters depending on the values of another attribute. It usually indicates partially dependent attributes and can be translated into conditional domain constraints. Value clustering is very common when a single data field is used to store different logical attributes, such as weekly and annual pay rates.

Consider the distribution of values of attribute PayRate shown in Figure 8-3. It clearly has two distinct clusters – one with rather small values and the other with values between $14,000 and $84,000.

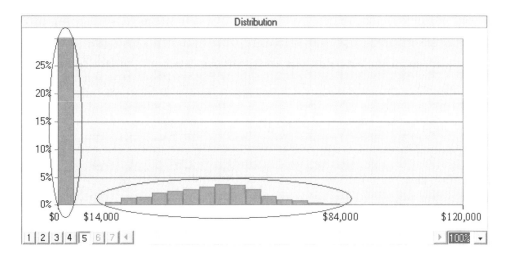

Figure 8-3: Value Clustering for PayRate Attribute

Whenever you observe such value clustering, further analysis is warranted. The objective is to identify a discriminating variable, that is, an attribute or collection of attributes whose values drive clustering for each record. Some sophisticated pattern recognition techniques can be utilized, but often a simple investigation will provide the answer. In case of the example from Figure 8-3, it was rather easy to identify that attribute PayPeriod made a perfect discriminating variable: code *A* ("annual") correlated with high PayRate amount, while code *W* ("weekly") correlated with low amounts.

As with other dependency profiling techniques, value clustering can be expanded to search for complex clusters of values in a multi-dimensional attribute space. Again, these techniques are outside of the practical capabilities in most projects, and we will not address them in this book.

8.4. IDENTIFYING DEPENDENCIES ACROSS DATA SOURCES

The explosion of software development in the last two decades forever changed the structure and complexity of the information universe. Organizations, large and small, routinely have hundreds of systems and thousands of smaller databases, files, and spreadsheets storing incomprehensible volumes of data.

It is important to recognize that the data for the same real world object such as company employee, customer, or product – is often stored in several systems. Since most characteristics and behaviors of a complex object are somewhat interrelated, so are the data elements across various databases. In fact, some of the data may even be totally redundant. While database designers growl about the inefficiencies and costs of data redundancy (and make no mistake, they are right!), I must point out that the redundancy across various databases is a gold mine for data quality initiatives.

Designing data quality rules that span across multiple data sources is quite a difficult task and should not be undertaken without forethought. While such data quality rules are invaluable in data cleansing and data consolidation, their usefulness is more marginal in pure data quality assessment. For that reason, we will discuss it only briefly in this chapter. I am planning to include detailed treatment of the topic in the "Data Conversion and Consolidation" volume of this book series.

For clarity we will refer to the databases whose data quality we measure as *primary data sources*. In a simple project, e.g. data quality assessment of a payroll database, we have only one primary data source. When the initiative is enterprise-wide, say data quality assessment of all employee data in the organization, then all databases with some data-of-record are primary data sources. All other databases containing potentially related data are referred to as *secondary data sources*.

8.4.1. Step 1 – Identifying Secondary Data Sources

The first step towards designing cross-database data quality rules is to identify relevant secondary data sources. This is not always trivial. Many useful databases may not be readily known to all but their immediate users. It takes several interviews with various business users and IT staff to identify all possibilities. The following is a list of potential categories:

- Corporate operational systems manage day-to-day business transactions and contain atomic level operational data-of-record. These are arguably the most trusted sources of information used by business.

- Old legacy systems are inherited from past generations of software design and often kept alive mostly due to the high replacement costs. Legacy systems are ugly behemoths that often lack documentation and use mind-boggling data structures. Ironically though, legacy systems have one big advantage over modern applications – they are not well suited for data editing and purging and thus typically contain a wealth of historical data.

- "Ad-hoc" databases are systems and documents created by business users for their internal purposes. They are a hidden treasure for data quality projects since they almost always contain highly reliable data. Why? Simply because people who create them are at the same time their users and so are likely to be very diligent, motivated, and detail-oriented.

- Backups are point-in-time images of the database. They are frequently created as a part of disaster recovery programs or due to the IT fiduciary policies. Frozen databases are old systems that have been shutdown and are no longer updated or even maintained. Backups and frozen databases are usually stored much longer than one would anticipate, often hidden in the far corners of corporate tape libraries. They often contain a wealth of the data not found anywhere else.

- External databases from various vendors are managed outside of the business and often have much information overlap with internal databases.

- Hard copies are data stored in a non-electronic format. They include paper forms, images, and microfiche. While these data cannot be directly used in data quality assessment, it is often rather easy and inexpensive to key the data into an electronic format and then use it in a data quality initiative.

8.4.2. Step 2 – Qualifying Secondary Data Sources

A large organization may have hundreds of possible candidate databases, and it would be impractical and imprudent to use all of them. The next step is to qualify selected candidate data sources and choose which ones to use. This is based on their utility to our initiative. First and foremost, we need secondary data sources with redundant data to our primary data source. For instance, if the primary data source is an HR database, we need more data about the company employees. If the primary data source is the customer data warehouse, then we need more data about the company customers.

Data redundancy, though, does not guarantee high utility for the data quality assessment project. Ideally we want redundant data that was collected independently. They have the highest utility. Databases that feed data to the primary data source (i.e. upstream data sources) have reasonably high utility. They are used to identify data errors that were introduced in the primary data source by bugs in the incoming data feeds. Finally, databases that are fed from the primary data source (i.e. downstream data sources) are mostly useless.

8.4.3. Step 3 – Subject Matching

Subjects are the high-level business objects whose data are stored in the database. For example, employees and positions are among the subjects of common HR databases. In order to compare the data across data sources, we need to be able to match subjects in them.

To match subjects we first need to identify the main subject table in each data source. We then compare primary keys of these tables. If the primary keys coincide, then direct one-to-one matching by key is possible. For example, if different systems identify employees by Social Security Number, employee matching is rather trivial.

When primary keys of the main subject tables differ, matching must use common attributes. For instance, people can be matched using a combination of name and birth date. The result may not always be a one-to-one correspondence. For instance, the same person may be listed with several values of PayrollIdentifier in a payroll system if that person worked at several divisions.

Subject matching gets complex when matching attributes are in a free-flow text format. For instance, matching people by name is more difficult than by social security number. Various fuzzy matching techniques can be used, and numerous tools exist on the market to do the job.

If the subjects in question are identified differently on different systems, we need to create a *subject master list*. This list inventories all subjects from all different systems and gives each subject a unique master identifier. Then various lookup tables are populated matching subject keys used by various systems to the identifier in the master list.

Many databases store data about subjects of various types (often referred to as subject classes). For instance, shipping database can track orders, customers, and products; an HR database will have data for employees, positions, and beneficiaries. Subject master lists must be created for all subject types.

8.4.4. Step 4 – Identifying Related Entities and Attributes

Once the data across data sources is matched, you can use all techniques discussed previously in this chapter to identify attribute dependencies. You can start by comparing the data models. In theory an integrated data model can be built that incorporates entities from all data sources and indicates which of them are redundant. In practice a simple review of the entities is enough to discover the relationships in a more informal way. Data gazing is very helpful if you can look at the data for the same subject side by side, or if you can bring all the data into a common staging area. Dependency profiling techniques discussed in Section 8.3 are extremely useful.

One point to keep in mind is that attribute dependencies are only useful when the data in different systems has significant overlap in subjects and time periods. Consider payroll systems for two divisions of the company. Both have data for company employees. However, if the number of transfers between the divisions is small, we are dealing with data for two largely non-overlapping groups of employees, and no data quality rules can be implemented. Similarly, if the two databases have data for the same employees but cover different years, no data validation can be performed.

The extent of actual data overlap between data sources is found through a process of *subject profiling*. The objective of subject profiling is to identify which data is available for which subjects. It starts with building the master list of all subjects from all data sources. Then flags are added to the master list – one for each entity in each data source. These flags are set to *True* for all subjects with data in the corresponding entity. For example, flag SystemA_Address will have value *True* for all employees who have an address stored in System A. These flags can now be queried in order to find subject overlaps between any pairs of entities. The entities from various data sources that contain logically dependent attributes and have significant subject overlaps can be used to design powerful data quality rules.

SUMMARY

We say that two attributes are dependent when the value of the first attribute influences possible values of the second attribute. Attribute dependencies generally fall into five broad categories.

Historical data comprise the majority of data in both operational systems and data warehouses. They are also most error-prone. In this chapter we discussed various types of data quality rules for historical data, specifically:

- Redundant attributes are data elements representing the same attribute of a real world object. Theoretically the values of redundant attributes must always coincide. This requirement translates into a simple attribute redundancy rule.

- Values of derived attributes are calculated based on the values of some other attributes. Obviously the values of derived attributes must be in sync with the attributes used in the calculation. One of the most common cases of derived attribute constraints is a balancing rule, which requires an aggregate attribute to equal the total of atomic level attribute values.

- Often the value of one attribute will restrict possible values of another attribute to a smaller subset, but not to a single value. We call such attributes partially dependent. A very common special case of partially dependent attributes is conditional optionality. It represents a situation where values of one attribute determine whether or not the other attribute must take a Null or not-Null value.

- Occasionally values of one attribute can change the likelihood of values of another one, though not firmly restricting any possibilities. We call such attributes correlated. Knowledge of attribute correlation patterns helps identify unlikely value combinations and implement data quality rules.

There is no exact recipe to discover complex attribute dependencies. However, many analytical techniques can be used, including gathering expert knowledge, in-depth investigation of data relationships, and data gazing. Also, formal dependency profiling methods use data mining, statistical models, and pattern recognition techniques to discover hidden data relationships.

PART III – DATA QUALITY ASSESSMENT

The reader might remember an example we discussed in the introduction to Part II – a baseball umpire who does not fully understand the rules is a disaster in the making. However, the reader will certainly agree that it takes more than just knowing the rules to be a good umpire. One needs to also appreciate the nature of various individual plays, roles of different players, and many other aspects of the game. Similarly, the data quality assessment process involves more than just design of the data quality rules. In the following four chapters, we will discuss all aspects of this process.

In Chapter 9 we talk about the design, cataloguing, and coding of the data quality rules. We outline the structure of the rule catalogue and discuss the architecture of the rule engine.

Chapter 10 is devoted to rule fine-tuning – the process of identifying and eliminating rule imperfections. This step is very important because without fine-tuning, data quality rules tend to suffer from the same malady as the data itself – poor quality.

Chapter 11 presents the architecture of the error catalogue. It is a collection of tables that store error reports and manage the links between the errors, the rules that identify them, and the erroneous data records. Without a well-organized error catalogue, it would be impossible to make any sense of the ocean of errors.

Chapter 12 introduces aggregate data quality scores that provide high-level estimates of the data quality. Each score aggregates errors identified by the data quality rules into a single number – a percentage of good data records among some target data recordset. Wise design of aggregate scores allows us to measure data fitness for various purposes, indicate quality of various data collection processes, and make better decisions about data quality improvement.

Throughout the text, we will take a dual perspective of data quality assessment. From one side we look at the steps, procedures, and techniques of data quality assessment. From the other side we see various categories of the data quality meta data used or created in the process. This second perspective is very important because these meta data are the real product of the data quality assessment; thus the better we understand and organize them, the more valuable our result. In Chapter 13 we summarize the data quality meta data model and present the design and functionality of the data quality meta data warehouse, including architecture of the data quality scorecard.

It is a rather common situation when we want to reassess quality of the same data periodically in order to understand data quality trends and identify new errors. Adding the time dimension to data quality assessment requires making adjustment to many of its aspects. Chapter 14 describes the solution in detail.

The content of the upcoming chapters will get progressively more technical as we cover more advanced topics in data quality assessment. Chapter 11 and Chapter 12 are especially difficult as we venture into the areas of complex data manipulation and even some mathematical and statistical analysis. However, I recommend even the less technically inclined reader to not skip any of them entirely.

Each chapter is designed in layers from a simple general overview of the topic more detailed and advanced areas. You can choose to stop at the point that you feel is beyond your level of interest and still get the general idea.

Most importantly, Chapter 13 is not technical or difficult at all. It provides a good overview of the material from the previous four chapters and culminates in the discussion of the central product of data quality assessment – the interactive dimensional data quality scorecard.

CHAPTER 9
IMPLEMENTING DATA QUALITY RULES

Data quality rules are the main tool of a data quality professional. In Chapters 4 through 8 we have learned how to discover data quality rules of various types through meta data analysis, data profiling, and various analytical techniques. However, this knowledge must be applied wisely to achieve any success.

I used to play soccer with friends. Every Sunday some of us got together, split into two teams, and the battle began. Sometimes only five people showed and the game was not pretty. We got exhausted after ten minutes and stopped running. Other times 15 or more people came, and the game got really ugly we were a swarm following the ball; something you normally observe when watching kindergarteners play. Even when we had the right number of players, it did not always work out well until we figured out how to split into well-organized teams: five big slow guys do not make much of a soccer team, neither do five defensemen. The point being, it takes the right number of well-matched players to make a team.

The same phenomenon works for data quality rules. Not enough rules means we cannot find all of the errors, but with too many rules the results are unnecessarily difficult to comprehend. Poorly designed rules identify immaterial errors or find the same errors in many different ways. It is possible to design data quality rules in many different ways, and the success of the assessment project is greatly influenced by the rule design. This chapter offers comprehensive treatment of this topic.

- Section 9.1 describes how rule design is affected by the project scope.

- Section 9.2 describes rule aggregation and specialization techniques.

- Section 9.3 discusses the challenges of building the rule catalogue – a group of entities that collectively stores definitions of data quality rules.

- Section 9.4 presents a high-level overview of the techniques for coding rule validation algorithms.

A special topic in implementing data quality rules is organization of the error reports. It is the challenge that ruins many a data quality assessment project. To give it justice, we will dedicate the entire Chapter 11 to this subject.

9.1. PROJECT SCOPE AND RULE DESIGN

The purpose of using data quality rules is to identify data errors. This leads to an obvious question: "What constitutes a data error?" The fact is, there is no absolute in data quality, and it is impossible to define data accuracy in vacuum. This is nothing unique to the world of data. Quality is generally defined as "fitness for the purpose of use." I like going to old castles and forts. The tour guide will tell you all about who built the castle, why it was built, and when. He will also mention who attacked the castle, why and when it was attacked, and how many times it was sacked. Finally, the guide will often say something like, "This 14th century castle is still in great condition." Seeing the cracks, holes, and gaps, however, tells me otherwise. I clearly see why the visitors are not allowed into some portion of the building. Yes, it is a great historical monument and from that perspective the walls are still of highest quality. But even a child could bring down these walls, so their quality from the perspective of the original builders would be suspect at best.

Data quality is measured by its fitness to the purpose of use. For instance, employee compensation amounts used for tax reporting must be accurate to the nearest $1. The same compensation amounts used to calculate retirement benefits must only be precise to the nearest $100. Further, annual compensation will suffice for tax reporting, while monthly amounts are used in benefit calculation. Thus, if the January amount is short by $500, while the February amount is $500 too high, the data is still perfectly fine for tax purposes but inaccurate for benefit calculation. Finally, only data for the last three years may be required for tax reporting, while amounts for the last five years might be used in retirement calculations.

To conclude, data precision, granularity, and completeness requirements are all determined by the way the data is used. Therefore, the first step in data quality rule design is to determine how the data is used and what the quality requirements are.

Defining data quality requirements is easy when the assessment project is initiated by the need to understand data quality implication on some data-driven process or initiative. Business users instigate projects with such specific scope if they have a concern that the data quality may not adequately support some business process. For instance, I often find employee benefits administrators demanding an HR data quality assessment project when they believe the benefit amounts are not calculated accurately. In all such cases, it is immediately clear which data elements and records must be validated – the ones that are used. Also, data quality itself is clearly defined in terms of the data usage – data is good when the results of its use are acceptable and bad otherwise.

Defining data quality requirements is more difficult when the impetus for the assessment project is an overall desire to measure quality of data in a particular database. This may be just a part of due diligence and IT audit procedures. Also, such projects can be requested by the business users who regularly come in contact with the data and see data problems. Alternatively, full database quality assessment can be done in anticipation of the database conversion or a new system implementation. This case is more complex because the same data elements may be used for a variety of purposes (including some unknown future uses), and it may not be trivial to define accurate vs. inaccurate data. In fact it is often necessary to design multiple versions of the same rule, one for each data quality definition (or to use error-grouping techniques discussed later in this chapter to distinguish errors within a single rule).

Another question is which of all possible rules should be implemented in a particular project. It is rather intuitive that not all data quality rules may be relevant, e.g. it seems logical to only validate the data elements that are included in the project scope. In reality, the project objective influences rule selection in a more subtle way.

Let's start with a simple data quality assessment project. Most HR databases are used (among other things) to manage employee life insurance benefits. A typical program may provide each employee with an annual term life insurance policy in an amount equal to three times annual base compensation rate, effective at the beginning of the calendar year. Let's assume for simplicity that on January 1 of each year, the employer purchases all policies based on the compensation rate data. Benefits are then communicated to all employees on nicely printed colorful statements.

Obviously, the policy amounts will be incorrect any time the compensation rate is incorrect. A typical employee receives the statement, verifies the policy amount, and discovers one of three things:

- The policy amount is correct, and the employee sends the statement to straight to the wastebasket.

- The policy amount is lower than it should be (because the compensation rate was inaccurate on the low side), and the employee phones the call center in a fury. A services specialist must research and fix the problem, the policy must be re-issued, and benefit statement must be re-sent to the employee. Even ignoring the intangible cost of hurt feelings, the cost of re-work might be $250 per case.

- The policy amount is higher than it should be (because the compensation rate was inaccurate on the high side), and… the employee still happily sends the statement to the wastebasket. Actually, this would be a desirable outcome since the overpayment for a higher policy limit is probably less than the cost of re-work. However, a good and honest employee will still phone the call center, and the service cost will again run at $250 per case.

Thus the overall annual cost of inaccurate compensation rate data is $250 times the number of employees with data errors. For a company with 10,000 employees, a 4% error rate would then translate into $100,000 a year. This is certainly a significant amount to justify a recurrent data quality assessment project if any concern about data quality exists.

The objective of the project is defined very clearly – to identify erroneous compensation rates as of January 1 for all employees eligible for the life insurance benefit. The question now is, "Which data quality rules should we design?" Of course, we want rules that validate compensation rate records. Some rules are immediately obvious. We must check that one and only one record exists for each employee and that the compensation rate itself is not Null and is reasonable (e.g. positive). However, such trivial constraints will miss many errors.

The next step is to design more sophisticated rules. For instance, we could compare the compensation rate as of January 1 with the previous record for the same employee (presumably before the last pay raise) to see that the change is reasonable. We could also validate the compensation rate against the customary salary range for the position occupied by the employee. We could even reach out to the payroll database and verify that the compensation rate is consistent with actual paycheck data.

There is certainly a benefit in designing more rules, as we are likely to identify more errors. However, there is also downside. Any comparison that involves several data elements creates an uncertainty of which one is erroneous if a discrepancy is observed. For instance, if the compensation rate is $50,000, and the employee occupies an "Assistant Vice-President" position with the salary range between $70,000 and $90,000, it is premature to deem the compensation rate incorrect. It is possible that the position is mislabeled and, in reality, the employee's job is "Administrative Assistant to Vice-President" with the salary range between $45,000 and $55,000. Or maybe the range for this position is listed incorrectly.

In order to make accurate decisions about data quality when multiple data elements are involved in the data quality rule, we need to analyze all of them. This requires a lot more work, as we need to understand and profile many more data elements than are immediately relevant to our objective. More importantly, we now need to make judgments about the quality of the data we use in comparison, such as employee position in the example above. The only good way to accomplish that is to design more data quality rules that validate these additional data elements. However these rules will involve more data elements, which in turn will require more rules. The rule set can be viewed as made of many layers, with the innermost layer validating the target data elements, the next layer validating the data elements used to validate target data elements, and so on.

This is a lot more work! At the same time, we get a lot more results. Indeed we are measuring the quality of many more data elements than we initially planned. Also, the accuracy of data quality assessment is proportional to the number of layers in the rule set and the amount of crosschecking between various data elements. As a result, both accuracy and ROI of the data quality assessment for an entire database (made of many interdependent data elements and used for many purposes) are far greater than those for quality assessment of a data subset.

Of course, in reality we sometimes have to conduct data quality assessment projects with a narrow scope, such as the life insurance example above. It could be due to budget constraints or simply because it is often easier to "sell" a more specific project to the management. In that case, the question becomes, "How many layers do we incorporate?"

The solution is to implement data quality rules iteratively rather than commit to the set of rules from the beginning. We start by designing and implementing the rules that involve only the data elements within the project scope. We then add the second layer with rules validating target data against other data elements. In our example, we could implement the rules comparing the compensation rate as of January 1 against historic values and against position salary information.

The next step is to analyze the results and see if the rules from the second layer produce potentially useful findings. Have we found a significant number of errors? If no, then we can stop with this line of questioning. Do the errors overlap with the ones found by the rules in the first layer? If yes, then again the new rule probably adds little value (although it may be used at a future point to confirm that these are truly errors). When many new erroneous records are found, it is worth checking that the errors affect the target data element rather than the ones we use in comparison. This can be done quickly through a sample review. For instance, we can take 10 records with discrepancies between compensation rate and position salary range and manually check which ones are actually incorrect. If we find that a rule helps identify a meaningful number of otherwise missed errors in the target data, it certainly deserves to be a part of the data quality assessment.

Then there comes the question of adding another layer, i.e. additional rules validating the non-target data used by the rules in the previous layer. In our example, we could design further rules to test position information. The results would help decide which data is incorrect when our compensation rates are inconsistent with position salary ranges.

A noteworthy question is when to utilize the data from other databases. It is often helpful to compare redundant or related data across databases; however, it is usually time-consuming and expensive. The decision to use external data sources in data quality assessment is rather subjective. My typical recommendation is to start the assessment using rules within the database and add external data sources if such rules cannot find the majority of errors. There are, however, three major exceptions.

First, if data cleansing is planned to follow data quality assessment, then additional data sources should be incorporated immediately since they will be necessary during data cleansing anyway. Secondly, if it is known that the data in the external data source is reliable, it must be used. For instance, we would be justified to use payroll data to validate compensation rates if we believed that paycheck numbers were generally very reliable. Finally, if an enterprise-wide data quality assessment is planned, it is always better to prioritize and schedule it in such a way that related databases are assessed one after another. This makes data crosschecking easier.

9.2. SELECTING OPTIMAL RULE DESIGN

Any given set of rules can be implemented in many different ways. A way of visualizing the problem is to first imagine all rules combined in one enormous super-rule, testing every possible aspect of data quality. On the other end of the spectrum, we can picture thousands of the most trivial atomic rules, each testing the simplest possible condition and looking for a unique type of errors under unique circumstances. In the practice of rule implementation, both approaches may be undesirable, and the middle ground must be found. However, there are many ways to find the middle ground as the atomic rules can be combined into many sets of (possibly partially overlapping) rules.

Consider a simple example. Data elements A, B, and C are all redundant (i.e. they must have equal values). This condition can be used to implement a single super-rule, which gets tripped if any two of the three elements differ. Alternatively, we can implement three distinct atomic rules, comparing individual pairs of elements (A against B, B against C, and A against C). We could also use a combination of two rules instead of three, e.g. rule #1 could compare A against B, while rule #2 would test C against A and B. All of these options assume that these data elements are all part of the project scope. But what if only A is important? Of course, it is still valuable to compare A with B and C; yet again there are many ways of doing it. For instance, we could use rule #1 to compare A against B and rule #2 to compare A against C. Another option is to only validate rule #2 if A and B are the same.

Clearly there are many ways to implement the same rules even in this trivial case. Things get far more complex when we look at more sophisticated rules, such as rules for state-transition models. The reader might ask, "Is there any difference?" Indeed, rule decomposition and aggregation do not affect our ability to find errors. However, this impacts the ease of error analysis in the data quality scorecard. For example, many rules are interdependent, i.e. get tripped by the same data problems. In some cases, it is beneficial as it helps to confirm the nature of the problem. In other cases, it simply leads to unnecessary duplication of errors in the reports and makes analysis more cumbersome.

Keep in mind that designing data quality rules and creating error listings is not the ultimate goal of the data quality program. Rather, it is a step towards understanding and improving data quality. To achieve that objective we will eventually need to identify the true causes, nature, and location of the errors. Well-designed data quality rules clearly separate errors of different kinds and eliminate unnecessary duplication. We will now discuss the main reasons for and against rule aggregation and decomposition.

9.2.1. Rule Aggregation

Let's start our discussion with a simple example of reference rules for the data model presented in Figure 9-1. The data model shows four entities: strong entity E_EMPLOYEE_PROFILE and three dependent entities. Each of the dependent entities has a foreign key to E_EMPLOYEE_PROFILE.

Assuming that the database does not enforce referential integrity, we would immediately use the data model to design three foreign key rules. The first rule requires that each record in entity E_STATUS_HISTORY has a corresponding parent record in E_EMPLOYEE_PROFILE with the same value of key attribute EmpID. The other two rules have similar requirements for entities E_PAY_RATE_HISTORY and E_PAY_SPECIAL_HISTORY.

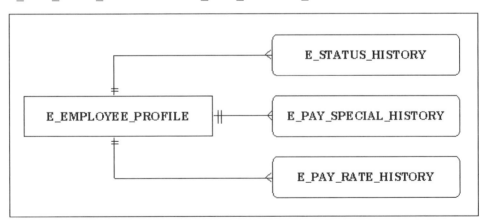

Figure 9-1: Data Model with Three Foreign Key Constraints

Figure 9-2 shows records violating our data quality rules. Altogether we found eight records violating these three rules. We clearly did not miss any bad records. However, there is a significant problem with our approach. Observe that seven of the records have the same value of EmpID equal to 114603. It is pretty obvious that the real error is a missing (or mislabeled) record for employee #114603 in the main E_EMPLOYEE_PROFILE table. On the other hand, the record with EmpID equal to 483 in table E_STATUS_HISTORY is most likely erroneous. Further analysis would show that it is miscoded and in reality belongs to employee #484. So rather than having eight erroneous records, we really have one incorrect and one missing record – for the total of two.

Figure 9-2: Reference Rule Violations

Why is this distinction so important? From the data quality perspective, there is a big difference between eight erroneous records and two erroneous records. Further, the missing main employee record in E_EMPLOYEE_PROFILE table is probably far more significant than having a mislabeled E_STATUS_HISTORY record.

Since we designed the three foreign key rules separately, the resultant error reports do not tell us about this pattern. We would have to get lucky to find the error overlap between the three rules and recognize its significance. Indeed, while it seems obvious when laid down side-by-side in Figure 9-2, remember that in data quality assessment projects we routinely use hundreds of rules; and many of them have some overlapping errors.

Obviously, the proper design for reference rules is to combine all foreign key constraints pointing to the same parent table into a single data quality rule. One error for this rule will include all orphan records with the same foreign key value. Such a rule will find two errors in our example: the first one for EmpID equal to 483 affecting one record, and the second one for EmpID equal to 114603 affecting seven records.

In this example, aggregation makes sense because different rules were tripped by the same error. Aggregation allows us to see the true nature and location of the error. Such commonality of the error causes is the main factor influencing rule aggregation decisions. We definitely do not want to have the same problem identified many times by different rules. It is simply a lot of work to seek rule redundancies through analysis and profiling of the error reports. We still need to do it to find subtler rule dependencies (and we will discuss how to do it at length in Chapter 10, which is dedicated to rule fine-tuning). But at least let's not unnecessarily increase our workload. When conceptual analysis indicates that two or more rules will find violations caused by the same problems, you should seriously consider combining the rules.

Of course, rule aggregation is no exact science. There is no way to know in advance how many errors we will find and what causes them. In fact, the whole purpose of data quality assessment (and later data cleansing) is to answer this question. So the decisions are all preliminary. We will fine-tune the rules at the later stage of the project. All we are really trying to do in the initial rule design phase is simplify the fine-tuning.

9.2.2. Rule Specialization

Rule aggregation makes sense when a large portion of errors is expected to have the same cause. At the same time, we do not want to needlessly aggregate the rules. Consider the following example. Table E_EMPLOYEE_INFO is expected to have one record for each employee. Attribute HireDate in this table stores the employee's original date of hire. Table E_STATUS_HISTORY contains state-dependent employment history, which is expected to start from the original hiring event. Naturally, the employee's original date of hire must coincide with the effective date of the earliest record in the employment history. To validate this condition we can implement an attribute redundancy rule as follows:

For each EmpID:

[E_EMPLOYEE_INFO].[HireDate] = Min([E_STATUS_HISTORY].[EffDate])

Let's assume that we implemented this rule and, among others, found four errors shown in Figure 9-3 (the left panel shows HireDate values while the right panel shows the earliest record in E_STATUS_HISTORY). It is pretty obvious that we are dealing with four absolutely different types of problems. Look closer at the errors.

- Employee #112 has HireDate of 10/24/1955 but does not have any records in E_STATUS_HISTORY.

- Employee #5247 has Null value in HireDate, while the effective date of the earliest employment history record is 4/17/1997.

- Employee #202 has HireDate of 2/28/1986, while the effective date of the earliest employment history record is 2/1/1982.

- Employee #1302 has HireDate of 11/5/1973, while the effective date of the earliest employment history record is 4/15/1985. However, the employment history begins with *TERM* action rather than *HIRE* action.

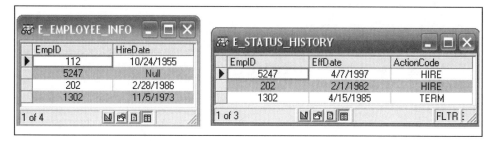

Figure 9-3: Violations of the Attribute Redundancy Rule

It makes little sense to pack all these problems into a single data quality rule. We accomplish nothing except making error analysis more cumbersome. For instance, the first error is the case of missing employment history. The complete lack of employment history data is a major problem with implications far beyond the simple mismatch with HireDate attribute. It must be tested separately by a relation optionality rule. Similarly, the last error is caused by incomplete employment history. It belongs to the terminator constraint and not the test of HireDate attribute.

The correct approach would be to only apply the above attribute redundancy rule to the data (that is values of EmpID) meeting the following conditions:

- EMPLOYEE_INFO has only one record.

- HireDate value in the E_EMPLOYEE_INFO record is not Null.

- Employment history in E_STATUS_HISTORY table has at least one record.

- Employment history starts with *HIRE* action.

Thus the rule <u>would not apply</u> to employees #112, #5247, and #1302 in Figure 9-3. The only remaining error in Figure 9-3 would be for employee #202 whose data satisfies all four conditions above.

But what about the other three errors in Figure 9-3? We are not ignoring them. Instead, we use other data quality rules to find them. In fact every condition from (a) to (d) translates into a data quality rule:

- Condition (a) is the primary key constraint for E_EMPLOYEE_INFO.

- Condition (b) is the attribute optionality constraint for HireDate.

- Condition (c) is the relation optionality rule for E_STATUS_HISTORY.

- Condition (d) is the terminator constraint for employment history.

These four rules are pre-conditions for the attribute redundancy rule comparing the employee's original date of hire with the effective date of the earliest record in the employment history.

This is an example of rule specialization, opposite of previously discussed rule aggregation. Rule specialization ensures that rules do not get tripped by unrelated errors. The atomic structure of the rules significantly simplifies error analysis. Also, atomic rules are easier to understand, code, and maintain.

9.2.3. Derived Rules

It is natural to ask whether or not rule design should be driven by coding complexity and processing efficiency. For example, simple foreign key violations can be identified by a rather trivial query, while validating an aggregated reference rule requires a creative solution. I have seen people choose not to aggregate rules just because it makes coding more complex.

This logic is wrong. The complexity of programming the rule validation algorithms should play no significant part in rule design. Whatever you save during coding will be paid back exponentially once you start analyzing data quality assessment results. Remember that the value of data quality assessment is not in the efficiency of the rule implementation programs, but in the accuracy and usability of the data quality scorecard and detailed error reports.

I always recommend using *derived rules* in order to mitigate coding complexity. Derived rules do not operate on the actual data but rather manipulate and aggregate the results of other rules. Consider again the foreign key rules example. Rather than trying to aggregate individual foreign key rules immediately, we could keep them separately. Thus we have three primary foreign key rules:

- Rule *FK.E_STATUS_HISTORY* finds three errors.

- Rule *FK.E_PAY_RATE_HISTORY* finds three errors.

- Rule FK.E_PAY_SPECIAL_HISTORY finds two errors.

Each error identifies an individual orphan record.

Now we design a derived rule *REFERENCE.E_EMPLOYEE_PROFILE* that takes all errors from the primary foreign key rules and processes them into aggregate level errors. This derived rule finds and aggregates all errors referencing records with the same EmpID. Naturally, it will find two errors – one for employee #483 affecting one record, and the second one for employee #114603 affecting seven records.

Using derived rules simplifies rule coding and makes rule aggregation decisions less painful. In essence, derived rules allow the application of common concepts of structural programming to data quality assessment. We start by decomposing rules into simple sub-rules that are easy to implement and test. Then we use derived rules to manipulate the results and build the logically desired aggregated rules.

9.2.4. Error Grouping

More often than not, a single data quality rule will find errors of different kinds. Consider again the aggregated reference rule discussed above. The rule clearly yielded two distinct types of errors – those with a parent record missing and those with a child record mislabeled. It can be very important to know which error cause is more likely to make proper judgments about data quality.

The rule specialization view would be to split the rule into two sub-rules. But can we determine for sure which error is of which type? The answer is probably no. In practice, there is usually no reliable way to determine the exact nature of each error, at least not at the beginning of the project and not without extensive analysis. But we have some clues that indicate which cause may be <u>more likely</u> for each error.

For instance, if we find complete employment history and pay rate history but no parent employee profile record, we can conclude that the latter is most likely missing. Similarly, if we only find one orphan pay rate record with no parent employee profile record and no records with the same EmpID in other tables, we can deduce that the record is probably mislabeled.

In order to accommodate this important knowledge, we use ***error grouping*** – creation of multiple sub-groups of errors identified by a single rule. For instance, we can categorize all errors into three groups:

- Errors with orphan records in two or more tables.

- Errors with several orphan records confined to a single table.

- Errors with only one orphan record.

This allows us to keep the errors together for easy aggregated analysis, and yet provides enough decomposition to account for these errors differently when building aggregated data quality scorecards.

Error grouping is one of the most important techniques in error analysis, building the data quality scorecard, and data cleansing. In practice, rare data quality rules will not benefit from the introduction of error groups. We will talk more about error grouping in Chapter 10 in light of rule fine-tuning.

9.3. RULE CATALOGUING

Data quality rules number in the hundreds for even a small database, and reach into the thousands for larger projects. An enterprise-wide collection of data quality rules can be truly staggering. Before implementing, it is necessary to organize the rules in an efficient manner. Indeed, data quality rules form specifications for the data quality assessment. As with any project, if specifications are not well organized, the results will be disastrous.

A *rule catalogue* is a group of entities that collectively store definitions of data quality rules. Maintaining a rule catalogue is probably the easiest yet the most neglected of all tasks in data quality initiatives. It is boring indeed to write detailed descriptions for hundreds of data quality rules – seemingly trivial in many cases. In my experience, an up-to-date comprehensive rule catalogue is maintained in about one out of 10 projects. Usually this is done because someone on the project team is meticulous beyond reason, rather than due to recognition of its importance.

As is the case with any documentation on a large project, it eventually pays off when you maintain a comprehensive rule catalogue and bites back when you don't. I strongly recommend creating a convenient interface for editing the rule catalogue and setting up a process whereas all rules are neatly described.

9.3.1. Rule Catalogue Components

Rule listing is the centerpiece of the rule catalogue. It enumerates all designed data quality rules and provides their detailed descriptions. Table 9-1 summarizes the structure of the rule listing.

Attribute Name	Attribute Description
Rule Identifier (PK)	Unique identifier for each data quality rule
Rule Name	Unique descriptive rule name
Formal Definition	Unambiguous rule definition using standard templates
Informal Description	Natural language description for a non-technical user

Table 9-1: Structure of Rule Listing

Every rule in the rule listing must be given a unique rule name. This name will be referenced in communications by the developers and business users. Rule names that are relatively short, descriptive, and follow some common naming convention are easier to remember.

Separately, each rule must be given a unique rule identifier – a surrogate key. It is a bad practice to use rule names for internal identification and referencing since the rules often change over time. A name that fits the description of the rule when it is initially thought of may become totally misleading after the rule is changed during fine-tuning. Thus, we want to retain the ability to change rule names at will without having to change all records referencing the rules in the error reports.

It is important to ensure accurate implementation of the data quality rules. This leaves no room for ambiguity and requires each rule to have a clear formal definition using standard templates and terminology, as well as exact data element names.

The formal definitions are great for the purpose of accuracy. They also are easy to follow when coding rule validation algorithms. However, experience shows that the natural language is more suitable for the business users despite potential ambiguity. In that regard, it may leave less room for misinterpretation than the formal rules of grammar! Since rule specifications are typically shared with and approved by the non-technical business users, it is important to augment the formal rule definitions with informal descriptions.

Begin/end date stamping of rules may be needed in some projects. Knowing the span of time for which a rule is in effect is critical for recurrent data quality assessment, but would also be necessary in assessment of time-variant data in a data warehouse. We will discuss this issue in detail in Chapter 14.

Table 9-2 shows how a simple data quality rule – an attribute domain constraint – is stored in the rule listing. The rule has numeric identifier (1) and descriptive name (*DOMAIN.E_STATUS.EMP_TYPE*) referencing rule type and the attribute to which the constraint applies. Its formal definition allows immediate coding, while the informal description can be understood and verified by non-technical users.

Rule #1. *DOMAIN.E_STATUS.EMP_TYPE*

Formal Definition:

[E_EMPLOYEE_STATUS].[EmployeeType] In ('O', 'RF', 'RP', 'TF', 'TP')

Informal Description:

Employee type must either be *O* ("occasional") or consist of exactly two characters, with the first one as *R* ("regular") or *T* ("temporary") and the second one as *F* ("full-time") or *P* ("part-time"). All other values are invalid.

Table 9-2: Simple Data Quality Rule

As we discussed in the previous section, many rules find errors of different types. We use error groups to differentiate such errors. Each group must be given an identifier, a descriptive name, and a definition. We do not require distinguishing between formal and informal descriptions since group definitions are typically rather simple. Table 9-3 shows two error groups for rule #1 from Table 9-2.

Rule #1. *DOMAIN.E_STATUS.EMP_TYPE*

Group A. MissingValue.   *EmployeeType Is Null*

Group B. InvalidValue.   *EmployeeType Not In (O, RF, RP, TF, TP)*

Table 9-3: Error Groups for Simple Data Quality Rule

Each data quality rule can apply to one or several attributes from one or several data entities. We use the term ***rule domain*** to describe a collection of data elements to which the rule applies. The basic rule listing does not define rule domains, though the domains can be deduced from the formal definitions. A more advanced rule catalogue provides structured information about data entities and attributes to which each rule applies. This information can be queried to construct a list of all data quality rules created for a specific subset of data elements. Such reports allow us to keep track of all data elements validated in a project. They are also invaluable for the purposes of change management.

9.3.2. Rule Catalogue Data Model

Figure 9-4 shows a data model for a comprehensive rule catalogue. Consider the key features of this data model. RULE table contains the rule listing. Each data quality rule is represented by a single entry. RULE_GROUP lists error groups. RULE_ENTITY and RULE_ATTRIBUTE define rule domains. One data quality rule may have a domain consisting of one or more attributes in one or more entities. Theoretically the RULE_ENTITY table is unnecessary. All distinct entities affected by a rule can be obtained by querying the RULE_ATTRIBUTE table. However, in practice it is more convenient to maintain both tables.

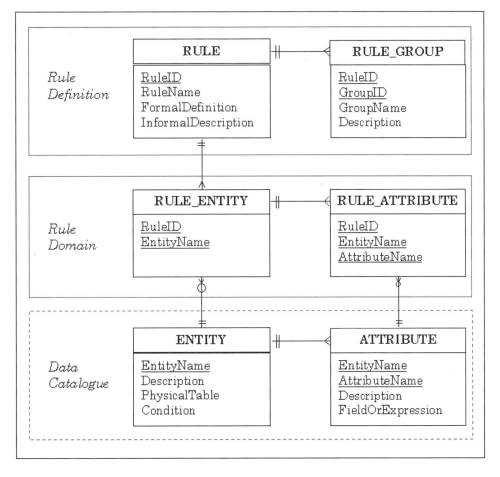

Figure 9-4: Rule Catalogue Data Model

Rule domain tables in Figure 9-4 also reference data catalogue tables ENTITY and ATTRIBUTE. This data catalogue serves two purposes. First, it provides a comprehensive listing of all entities and attributes of the actual data, which can be used in various data quality reports. Secondly, it offers a link between logical and physical data models. This link is used by the rule engine to validate rules expressed in terms of logical data elements against actual physical data.

Figure 9-5 shows several rule catalogue entries. Consider, for instance, the domain constraint for EmployeeType in entity E_EMPLOYEE_STATUS (rule #1 from Table 9-2). The rule catalogue has the following entries for RuleID equal to 1.

- One RULE entry with attributes populated as described in Table 9-2

- Two RULE_GROUP entries for groups described in Table 9-3

- One RULE_ENTITY entry and one RULE_ATTRIBUTE entry indicating that the rule affects attribute EmployeeType in entity E_EMPLOYEE_STATUS

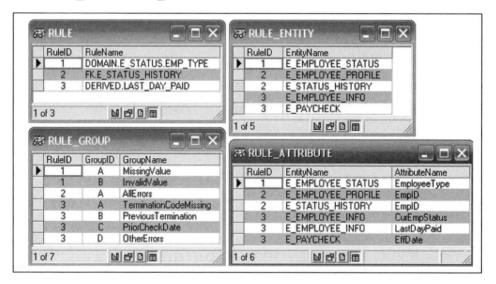

Figure 9-5: Rule Catalogue Examples

In general, multiple RULE_ENTITY and RULE_ATTRIBUTE entries can be created for one rule. For instance, rule #2 is a simple foreign key constraint for the E_STATUS_HISTORY entity. It compares attribute EmpID in two entities – E_EMPLOYEE_PROFILE and E_STATUS_HISTORY. Rule #3 applies to three attributes, including two attributes in entity E_EMPLOYEE_INFO and one attribute in entity E_PAYCHECK. Also, a rule can have one or several error groups. For example, rule #2 has one generic error group that holds all errors. Rule #1 has two groups, while rule #3 has four groups.

9.4. RULE CODING

We now know how to design and catalogue data quality rules. Through analysis and profiling, we have prepared and documented a comprehensive list of rules. It is time to consider the coding of rule validation algorithms.

It is a natural desire to look for a tool that can be used to quickly and easily implement all data quality rules. Unfortunately such yearning is totally unrealistic. No data quality tool on the market today can be used to easily define more than a tiny fraction of the data quality rules. Also, in recent years several commercial business rule engines have become available, which can be used to implement some data quality rules. However, these engines do not target data quality rules directly and so are not easy to use. Hopefully, functionality of the tools will expand in the future. In the meantime, we have to rely on more basic approaches, such as using SQL or general programming languages, to code the bulk of data quality rules.

Fundamentally, there are two approaches to coding rule validation algorithms. The first method is to simply write individual programs (in SQL or a programming language) for each data quality rule. The second method is to utilize a table-driven rule engine, which will use stored rule parameters to execute the rules. In practice, a combination of both works best. In this section we will offer an overview of these techniques.

9.4.1. Writing Individual Programs for Each Rule

Consider the attribute domain constraint for attribute EmployeeType. It restricts values of the attribute to {*RF, RP, TF, TP, O*}. A rather trivial Query 9-1 can be used to validate this data quality rule. All records returned by the query violate the rule, and thus we can simply process this query record by record and register data errors (we will discuss how to catalogue data errors in the Chapter 11).

```
SELECT     *
  FROM     E_EMPLOYEE_STATUS
 WHERE     EmployeeType NOT IN ('RF', 'RP', 'TF', 'TP', 'O')
    OR     EmployeeType IS NULL
```

Query 9-1: List of Records Violating Attribute Domain Constraint

The foreign key rule for E_STATUS_HISTORY entity requires a more complex query. Still, with little effort we can come up with Query 9-2. It returns all records from E_STATUS_HISTORY table that have no counterpart in the parent E_EMPLOYEE_PROFILE table. All such records violate the foreign key constraint.

```
SELECT     E_STATUS_HISTORY.*
  FROM     E_EMPLOYEE_PROFILE RIGHT JOIN E_ STATUS_HISTORY
    ON     E_EMPLOYEE_PROFILE.EmpID = E_STATUS_HISTORY.EmpID
 WHERE     E_EMPLOYEE_PROFILE.EmpID IS NULL
```

Query 9-2: Records Violating Foreign Key Rule

As we continue implementing various types of data quality rules, the validation code will get more and more complex. Soon enough we will need to write stored procedures in SQL or use a programming language. In my experience, about half of the rules can be coded using rather simple queries and stored procedures, while the other half will require more sophisticated programming. In any case, you can create an individual routine for each data quality rule.

For example, consider the derived attribute constraint for the LastDayPaid attribute defined in Table 9-4. The first part of this constraint can be validated by a simple query; the second part is much more complex and requires a nested aggregated query with an outer join, or a stored procedure. I will let the technically inclined readers design these queries themselves or trust me that it can be done with relative ease.

Rule #3. *DERIVED.LAST_DAY_PAID*

Formal Definition:

If   *[E_EMPLOYEE_INFO].[CurEmpStatus] In ('A', 'L')*

Then   *[E_EMPLOYEE_INFO].[LastDayPaid] Is Null*

Else   *[E_EMPLOYEE_INFO].[LastDayPaid] = Max([E_PAYCHECK].[EffDate])*

Informal Description:

"Last day paid" is a derived attribute. It is populated with the effective date of the last paycheck for terminated employees. For all other employees, "last day paid" must be blank.

Table 9-4: Derived Attribute Constraints for LastDayPaid

9.4.2. Using Parameterized Rule Engine

It is quite obvious that rules of similar type will have very similar implementations. For instance, all attribute optionality constraints can be implemented by a generic Query 9-3. The query takes three parameters: *EntityName* and *AttributeName* reference the attribute to which the rule is applied, while *DefaultValueList* is a comma-separated list of default values used as substitutes for Null values. Of course, the "OR" part of the "WHERE" clause in the SQL is not necessary when no default values exist. We could write a program that takes *EntityName*, *AttributeName*, and *DefaultValueList* as parameters, builds the appropriate SQL statement, executes it, and catalogues all errors. Such a program could then be used to validate all attribute optionality constraints.

```
SELECT    *
   FROM   EntityName
  WHERE   AttributeName IS NULL
     OR   AttributeName IN (DefaultValueList)
```

Query 9-3: Generic Statement for Validating Optionality Constraints

Similarly, all foreign key rules on a single attribute can be validated using generic Query 9-4. It has four parameters: the two names of the related entities (*ParentEntity* and *ChildEntity*) and the two names of the linked key fields in the respective entities (*ParentKeyField* and *ChildKeyField*). We could write a program that uses these four parameters to validate all simple foreign key constraints.

```
SELECT      ChildEntity.*
   FROM     ParentEntity RIGHT JOIN ChildEntity
     ON     ParentEntity.ParentKeyField = ChildEntity.ChildKeyField
  WHERE     ParentEntity.ParentKeyField IS NULL
```

Query 9-4: Generic Statement for Validating Foreign Key Rules

Now, in order to use our rule engine to validate all parameterized rules, we simply need to store various parameters in the rule catalogue. Figure 9-6 shows the data model for an extended rule catalogue incorporating parameters for attribute optionality and simple foreign key constraints.

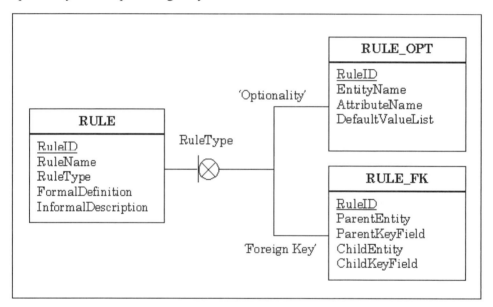

Figure 9-6: Extended Rule Catalogue with Rule Parameter Entities

A new field RuleType is added to the RULE table. It is the discriminating attribute for various parameterized rule sub-types. It uses value *Optionality* for all optionality constraints and *Foreign Key* for all simple foreign key constraints on a single attribute. For all other rules, RuleType is Null.

The new entity RULE_OPT stores parameters for all optionality constraints. Another new entity RULE_FK stores parameters for foreign key constraints on a single attribute. Both of these entities are subtypes for the main RULE entity. We

196

can continue extending the set of parameterized rule validation programs and incorporate parameters of many different rule types into the rule catalogue.

9.4.3. Combining Two Approaches

An obvious question is when to write individual rule validation programs and when to develop general parameterized ones. There is no simple answer to this question. Individual programs are much easier to develop. As you try to generalize various rules into parameterized validation programs, they become more and more complex. The advantage, of course, is elimination of redundant code. The less code we must write, the fewer bugs we will have. Also, parameterized programs can be reused in all future data quality assessment projects. So if we can generalize a dozen rules in one parameterized program with relative ease, it is certainly worthwhile.

The common mistake is to try making generalized solutions fit all possible cases. For instance, it is rather easy to generalize some attribute valid value constraints but extremely difficult to generalize all of them. When the domain is made of a discrete set of values, a simple list or a lookup table can be stored in the rule catalogue (or data catalogue). It is also easy to parameterize constraints with domains made of one or several value ranges. But some domains can be very complex and involve complicated masks or range combinations. It is typically better to implement such cases in individual routines and only generalize the more common simpler ones.

SUMMARY

In this chapter, we have discussed various techniques for rule design and implementation along with the architecture of the rule catalogue. Here are the main takeaways from this chapter:

- Data precision, granularity, and completeness requirements are all determined by the way the data is used. Therefore, the first step in data quality rule design is to determine how the data is used and what the quality requirements are.

- Defining data quality requirements is easy when the assessment project is initiated by the need to understand data quality implication on some data-driven process or initiative. It is more difficult when the impetus for the assessment project is an overall desire to measure quality of data in a particular database. In the latter case, the same data elements may be used for a variety of purposes (including some unknown future uses), and it may not be trivial to define accurate vs. inaccurate data. In fact, it is often necessary to design multiple versions of the same rule, one for each quality definition.

- It is rather intuitive that not all data quality rules may be relevant in a project, e.g. it seems logical to only validate the data elements that are included in the project scope. Further, while there is a benefit in designing more rules (as we are likely to identify more errors), there is also a downside. Any comparison that involves additional data elements creates an uncertainty as to which one is erroneous if a discrepancy is observed.

- Designing data quality rules and creating error listings is not the ultimate goal of the data quality program. Rather, it is a step towards understanding and improving data quality. To achieve that objective we will eventually need to identify the true causes, nature, and location of the errors. Well-designed data quality rules clearly separate errors of different kinds and eliminate unnecessary duplication. We use rule aggregation, specialization, and error grouping to design the best set of rules.

- A rule catalogue is a group of entities that collectively stores definitions of data quality rules. It consists of the main rule listing, rule groups, rule domains, and (optional) parameters used by the rule engine for rule execution. A rule listing enumerates all designed data quality rules and provides their detailed descriptions. A rule group table stores definitions for all error groups. A rule domain specifies data elements (entities and attributes) affected by the rule.

- Fundamentally, there are two approaches to coding the rule validation algorithms. The first method is to simply write individual programs (in SQL or a programming language) for each data quality rule. The second method is to develop a table-driven rule engine, which will use stored rule parameters to execute the rules. In practice, a combination of both is most effective.

CHAPTER 10
FINE-TUNING DATA QUALITY RULES

The objective of the data quality assessment is to identify all data errors. Considering the volume and structural complexity of a typical database, this is a daunting task. Our optimism in tackling the problem should certainly cause any normal person to question our sanity. The reason we accept the challenge has nothing to do with our state of mind or youthful abandon. Instead, we possess the most powerful tool – data quality rules. They can be designed and implemented by hundreds; they can validate millions of data pieces in minutes; and they can find even the sneakiest data errors!

However, there is a catch. It is very hard to design perfect data quality rules. The ones we come up with will often fail to spot some erroneous records and falsely accuse others. They may not tell you which data element is erroneous even when the error is identified. They may identify the same error in many different ways. This imperfection, if not understood and controlled, will overrun and doom any data quality assessment effort.

But do not despair – there is a solution! Most rules can be "fine-tuned" to near perfection. This problem can hardly be addressed at the onset of the project. Instead, we start by designing and implementing the most complete set of data quality rules within the project scope as discussed in the last chapter. We then analyze the results to find and eliminate rule imperfections as best we can. This process of rule fine-tuning is the subject of this chapter.

- Section 10.1 offers an overview of possible rule imperfections.

- Section 10.2 introduces four steps of the rule fine-tuning process.

- Section 10.3 describes how to identify rule imperfections.

- Section 10.4 shows how to analyze rule imperfections and find patterns in them.

- Section 10.5 discusses methods for eliminating *false positives* – rule violations that under close examination prove to be correct data.

- Section 10.6 presents techniques for dealing with *false negatives* – errors missed by all data quality rules.

- Section 10.7 outlines ways for using error groups to eliminate situations when errors of different types are found by the same rule.

10.1. RULE IMPERFECTIONS

Data quality assessment relies on our ability to use data quality rules to accurately identify all data errors. By that we mean finding and identifying each and every erroneous record. However, this proves to be a major challenge. Data quality rules often fall short in at least three departments.

First, the fact that the data are tested by hundreds or even thousands of data quality rules does not guarantee that all errors are identified. The data might conform to all applied rules and still be inaccurate. With the increase in the number and variety of the rules more errors will be found. Yet the question remains: "How many errors did we miss?"

Secondly, while well-designed rules can identify data errors *en masse* they will often yield numerous false positives. Without a systematic approach to weeding out the false positives, they tend to overrun the error reports and doom the entire effort of data quality assessment.

Finally, most data quality rules test several data elements against one another. When a rule violation is identified, it is often not obvious which of the data elements is incorrect. Knowing the exact location of the error is critical since the quality of different data elements may have different importance. The error may be critical in one of them but negligible in the other one.

Consider, for example, the attribute redundancy rule for HireDate attribute. It requires the employee's original date of hire (HireDate in E_EMPLOYEE_INFO table) to coincide with the effective date of the earliest record in the employment history (EffDate in table E_STATUS_HISTORY).

Figure 10-1 shows relevant data for two employees. The left panels show HireDate values while the right panels show employment history data in E_STATUS_HISTORY table.

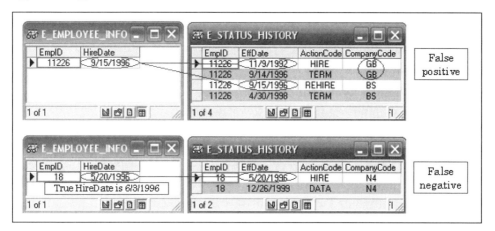

Figure 10-1: Examples of False Positives and False Negatives

Obviously data for employee #11226 (top tables) violates the rule and thus will be identified as an error, while data for employee #18 (bottom tables) will pass the rule. Now let's compare these results with the truth (assuming that we have done research and found out when each employee actually was hired).

- Employee #11226 is actually part of an acquired company (coded as GB in CompanyCode field). Employment with this acquired company does not count for any HR purposes. Thus employee #11226 was assigned HireDate as of the acquisition date 9/15/1996. The original employment history with the acquired company was loaded into the E_STATUS_HISTORY table during data consolidation for informational purposes only. Our rule does not account for this special case and produces the false positive.

- Employee #18 has an original hire date recorded as 5/20/1996 in both HireDate field and employment history. Our rule will, therefore, not get tripped. In fact, none of the designed rules identifies it as erroneous. However, the data is wrong! The actual date of hire is 6/3/1996.

These are very important deficiencies. Our rule is simply inaccurate and must be improved before we can rely upon its results to evaluate the data quality.

Figure 10-2 shows two more data examples in the same format. Data for both employees is truly inaccurate and it does violate the hire date attribute redundancy rule. Thus the rule correctly finds two errors. However, it does not indicate which of the data elements is erroneous.

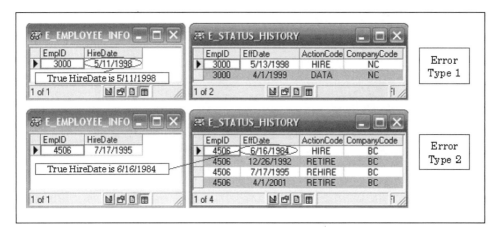

Figure 10-2: Examples of Errors of Different Types Found by the Same Rule

Now, imagine again that we have conducted research and found out when each employee actually was hired. Below are our findings:

- Employee #3000 was actually hired on 5/11/1998. However, his data were not entered into the system until 5/13/1998. During data entry the initial employment history record automatically defaulted to the then date, and the HR administrator forgot to make the correction. Therefore in this case, the erroneous data element is the employment history record.

- Employee #4506 was actually hired on 6/16/1984 and worked for 8.5 years until retiring on 12/26/1992, all in accordance with employment history. Two years later she returned as a temporary employee and worked from home until 4/1/2001. Due to a software glitch, HireDate value for all rehired retirees was changed to their rehire date. Thus HireDate for employee #4506 was reset to 7/17/1995 and became incorrect.

In this example the rule correctly indicates presence of an error, but it cannot tell which record is incorrect. It may be acceptable for preliminary data quality assessment, but this must be improved before a serious data cleansing initiative can be undertaken. Even for data quality assessment, such imprecision may be significant. Imagine, for example, that we have a process that uses HireDate but not employment history. If we are asked whether or not the data quality is adequate for this process, we cannot provide a reliable answer.

10.2. RULE FINE-TUNING PROCESS

The examples of rule imperfections presented in Figures 10-1 and 10-2 make data quality assessment results incomplete and partially inaccurate. The objective of rule fine-tuning is to identify such imperfections and enhance the rules as much as possible.

Rule fine-tuning relies largely on manual verification of the sample data and comparison of the results with the errors identified by the data quality rules. The discrepancies must be addressed through rule redesign, error grouping, and other techniques. Any rule imperfections that cannot be eliminated must at least be understood and accounted for in the data quality scorecard. The process of rule fine-tuning involves four steps shown in Figure 10-3.

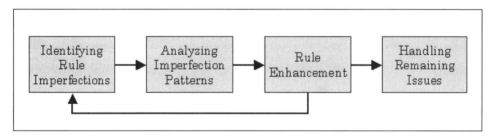

Figure 10-3: Steps in Rule Fine-Tuning Process

The objective of the first step is to identify rule imperfections. The second step is devoted to the analysis of our findings and the search for patterns. On the third step we enhance the rules in order to eliminate as many flaws as possible. These three steps are repeated iteratively until we are satisfied with the results, cannot make further improvements, or simply run out of resources. Ideally at that point we have a set of rules that accurately identify and locate each and every data error. In reality we usually stop short of this objective. On the final step we estimate percentages of residual false positives and false negatives, as well as quantify other error uncertainties.

The first two steps are common for all types of rule imperfections; we will discuss them in Sections 10.3 and 10.4. The last two steps vary significantly by types of problems. We address false positives in Section 10.5, false negatives in Section 10.6, and error types in Section 10.7.

10.3. IDENTIFYING RULE IMPERFECTIONS

The only way to identify rule imperfections is through manual verification of the sample data by the data experts. It usually involves data comparison with "trusted," often non-electronic sources. At the end of the first step, we expect to have a representative list of true data errors that can be compared with the errors found by data quality rules to produce a reliable sample of rule imperfections.

10.3.1. What to Validate?

The first question we must answer is, "What exactly do we want data experts to validate?" On the surface what we mostly need is for someone to validate our error reports. We could simply provide data experts with samples from each error report and ask them to identify the location or each error (or reject some as false positives).

However, this approach proves very inefficient in practice. First of all, it requires an expert to understand each and every one of the data quality rules. Secondly, several rules often find errors in the same record, which makes validating individual error reports inefficient. Finally, human data specialists rarely think of individual data records and errors. Rather, they perceive databases as consisting of the data for various subjects, such as employees. An HR data expert would have a hard time verifying individual data records or attributes without looking at the big picture of all data for the employee. Thus validating a sample of 200 rule violations in 200 individual records would translate into a rather comprehensive analysis of all of the data for 200 employees.

This sounds like too much work for too little result. This is true. A much more efficient approach is to simply ask data experts to validate all data for a sample of subjects. Now, with the same sample of 200 employees, we get far superior results. First of all, many employees have more than one data error, thus we will get more errors validated with the same amount of work. Secondly, now experts also look for errors that the data quality rules possibly missed. Finally, experts do not need to understand anything about the rules. Instead, they simply follow their normal data validation routine – indeed most data experts have to validate data from time to time as a part of their everyday work.

In fact, an even better idea is to have data experts cleanse the data from the selected sample. At this point, it will take them no more work to make the corrections once the investigation is done. As a result, the work is not just a step in our rule fine-tuning exercise, but simultaneously a data improvement effort. Under this banner you may find it easier to conscript the data experts to help in the project.

Of course, once the experts are done with data validation we can simply compare their findings with the errors identified by the data quality rules and produce lists of confirmed errors as well as any discrepancies. This is the same information we would have obtained if the data experts were directly validating the error reports in the first place.

10.3.2. How to Select Validation Sample?

The second question is, "How to select subjects for manual validation?" Of course, it is impractical to have an expert verify every error. Fortunately, it is also unnecessary. All we need is to validate a rather small sample. A sample made of a few hundred subjects is typically enough to identify all rule imperfections that impact many errors.

Indeed, imagine a data quality rule that initially yields 100 false positives out of 1,000 errors (10% rate). It can be shown statistically that after reviewing only seven sample errors, the odds of finding a false positive are over 50/50. The odds grow to over 9 against 1 after only 22 samples. Thus, for a rule with a reasonably large fraction of false positives, we only need to validate a small sample before we find a representative problem. Since rule imperfections are typically systemic, finding even one or two false positives would often be enough to see the pattern, enhance the rule, and eliminate the problem.

On the other hand, if a rule has 10 false positives out of 1,000 errors (1% rate), it is unlikely that we will hit one of them even from a large sample. Indeed, we need

70 errors reviewed to have a 50/50 chance of hitting one false positive. This basically means that we are unlikely to identify such minor problems in practice. The good news is that data quality assessment does not reach for the stars with ultimate perfection. There is not much practical difference between having 1,000 or 990 errors. So even if our rules have a few false positives and false negatives here and there, we do not need to be concerned with the overall results.

The sample size is typically perceived as an all-important question on many projects and is covered in mysteries. For instance, it is a common misconception that the sample needs to be proportional to the size of the database. It is also a misconception that mathematics offers an exact formula for optimal sample size. The typical result of these misconceptions is that project teams end up with a much bigger sample (and thus much more work) than really necessary. Even more disappointing is that you can get marginal results from the verification of a large sample if the sample records are not properly selected.

The truth is that how the sample is selected is far more important than how big it is. For now let's ignore the question of the ultimate sample size. Instead, we will address the issue of how to select subjects into the sample. Fundamentally, we need a sample that meets two criteria:

- It allows us to make safe conclusions about the numbers and types of inaccuracies in the data outside of the samples.

- It yields as much information as possible about rule imperfections, so we can use it to fine-tune the rules.

The second objective is far more important. Indeed, if we find rule imperfections we stand a good chance of eliminating most of them. Our error reports will then be very accurate, and estimating the number of residual inaccuracies becomes a somewhat mute point.

The first objective is achieved by using a <u>random sample,</u> i.e. when the selection criteria are not biased towards certain types of subjects. An ideal method uses a computer-generated randomizer to pick sample subjects. This principle is rarely followed in practice. For instance, I often see sample selection delegated to the data experts, who are usually biased towards what they know about the data and tend to select known "special cases." Their samples, then, do not randomly represent all data problems and are of limited value. While it actually helps to let the experts pick sample subjects in addition to the baseline sample, the baseline itself must be created more randomly.

The second objective is achieved by using a representative sample, i.e. a sample in which all relevant types of subjects are represented. But how do you identify relevant types of subjects? In this context, subject types are defined as groups of subjects with similar types of errors. And of course (as is typical in all methods relying on sampling), if we knew all about error types we would not need to build the sample and work on the rule fine-tuning in the first place. So this definition does not help us.

Mathematical statistics suggests that a large enough random sample would most certainly be representative due to the law of large numbers, but we do not want a large sample. Further, a sample selected totally at random will be biased towards larger groups of errors. This would work well if the errors themselves were random, but in reality most errors are systemic. Thus we only need to find a few rule imperfections of any kind to make general conclusions. The bottom line is that we need a few samples of every kind, rather than a lot of samples from a few rules with the majority of errors.

Let's say we want to end up with 10 sample subjects with errors for each rule. How can we build such a sample? It seems trivial on the surface – just select randomly 10 subjects for each rule, right? Wrong! This would work if there was no overlap between populations of subjects with errors found by different rules. However, in reality many subjects have multiple errors. And so when we select 10 samples from rule #1, one or more of them will likely have errors in other rules, say rule #2. Then if we selected 10 more subjects from rule #2, we would end up with 11 in total, rather than 10. In fact, if the overlap between every pair of rules was 10% and we selected randomly 10 subjects for each rule, we would end up with about 20 samples for each rule, rather than 10. This is actually good news. It means that we need a smaller overall sample than initially thought. In other words, to get 10 samples from 30 rules we typically need much less then 300 sample subjects, likely as few as 150-200.

The actual algorithm for selecting 10 sample subjects with errors for each rule is rather tricky. In fact, there is no exact method. I use a simple, rather informal procedure. I start with a much smaller number of samples than is desired, say five (one half of the desired 10), and make the random selection. Then I count how many samples for each rule I <u>really</u> have. Most likely I will have more than five for most rules, may be 10 or more for some. Now I just go through these rules and add more samples until I reach the desired number 10. After every step I refresh the sample counts. At the end of the procedure, you will end up with 10 or slightly more samples for each rule.

Of course, I do not do this manually, but rather I have written a program that does sampling according to this algorithm. To be quite honest, my program is a bit more sophisticated. It also takes into account correlations between errors for different rules in order to select samples with minimum overhead. But the gist is as described.

Lastly, here are a few more suggestions, to assist you in selecting a validation sample. I usually set aside rules with less than some minimal number of errors (e.g. 50) and select samples for these rules at the end. For such rules it is usually sufficient to get a few cases, not 10-15 desirable from rules with many errors. Also, it is a good idea to add a few special groups to the baseline sample. These would include:

- A few subjects representing problem groups with many different errors since data quality rules tend to break down more often in such cases

- Special cases recommended by the data experts

- A relatively small totally random sample (I recommend about 25% of the entire sample to be totally random)

10.3.3. How to Perform Validation in Iterations?

Now we are ready to proceed with sample validation. One important point is to keep the validation interactive. In other words, we do not want data experts to simply go away with the 300, or whatever number, of sample subjects and spend the next month validating them all. Rather, we need to regularly compare their findings with our error reports in search for rule imperfections. Once any rule imperfections are found, it is better to eliminate remaining subjects with the same errors from the sample while we try to enhance the rule. As soon as the rules are changed, the sample must be updated to reflect the changes.

Thus I basically think of the sample list as a work-in-progress document used by the project team and data experts doing manual validation. The list is sorted, and data experts pick subjects from it for validation. As we go through their findings and make rule changes, the list itself gets re-sorted and updated.

When do we stop the iterations? First of all, we can stop when the total sample reached the size where we can make accurate data quality conclusions using statistical methods. More likely, we stop when we find that the last iteration or two did not yield any new knowledge useful for rule fine-tuning. Finally, the reality of data quality assessment projects is that we have limited timeframe and resources. Thus, the number of fine-tuning iterations will naturally be limited by these constraints.

10.4. ANALYZING IMPERFECTION PATTERNS

The next step in rule fine-tuning is to analyze rule imperfections and identify patterns in them. These patterns can be used to enhance the data quality rules. The objective is to match errors found by the data quality rules against manual verification results as best as possible. Typical enhancements include narrowing the rule scope and adding error groups. In addition, new rules sometimes must be designed, and some originally designed rules are eliminated.

The analysis starts with the investigation of findings by the data experts. We want to understand why their findings are any different from the errors identified by our rules.

An important word of caution is that data experts are human (though their patience while dealing with horrendous data often makes me wonder). Therefore, they also make mistakes. In my experience, an average data expert errs in about 3% of cases. The first step after identifying discrepancies between expert findings and our error reports is to ask the experts to review these discrepancies. Oftentimes experts will admit their guilt and agree with your results. This saves you from chasing the mirages and also increases experts' confidence in your work.

When the experts are correct, they usually can clearly explain their thought processes. In an ideal case we can replicate that process in an algorithm, which will then identify all other situations identical to the one found by the expert in the sample. Of course, we must somehow confirm that our algorithm is appropriate. We accomplish that by selecting a few more random samples from the newly found group and having the data experts verify those. If their findings match ours, then our enhancement is appropriate.

A word of wisdom: I usually prefer not to tell the data experts that they are re-validating a similar problem. Rather, I just add a few subjects to the overall sample. It is due to a simple human psychology trait. People get biased by what they expect to find. Thus, if I tell data experts that they are validating the same problem for new examples, they are likely to just confirm their findings without much extra checking. However, it is always possible that an unbiased review could identify other problems and special cases.

Sometimes the logic used by experts cannot be directly replicated in an algorithm. This involves situations when the experts rely on an information source outside of our database (such as a paper file, phone call, or just their "gut instinct"). Matching such logic in data quality rules is more difficult. A good start is to ask the expert if he/she can identify a few more similar cases. Or we just pick more random samples from the same rule in hopes of finding more examples of the same situation. Once we have a few similar cases, we use data gazing and analysis to identify anything common in the data for these cases. It sounds like an art, and it certainly is; but with experience, a good data analyst can usually find desired patterns rather quickly. We can then confirm our theories by having the experts review a few more samples. It is a very rewarding feeling to solve another data quality puzzle. In fact, this investigative part of data quality work is what keeps me so excited about my profession.

Keep in mind that even if we cannot match expert findings in all cases (and trust me, it is simply impossible), any improvement that decreases the number of false positives or better identifies data errors is beneficial. So we do not need to always be looking for a magic pill but rather for enhancements.

We will now discuss the specifics of analyzing imperfections and approaches to enhancing the rules for different types of problems.

10.5. ELIMINATING FALSE POSITIVES

Consider the false positive example from Figure 10-1 (shown again in Figure 10-4). A data expert could clearly communicate the reason why the error we found for employee #11226 is a false positive. The employee is actually part of an acquired company (coded as *GB* in CompanyCode field), and employment with this acquired company does not count for any HR purposes. The HireDate is correctly set to the first day of the employment with the parent company. The employment history shows previous employment with the acquired company for information purposes. In this case HireDate simply does not have to match the effective date of the earliest record in the employment history. Rather it must be set to the first day of employment with the main parent company (or one of its original subdivisions).

Figure 10-4: False Positive Example

We can now try to find the pattern that can be used to enhance the rule. First we need to determine all of the acquired companies that fall in this category and identify their company codes (found in the CompanyCode field). Secondly, we need to determine an algorithm for validating the value of HireDate for all employees from these acquired companies.

The expert may suggest using company acquisition dates, which can be found in COMPANY table. For instance, the acquisition date for company *GB* is listed as 9/15/1996. However, we cannot trust the experts blindly. No disrespect, but 9 out of 10 general rules suggested by data experts are wrong. It is not for the lack of knowledge, but rather because data experts are used to thinking about individual situations rather than in terms of general rules.

To check the acquisition date theory we could start by running a report showing HireDate value for all employees whose employment starts with an acquired company. Based on the expert's opinion, we expect to find all employees from *GB* to have HireDate of 9/15/1996. What we might actually find is that only about half of them do. Another 30% have HireDate of 11/1/1996, yet a smaller group has HireDate of 5/15/1997; and some employees have dates in between.

Armed with this knowledge, we go back to our data experts and promptly learn that employees from the company *GB* were transferred in stages, thus the many dates. The same is true for several other acquisitions. This situation is very typical of working with data experts. They have a tremendous amount of knowledge but usually cannot summarize it. You have to ask the right questions to get the right answers, and finding exceptions from the rules is the best way to ask the right questions.

So now we have determined that HireDate for employees from acquired companies does not have to fall on the acquisition date listed in COMPANY table. What do we do now? One suggestion is to simply assume that any of the dates during the acquisition period are acceptable. However, this is not a very accurate rule if the period extends over several years. We can easily miss many errors.

Data gazing gives us another alternative. A look at the data in Figure10-4 suggests that the acquisition was coded in the employment history as one-day termination on 9/14/1996 and rehire on the following day. We can use this pattern to match HireDate against the date of the *REHIRE* record. A report again is in order, checking that the technique was used for all acquisitions. More likely than not, the report will show some further kinks that require more investigation. I love my job!

The bottom line is that rule fine-tuning is a process that takes much data analysis and investigation. It also typically results in adding a lot of special logic to the rules to make them more accurate. The further you go, the more precise will be the data quality assessment. Fortunately, with reasonable efforts it is almost always possible to make rules quite precise.

With the best effort, it is often inevitable that some rules will still produce false positives. Therefore, we will always have somewhat inflated error counts. To adjust for this phenomenon we can estimate false positive fractions and use them when tabulating aggregate data quality scores (see Chapter 12). The best estimate for the false positive fraction is the ratio of the number of remaining false positives in the sample among all reviewed samples. In other words, if we validated 20 errors for a given rule and found one false positive, then the best estimate is 1/20 or 5%. Keep in mind that we are talking about the number of unresolved false positives. If we initially found three false positives but were able to enhance the rules and eliminate two of them, the final count is still one.

The estimated false positive fraction for each rule should be stored in the rule catalogue for further reference. The most practical place is to add an attribute to the RULE table.

In theory, this estimate may not always be accurate because we are using a relatively small sample. The good news is that the estimate is not biased. It will be a bit too high for some rules and a bit too low for other rules, all at random. Therefore, when we aggregate the information to look at the big picture of the data quality across many rules, individual inaccuracies will average out.

So far we discussed the techniques for handling the false positives we are able to find through sample validation. But what if we cannot find any? Or what if we enhanced the rule and eliminated all false positives that we have found? How do we know that there are no more false positives hiding out there? The answer is, there is no guarantee; but with a large enough sample, we can feel rather confident that we did not miss anything major. Mathematical statistics offers a rather simple formula for the number of samples we need to validate before we can feel comfortable about false positives in our rules.

Imagine that a rule finds N violations, out of which F are false positives and $(N-F)$ are true errors. Now we take a random sample of S errors. The odds of not finding any false positives among the sample are

$$[(N-F)/N]^S$$

i.e. the fraction of true errors raised in the power equal to the sample size S. Thus, if the rule finds 1,000 errors ($N=1000$) and 100 of them are false positives ($F=100$), then a sample of 15 ($S=15$) will miss all false positives with probability 0.9^{15}, or approximately 0.2. By the way, the formula does not depend on the total number of errors but rather only on the fraction of false positives. The result would be the same if we had a rule with 100 errors and 10 false positives, or 10,000 errors and 1,000 false positives.

Now we can use this formula to figure out the desired sample size. Say we have taken a sample of 15 errors identified by a rule and found no false positives (or at least we eliminated all that we found by fine-tuning the rule, which is the same thing for us). Now, we do not know how many false positives this rule really has, but we can bet 8 against 2 that the fraction of false positives among all identified errors is no more than 10%. These are good enough odds for me. Of course, the possibility of having even 9% false positives may be too unsettling. Then we need a slightly bigger sample. For instance, a sample size of 31 gives us the same 8 against 2 odds that the fraction of false positives among all identified errors is no more than 5%. We can tune the sample sizes to our desired level of comfort or simply accept the comfort level provided by a certain sample size.

One important thing to keep in mind is that this formula does not guarantee anything but only gives you the odds. If we apply the same logic to many different rules, it will work for most but not for all. Indeed, if you play a game with 8 against 2 odds over and over again, you will still lose sometimes. Thus, based on the formula we can say that <u>most</u> rules will have no more than 5% of false positives, but some will probably have over 5%. At the same time, many will have way less than 5%.

At the end of the day, let's remember that we are dealing with good records falsely accused by our data quality rules of being erroneous. Having a few of these is not as bad as having erroneous records sneaking in among the good citizens. So we are safe here even if we miss a few false positives. Once we finish data quality assessment and proceed to data cleansing, we will inevitably find these perpetrators.

10.6. HANDLING FALSE NEGATIVES

False negatives are data errors not found by any rules. Those are the most dangerous and sneaky criminals. Examples of false negatives are often identified during sample validation. The challenge is to design new data quality rules that will catch the missing errors. Sometimes the data experts can offer suggestions by describing how they were able to identify these errors. In other cases, data gazing helps find something unusual in the data. A common technique is to find an additional data source for comparison. Regardless, some false negatives are inevitable, and all we can hope to do is bring their numbers to a small fraction.

The good news is that we have overwhelming odds against missing any large pockets of errors even with a reasonably small sample. Say we have manually validated data for 250 subjects and found five false negatives for which we could not create any data quality rules even after fine-tuning. We can rather safely assume that the overall fraction of subjects with false negatives in the database is about 2% (5 divided by 250). It can be shown that with probability 0.95, the true fraction lies between 0.8% and 4.5%.

The numbers on the record level will usually come up even better. Indeed, data experts validate data for subjects, but each subject has many records. For example, employment history may have on average four records per employee. Then the sample of 250 subjects consists of 1,000 employment history records. Now if we found five erroneous records missed by all of our rules, we can conclude that overall the database has about 0.5% of such missed erroneous records (5 divided by 1,000). It can also be shown that with probability 0.95, the true fraction lies between 0.2% and 1.2%.

I am sure this statistical mumbo-jumbo may seem overwhelming to any reader without appropriate background. And we do not expect data quality experts to also be mathematical gurus. The truth is that statistical formulas are only important if we are trying to make data quality assessment estimates for the worst-case scenario. Normally all we are looking for are reasonable estimates. To get those we simply rely on direct findings of the sample review. If we found five false negatives in the sample of 250 subjects, then we expect our data quality rules overall to miss about 2% of errors, period! This is good enough as an estimate. We will get more accurate measurements if and when we proceed to data cleansing.

10.7. HANDLING UNCERTAINTY IN ERROR LOCATION

Consider the two examples from Figure 10-2 (shown again in Figure 10-5). Both are legitimate errors. However, in the first case HireDate is correct, while the effective date of the first employment history record is erroneous. In the second case employment history is accurate, while HireDate is incorrect.

Sample validation will identify this situation. Further investigation would hopefully provide the explanations. The first situation is an example of "delayed data entry" into the system. We can identify all similar situations rather accurately, though not with 100% precision. An adequate algorithm would look for all situations where HireDate precedes effective date of the earliest employment history record by less than two weeks.

The second situation is also rather simple. Due to a software glitch, HireDate value for all rehired retirees was changed to the rehire date. We could easily identify all rehired retirees and see that this is true. If fortunate enough to be in an organization that does formal software maintenance tracking, we may even be able to include in the rule the period of time for which the glitch existed.

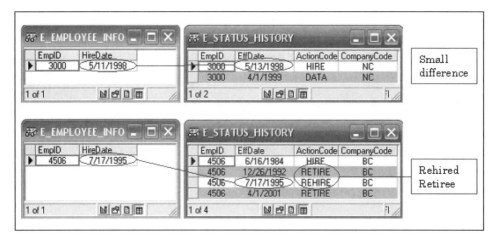

Figure 10-5: Examples of Errors with Different Locations

And what if we cannot find good error patterns? Often a good technique is to find additional data elements related to the data compared in the rule. We can use such data elements as "tie-breakers," who decide which of the data elements are more likely to be correct. For example, we can look up the earliest record in compensation history to see if the employee's first paycheck is consistent with the HireDate value or with the employment history.

Another useful technique is to look for error dependencies across data quality rules. Oftentimes violations of several rules are caused by the same underlying problem. Thus we can use a presence of an error in another rule for the same record (or subject) as the "tie-breaker." For instance, we can have a separate rule validating that compensation history is present all the way back to the original hire date. When that rule is also violated, we have good reasons to mistrust HireDate.

To find potential dependencies between rules, we use ***error profiling***. The simplest technique measures error overlap between two rules defined as the fraction of records (or subjects) identified as erroneous by both rules among records identified as erroneous by at least one of the rules. Say rule #1 identified 500 records in a certain table as potentially erroneous, rule #2 identified 700 records, and 100 of them are the same. Then the total number of records identified by at least one of the rules equals 1,100 (400 unique to rule #1, 600 unique to rule #2, and 100 common to both), and the overlap metrics equals about 9% (100 out of 1,100). This is relatively low. If 400 of the records are common to both rules, then a similar calculation yields overlap metrics of 0.5, which is rather high. These metrics can be calculated for all pairs of rules and for different data tables. It is even possible to set up a program that will calculate all such metrics and then report any that are above a certain threshold. We could then investigate rules with high error overlap and try to understand the reasons behind it. This knowledge always helps enhance the rules, which is why error profiling is a valuable fine-tuning technique.

Once we identify patterns, the next step is to enhance the rules. We can split them into sub-rules, but a better solution is to introduce error groups. In our case we have three groups:

- HireDate precedes the earliest employment history record by less than two weeks.

- HireDate coincides with the effective date of the *REHIRE* record in employment history for a rehired retiree.

- All other errors.

Note that we always have the last "unclassified" error group. Sample review by experts should always be focused on the errors from this group. As we find more patterns, we continue reclassifying errors from that group into the known patterns.

The reader may ask, "Aren't we going to far?" Indeed a more narrow view of data quality assessment is simply to identify errors, not explain their causes. Investigating the nature of the errors belongs to the data quality improvement initiative. This is partially true, which is why I defer further discussion of the error patterns and error grouping to my future book on data cleansing. Suffice it to say here that if you can find some error groups with different error types, it is very useful to create them.

It is also useful to estimate how often each of the records affected by a rule is erroneous among all identified errors. For example, say we reviewed 20 sample errors from the HireDate rule and concluded that in five of them HireDate was erroneous, while in the remaining 15 the earliest employment history record was inaccurate. Then our best estimate for the probability that HireDate is incorrect, given the rule violation, is 5/20 or 25%. This information can be used to build a more accurate data quality scorecard. We will discuss the topic further in the next two chapters.

SUMMARY

In this chapter we have discussed the process of rule fine-tuning. The purpose of fine-tuning is to identify and eliminate various rule imperfections, which generally fall into three main categories:

- False positives are rule violations that under a close examination prove to be legitimately correct data.

- False negatives are erroneous data not found by any data quality rules.

- Uncertainties in error location are situations when a rule compares two or more data elements and identifies an inconsistency but cannot tell which of the data elements is incorrect.

The process of rule fine-tuning involves four steps. The objective of the first step is to identify rule imperfections. The only way to accomplish this is through manual verification of the sample data by the data experts. The second step is devoted to the analysis of sample verification findings and the search for patterns. On the third step we enhance the rules in order to eliminate as many flaws as possible. Typical enhancements include narrowing the rule scope and adding error groups. In addition, new rules sometimes must be designed, and some originally designed rules are eliminated.

These three steps are repeated iteratively until we are satisfied with the results, cannot make further improvements, or simply run out of resources. Ideally at that point we have a set of rules that accurately identify and locate each and every data error. In reality we usually stop well short of this objective. On the final step we estimate percentages of residual false positives and false negatives, as well as quantify other error uncertainties.

CHAPTER 11
CATALOGUING ERRORS

The main objective of data quality assessment is to identify erroneous data. To that end we design numerous data quality rules and use them to produce an even greater number of lengthy error reports. While it seems rather simple to store these error reports, the task proves quite challenging in practice. I have seen many data quality assessment projects successfully produce hundreds of error reports and get subsequently totally lost in the meta data jungle. The sight of a 500-page printout or even of an electronic listing with 20,000 lines of error messages will make most data quality professionals duck for cover.

To get any significant value out of the data quality assessment initiative we need a well-structured, queryable electronic error catalogue. An ideal error catalogue would support the following functionalities:

- Aggregate, filter, and sort errors across various dimensions,

- Identify overlaps and correlations between errors for different rules,

- Identify data records affected by a particular error or a group of errors, and

- Identify all errors for a particular data record or a set of records.

This functionality can only be achieved if the error catalogue stores all error reports in a relational structure that links errors with rules that identify them and with erroneous data records themselves. In this chapter, we will discuss such architecture.

- Section 11.1 introduces basic error catalogue concepts.

- Section 11.2 presents methods for tracking potentially missing records.

- Section 11.3 introduces an important concept of error locations.

- Section 11.4 discusses error groups.

- Section 11.5 describes the mechanism for subject-level error tracking.

- Section 11.6 presents the structure of error messages.

11.1. ERROR CATALOGUE BASICS

An ***error catalogue*** is a group of entities that collectively stores information about all identified data errors. An error catalogue is the core part of data quality meta data. I will start the analysis of the error catalogue architecture from a simple example. Consider the attribute domain constraint described in Table 11-1.

Rule #1. *DOMAIN.E_STATUS.EMP_TYPE*

Formal Definition:

[E_EMPLOYEE_STATUS].[EmployeeType] In ('O', 'RF', 'RP', 'TF', 'TP')

Informal Description:

Employee type must either be *O* ("occasional") or consist of exactly two characters, with the first one as *R* ("regular") or *T* ("temporary") and the second one as *F* ("full-time") or *P* ("part-time"). All other values are invalid.

Table 11-1: Attribute Domain Constraint for Employee Type

Figure 11-1 shows two records in E_EMPLOYEE_STATUS table with invalid values of EmployeeType attribute. Rule #1 from Table 11-1 will identify both as erroneous. How do we record these errors in the error catalogue?

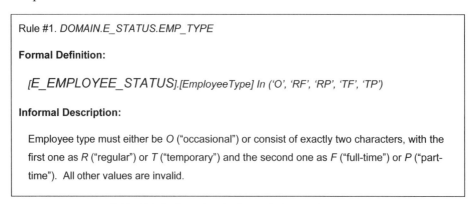

Figure 11-1: Records with Erroneous Employee Type

First of all, each error must be registered in a general error listing. At a bare minimum each entry in this listing must be given a unique error identifier and must also reference the data quality rule that found the error.

Additionally we want to be able to identify the data records where the errors are found. Consider the erroneous records in Figure 11-1. Each can be identified by the combination of the table name (E_EMPLOYEE_STATUS) and the value of the primary key field EmpID. In general, we can reference any record in the database by a combination of its table name and the value of a unique identity key. Such reference reliably distinguishes all records. The question becomes: which identity key to use?

The simplest solution is to add a surrogate key attribute to all tables and use it for referencing. Table E_EMPLOYEE_STATUS in Figure 11-1 has such a surrogate key field named RecordID. It is actually convenient to have a common name for the surrogate key in all database tables. Now we can easily reference all erroneous records using a simple identity key made up of the table name and RecordID value. For instance, records in Table 11-1 are referenced as {*E_EMPLOYEE_STATUS; 1662*} and {*E_EMPLOYEE_STATUS; 1904*}.

Figure 11-2 shows basic error catalogue architecture made of two tables. ERROR table simply lists all errors and provides reference to the data quality rules that found each error. ERROR_RECORD table references actual erroneous records. It must be a separate table because a single error will often affect multiple records.

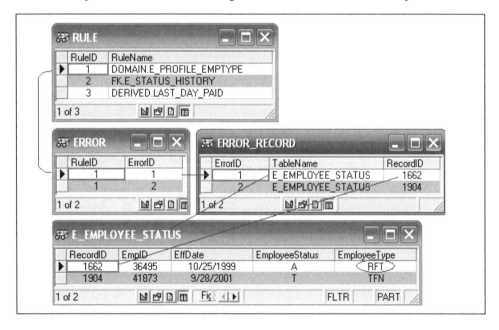

Figure 11-2: Basic Architecture of the Error Catalogue

Let's look at the way the errors are registered in Figure 11-2. Rule #1 finds an erroneous value *RFT* in EmployeeType for employee #36495. It logs a new entry with a unique ErrorID equal to 1 into the ERROR table. A linked entry is made in the ERROR_RECORD table. It has the same ErrorID and identifies the erroneous record as coming from E_EMPLOYEE_STATUS table with RecordID equal to 1662. The trace is now complete. We can use it to locate all erroneous records.

The reader may wonder, "Why are we using a surrogate key to reference erroneous records?" After all, most data tables have a primary key, which can be used for referencing. However, using actual primary keys may be undesirable for several reasons. First of all, primary keys are not always enforced by the databases (we even include identity rules to check primary key violations in the data quality assessment). When key duplications are possible, the key cannot be used for reliable record referencing. Secondly, some data tables may have composite keys made of multiple attributes with varying data types. Using values of such keys in the error catalogue presents significant challenges. This is why I recommend using surrogate keys in place of actual primary keys, even when the primary keys exist.

Surrogate keys are easy to create when data quality assessment is done in a staging area, rather than against the production database. I always recommend using a staging area when there are no plans to execute data quality assessment recurrently. On the other hand, when data quality assessment is done on a regular basis, we often have to run the rules directly against the production database; and thus we are stuck with the actual structure of the database. We will discuss this situation in detail in Chapter 14, which is dedicated to the specifics of recurrent data quality assessment.

11.2. RECORDING MISSING RECORDS

Now consider a slightly more complex foreign key constraint for E_STATUS_HISTORY entity (described in Table 11-2). Any time an orphan record is found in E_STATUS_HISTORY table with no matching record with same EmpID in E_EMPLOYEE_PROFILE table, an error must be recorded.

Rule #2. *FK.E_STATUS_HISTORY*

Formal Definition:

FK([E_STATUS_HISTORY].[EmpID]) = [E_EMPLOYEE_PROFILE].[EmpID]

Informal Description:

Every record in the employment status history must have EmpID referencing an existing employee listed in the main employee profile table.

Table 11-2: Foreign Key Constraint for E_STATUS_HISTORY

Figure 11-3 displays data violating this rule. It shows two records in E_STATUS_HISTORY table for employee #114603. There is no record of such an employee in E_EMPLOYEE_PROFILE table. The foreign key constraint (rule #2 from Table 11-2) will identify the error. How do we record it in the error catalogue?

The challenge here is that the error can be explained either by erroneous values of EmpID in E_STATUS_HISTORY records or as a missing record with EmpID equal to 114603 in E_EMPLOYEE_PROFILE table. We already know how to reference E_STATUS_HISTORY records in the error catalogue (by using table ERROR_RECORD). But how do we log a possibly missing record? We cannot reference what does not exist! Yet we cannot ignore the possibility. Missing records are as important as erroneous records and must find their way into the error reports and, ultimately, the data quality scorecard.

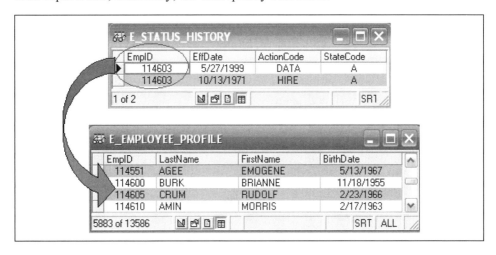

Figure 11-3: Records with Foreign Key Violation

The solution necessitates the introduction of an additional table into the error catalogue. The new ERROR_RECORD_MISSING table is used to track possibly missing records. Figure 11-4 illustrates the use of the new table.

Rule #2 is applied to the data from Figure 11-3 and finds a foreign key violation for records with EmpID equal to 114603. It logs the error with unique ErrorID equal to 2 into the ERROR table. Two linked entries are made into the ERROR_RECORD table. They reference the two orphan records (RecordID #33349 and #33350 in table E_STATUS_HISTORY). In addition, an entry is logged into ERROR_RECORD_MISSING table indicating the possibility of one record missing in E_EMPLOYEE_PROFILE. We can now use the error catalogue to locate all erroneous records and also to count potentially missing records.

Figure 11-4: Error Catalogue Incorporating Missing Records

11.3. ERRORS AFFECTING MULTIPLE RECORDS

Most data quality rules affect several records, often in several tables. Thus when an error is found, one or more of these records could be erroneous. We must log all potentially erroneous or missing records in the error catalogue so they can be later identified for further analysis. For instance, for the foreign key error shown in Figure 11-4, we catalogued both orphan records and a potentially missing parent record. Now when we decide to run an error report or build the data quality scorecard, all possible errors will be accounted for.

But what if we conclude that 75% of the time the foreign key violation is caused by a missing parent record, and 25% of the time orphan records are mislabeled? We catalogued them all, but how do we make sure that the errors are properly counted? Indeed, a query tallying all catalogued records will count three. In reality we have two erroneous records with probability 0.75, or one missing record with probability 0.25. Under no circumstance do we have three erroneous records.

This problem will persist for most data quality rules. We will inescapably overestimate the number of erroneous records. What we need to do is somehow assign error probability factors to the potentially erroneous records.

The first solution that comes to mind is to add ErrorProbability attribute directly to the tables ERROR_RECORD and ERROR_RECORD_MISSING and populate it during the rule execution. But it is very inefficient. First, we end up storing the same value with every error. More importantly, if we later concluded that our 0.75/0.25 probabilities were off and 0.9/0.1 were more precise, we would be forced to rerun the rule.

The proper solution is to introduce the concept of *error location* that marks records in similar circumstances. Error locations must be selected in such a way that for all records from the same location the probability to be in error is the same. For instance, a foreign key constraint would have two error locations:

- Orphan record.

- Missing parent record.

Figure 11-5 incorporates locations into the error catalogue from Figure 11-4. The list of locations along with error probabilities for each one is stored in a new table RULE_ERROR_LOCATION. We then record location for each erroneous record. Orphan E_STATUS_HISTORY records are properly assigned location A, while potentially missing record in E_EMPLOYEE_PROFILE table is designated with location B. We do not need to store error probabilities in ERROR_RECORD and ERROR_RECORD_MISSING tables as these can be accessed by queries, but we show them in Figure 11-5 for ease of understanding.

And what if we concluded that the error is always indicative of a missing parent record in E_EMPLOYEE_PROFILE table? Then, of course, we do not have to log orphan E_STATUS_HISTORY records into the error catalogue. However, if it was desirable to catalogue such records (for instance for reference purposes to know which records were used by the rule), we would list them under a special location "X" assigned error probability 0.

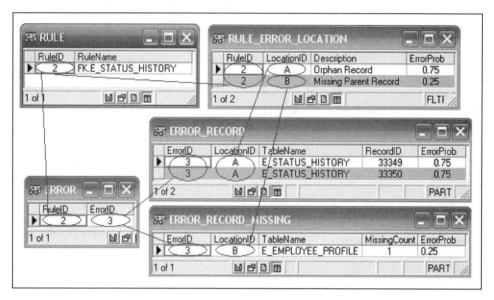

Figure 11-5: Error Catalogue Incorporating Error Locations

Keep in mind that the assignment of records to locations is driven by their likelihood of being in error, not by their physical location. For example, consider the aggregated reference rule that validates all foreign keys referencing E_EMPLOYEE_PROFILE entity. A single error will affect records in all dependent entities with the same value of the key attribute EmpID missing in the parent E_EMPLOYEE_PROFILE entity. This rule will still have two error locations. Indeed, we have only two possibilities: either a parent record is missing, or all child records are mislabeled. Therefore location A can be used to refer to all orphan records in all dependent entities.

Consider another example. State-transition rules limit valid pairs of states in sequential records. Each error will therefore impact two records in the same state-dependent entity. Analysis may indicate that the first record is more likely to be correct, say in 90% of cases, than the second. To incorporate this we would introduce two error locations:

- First (earlier) record.

- Second (later) record.

We will then assign appropriate probabilities to these locations. Now we have an error affecting records in the same table but assigned to different locations.

11.4. ERROR GROUPS

When a rule has multiple error groups, we need to categorize each error into its group. We also need to account for the possibility that error probabilities by location vary for different error groups.

Consider the example of the aggregated reference rule that validates all foreign keys referencing E_EMPLOYEE_PROFILE entity. Each error will affect all orphan records with the same EmpID in all dependent entities. We can categorize all errors into three groups:

- Errors with orphan records in two or more tables

- Errors with several orphan records confined to a single table

- Errors with only one orphan record

We can reasonably conclude that errors of group A are most likely caused by a missing parent record, while errors of group C are more likely explained by a mislabeled child record. Assume that the estimated error probability by location is as shown in Table 11-3.

	Group A	Group B	Group C
Location A: Orphan Record	0%	50%	80%
Location B: Parent Record	100%	50%	20%

Table 11-3: Error Probability by Error Group and Location

To fully incorporate error grouping into the error catalogue we must first add ErrorGroup attribute to the main ERROR table in the error catalogue. Further we must add a new table to store error probability data from Table 11-3.

Figure 11-6 illustrates this solution. The top four tables are technically parts of the rule catalogue. Observe the following:

- RULE table lists rule #4 REFERENCE.E_EMPLOYEE_PROFILE.

- RULE_GROUP table defines three error groups for rule #4.

- RULE_ERROR_LOCATION table describes two locations for rule #4.

- RULE_ERROR_PROBABILITY table stores error probabilities by error group and location as shown in Table 11-3.

The bottom three tables in Figure 11-6 are parts of the error catalogue. ERROR table lists two errors. The first error (ErrorID equal to 4) affects seven orphan records in three tables for the same employee. Observe how it is recorded:

- ERROR table assigns the error to group A of rule #4.

- ERROR_RECORD table references all seven orphan records. Lookup into RULE_ERROR_PROBABILITY yields the probability zero. Thus we are certain these orphan records are actually valid, though we decided to list them in the error catalogue for reference purposes.

- Entry in the ERROR_RECORD_MISSING table indicates that one record is missing in E_EMPLOYEE_PROFILE. Lookup in RULE_ERROR_PROBABILITY obtains the probability one, meaning that we are certain a record for this employee is missing.

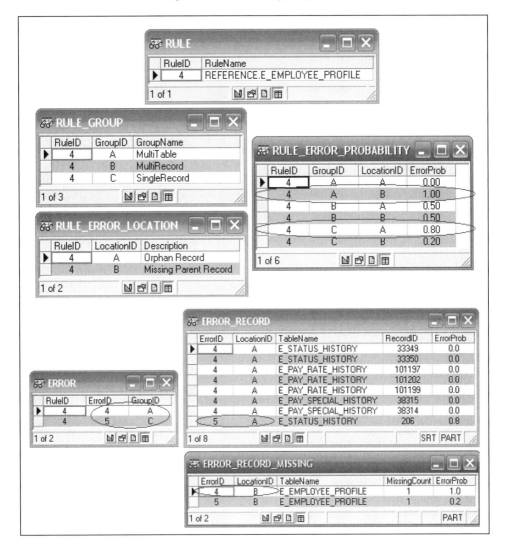

Figure 11-6: Error Catalogue Incorporating Error Groups

The second error (ErrorID equal to 5) involves a single orphan record. Accordingly, ERROR table assigns the error to group C of rule #4. ERROR_RECORD table references the orphan record (RecordID #206 in E_STATUS_HISTORY table) classified into location A. Lookup into RULE_ERROR_PROBABILITY yields the probability 0.8. This means that record #206 is erroneous with 80% probability.

Keep in mind that this technique assumes mutually exclusive error groups, i.e. a situation where each error falls into one and only one group. A solution for overlapping groups is also possible, but more complex. I recommend using mutually exclusive groups whenever possible for basic grouping purposes and for defining error probabilities. Additional groups can be defined as tags in the error message, as discussed in section 11.6.

11.5. SUBJECT-LEVEL ERROR TRACKING

In Chapter 8 we introduced the concept of *subjects* – high-level business objects whose data are stored in the database. For example, employees and positions are among the subjects in common HR databases; shipping database subjects would include orders, customers, and products. Subjects play a critical role in data quality initiatives.

First of all, data quality is more meaningful when defined on the subject level rather than the record level. Indeed, knowing that 10% of employees have incorrect HR data, or that 8% of insurance claims have material errors, is far more important than knowing that 4% of data records in the database are erroneous. Subject level quality measurements can be easier translated into the cost of bad data and ROI of data quality initiatives.

Secondly, many data quality rules operate on the subject-level data. For instance, state-transition rules really apply to subjects as a whole rather than to individual records. Even such simple rules as foreign key constraints are more meaningful on the subject level. Recall how we aggregated various foreign key constraints into a composite reference rule to see all orphan records for the same employee.

The error tracking mechanism discussed thus far does not provide subject-level view of the data quality. Figure 11-7 illustrates this point. It shows a portion of the data for employee #193585 in tables E_STATUS_HISTORY (storing state-dependent employment history) and E_PAY_RATE_HISTORY (storing the history of pay rate changes). The data has eight errors found by six different data quality rules.

- The first record in E_STATUS_HISTORY table has action *REHIRE*, but only action *HIRE* is allowed as terminator. This error is found by terminator constraint *TERMINATOR.EMP_HISTORY*.

- After resignation on 8/13/1971, this employee has some state-specific data change actions that are only allowed during active employment. This error is found by state-action constraint *ACTION.EMP_HISTORY*.

- There are three employment termination records with one-day duration. One-day records are usually the result of mistaken data entry and violate duration rule *DURATION.EMP_HISTORY*.

- There are two consecutive records in E_STATUS_HISTORY with *LOA* action, violating state-transition rule *TRANSITION.EMP_HISTORY*.

- The weekly pay rate of $84.5 in E_PAY_RATE_HISTORY table is too low – less than the minimum allowed weekly pay rate of $200. This error is found by conditional domain constraint *COND_DOMAIN.PAY_RATE.W*.

- Two records co-exist in E_PAY_RATE_HISTORY table with different pay rates but the same effective date 4/1/2000. This violates identity rule *PK.PAY_RATE*.

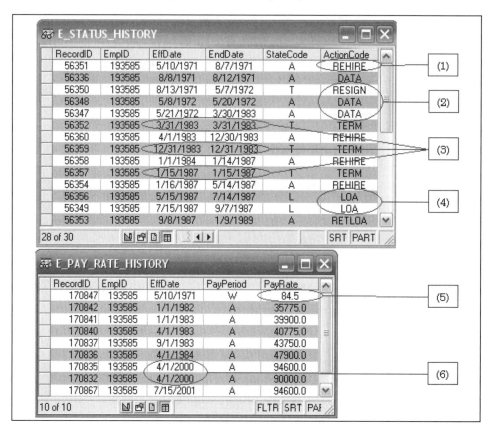

Figure 11-7: Multiple Errors for Employee #193585

Error catalogue tables ERROR and ERROR_RECORD provide us with complete record references. Each and every one of the 12 potentially erroneous records implicated by these eight errors will be logged. However, nothing in the error catalogue indicates that all these errors impact the same employee. To learn that directly from the error catalogue we would have to create a very complex and ineffective query. The task would be totally insurmountable if some errors indicated possibly missing records, since such situation does not provide any tangible record references.

The bottom line is that the structure of the error catalogue discussed thus far makes subject-level error analysis very difficult. We cannot efficiently build lists of employees with various types of errors, report all errors for a specific employee, analyze how many employees have errors of different kinds, and run numerous other useful reports. The necessary improvement involves explicit referencing of the subjects affected by each error.

How do we accomplish that? We cannot simply reference the subject from inside ERROR table since an error may impact multiple subjects. A proper solution is to add another error catalogue table ERROR_SUBJECT. Figure 11-8 shows this expanded error catalogue with errors (4) and (6) logged in.

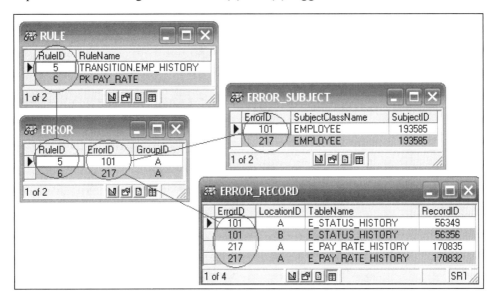

Figure 11-8: Error Catalogue Incorporating Subjects

Error (4) is logged with error identifier #101, while error (6) is logged with identifier #217. As you can see, ERROR_RECORD table references all four affected records (two for each error). At the same time ERROR_SUBJECT table indicates that both errors affect the same employee #193585. The trace is now complete. The data can be used to run subject-level data quality reports.

Note that in the general case of multiple subject classes and multiple heterogeneous databases, we would need to create a master subject list for each class. That is why we have attribute SubjectClassName in ERROR_SUBJECT table. We could also use these master lists to track the status of each data quality rule for each subject. For instance, we could add Boolean flags for each data quality rule to indicate whether or not each subject passed or failed this rule. This mechanism would tremendously speed up subject-level error reporting and also help us manage interdependencies between data quality rules.

11.6. ERROR MESSAGES

We have learned how to log an error in the error catalogue in a way that allows complete tracing of its origins. We can use this architecture to drill-down from error reports to the individual erroneous records. However, it is often desirable to merge error details for all or some errors into a single report. This helps analyze error patterns, fine-tune data quality rules, and identify possible correction approaches.

Consider for instance attribute domain constraint for EmployeeType (implemented by rule #1). It may be useful to see a report with all erroneous values of EmployeeType attribute. Of course, this can be easily accomplished by the error catalogue Query 11-1. Once executed the query would produce a report showing all erroneous records along with exact invalid values of EmployeeType attribute. Analysis of the report could give us possible clues to the nature of the problem. For instance, we may find that all erroneous values are 3-character codes, such as *RF1*, which add extra character at the end of legitimate 2-character combinations. Further investigation will find that such codes have been used in the past to indicate various types of regular full-time employment.

```
SELECT    E_EMPLOYEE_STATUS.EmpID, E_EMPLOYEE_STATUS.EmployeeType
  FROM    ERROR, ERROR_RECORD, E_EMPLOYEE_STATUS
 WHERE    ERROR.RuleID = 1
   AND    ERROR.ErrorID = ERROR_RECORD.ErrorID
   AND    ERROR_RECORD.RecordID = E_EMPLOYEE_STATUS.RecordID
```

Query 11-1: List of All Erroneous Values of EmployeeType

Now consider the aggregated reference rule that validates all foreign keys referencing E_EMPLOYEE_PROFILE entity. It is certainly beneficial to see a report listing all employees with some orphan records. This is far from trivial, as we need to join ERROR_RECORD table with many different data tables and then eliminate duplicates. Keep in mind that foreign key constraints are among the simplest data quality rules. More complex rules (such as rules for state-dependent objects) often involve multiple records from multiple tables. Merging record details for errors found by these rules into convenient reports might be extremely difficult and inefficient.

The conclusion is that our standard error catalogue architecture allows easy access to all potentially erroneous records as needed to build the data quality scorecard. However, it does not provide easy means for building custom data reports useful in error analysis and data cleansing. For that later purpose, it is useful to accompany each error with a "message" providing some relevant error details. Such a message can be formed during rule execution and stored in an additional attribute Message in the ERROR table.

You can build messages in a structured format, such as comma-delimited list of values or XML text. A structured format allows the access to error messages as tabular reports and provides a more efficient means for error analysis. I always recommend forming detailed messages with any and all attributes possibly relevant to the error analysis. Also, you can add Boolean flags to categorize errors into groups.

It is important to structure error messages with attention to those who will analyze the error reports. That sometimes means two kinds of message text for each error – one for a business-oriented audience and one for a technical audience. The former can be stored as readable free-flow text, while the latter organized in a structured format. Alternatively, the free-flow message can be built on the fly from the data stored in the structured message.

Figure 11-9 shows the error listing with detailed error messages for the reference rule that validates all foreign keys referencing E_EMPLOYEE_PROFILE entity. Each error is accompanied by two messages – a structured message stored in comma-delimited format and a free-flow text message. The structured message lists an employee identifier, the total number of orphan records, the total number of entities with orphan records, and counts of orphan records in each dependent entity.

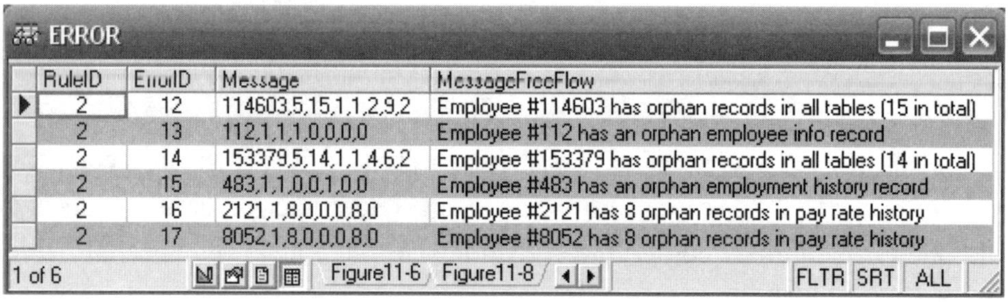

	RuleID	ErrorID	Message	MessageFreeFlow
▶	2	12	114603,5,15,1,1,2,9,2	Employee #114603 has orphan records in all tables (15 in total)
	2	13	112,1,1,1,0,0,0,0	Employee #112 has an orphan employee info record
	2	14	153379,5,14,1,1,4,6,2	Employee #153379 has orphan records in all tables (14 in total)
	2	15	483,1,1,0,0,1,0,0	Employee #483 has an orphan employment history record
	2	16	2121,1,8,0,0,0,8,0	Employee #2121 has 8 orphan records in pay rate history
	2	17	8052,1,8,0,0,0,8,0	Employee #8052 has 8 orphan records in pay rate history

1 of 6   Figure11-6 Figure11-8   FLTR SRT ALL

Figure 11-9: Error Messages for a Reference Rule

For instance, message for the first error (ErrorID #12) tells us that for employee #114603 a total of 15 orphan records were found in five entities. Specifically, one record in E_EMPLOYEE_INFO, one record in E_EMPLOYEE_STATUS, two records in E_STATUS_HISTORY, nine records in E_PAY_RATE_HISTORY, and two records in E_PAY_SPECIAL_HISTORY. This clearly indicates that a comprehensive set of records exists for this employee in all but the main E_EMPLOYEE_PROFILE table. A similar situation applies to employee #153379 (third row for ErrorID #14).

On the other hand, the message for the last error (ErrorID #17) shows that for employee #8052 there are eight orphan records, all in a single table E_PAY_RATE_HISTORY. The next to last error has identical message for employee #2121. These errors likely have the same cause but still different from that for the first two errors. This conclusion would be difficult to arrive without comprehensive error messages.

SUMMARY

In this chapter we have discussed the structure of the error catalogue – a group of entities that collectively stores information about all identified data errors. These are key components of the rule catalogue:

- Each error must be registered in a general listing ERROR. Each entry in this listing must be given a unique error identifier and must also reference the data quality rule that found the error.

- We use ERROR_RECORD table to reference erroneous records. Each record can be referenced by a combination of its table name and the value of a unique identity key. It is preferable to use simple homogeneous surrogate keys for referencing.

- Missing records are as important as erroneous and must find their way into the error reports and ultimately the data quality scorecard. The solution necessitates introduction of an additional table into the error catalogue. The new ERROR_RECORD_MISSING table is used to track possibly missing records.

- Error locations are used when the error probabilities vary for different records affected by the same error. Error groups allow us to address the situation when the error probabilities further vary for errors of different kind found by the same data quality rule.

- Subjects are high-level business objects whose data are stored in the database. Subject level quality measurements are very important because they can be easier translated into the cost of bad data and ROI of data quality initiatives. Error catalogue table ERROR_SUBJECT provides a direct link between errors and subjects affected by them.

- It is often desirable to bring error details for all or some errors into a single report. This helps analyze error patterns, fine-tune data quality rules, and identify possible correction approaches. For that purpose it is useful to accompany each error with a "message" providing some relevant error details. Such a message can be formed during rule execution and stored in an additional attribute Message in the ERROR table.

Chapter 11 – Cataloguing Errors

CHAPTER 12
MEASURING DATA QUALITY
SCORES

Error reports produced by data quality rules provide detailed information about data quality. Aggregate scores help make sense out of the jungle of numerous and lengthy error reports. They provide high-level estimates of the data quality. Each score aggregates errors identified by the data quality rules into a single number – a percentage of good data records among all target data records.

By selecting different groups of target data records, we can create many aggregate scores for a single database. Well-designed scores are goal driven and allow us to make better decisions and take actions. They can measure data fitness for various purposes, indicate the quality of various data collection processes, and serve many other purposes. Poorly designed aggregate scores are just useless numbers.

Score tabulation is arguably the most complex and technically challenging part of data quality assessment. Eventually I hope that future data quality tools will perform the advanced technical work and allows us to focus on the data quality analysis. In the meantime, we must deal with score tabulation as best as we can because accurate aggregate scores are the most important results of our work. They help translate data quality assessment findings into the cost of bad data, ROI from data quality improvement initiatives, and expectations from the data-driven projects. So the effort in accurate score tabulation is not wasted.

This chapter describes how to define and tabulate aggregate data quality scores. Since the topic is rather complex and technical, I tried to address it in layers so that the most technically advanced parts come after we achieve a more basic understanding of the problem.

- Section 12.1 introduces aggregate data quality scores and provides an overview of different score types.

- Section 12.2 offers an overview of the score tabulation process.

- Section 12.3 presents a score catalogue and discusses how to define score objective and relevant data elements.

- Section 12.4 shows how to tabulate record-level scores.

- Section 12.5 describes algorithms for dealing with rule imperfections.

- Section 12.6 addresses the tabulation of subject-level scores.

12.1. INTRODUCTION TO AGGREGATE SCORES

Aggregate scores provide high-level estimates of the data quality. Each score aggregates errors identified by the data quality rules into a single number – a percentage of good data records among all target data records. It is possible to build many different aggregate scores by selecting different groups of target data records. Aggregate scores help make sense out of the numerous error reports produced by data quality rules.

There are two conflicting schools of thought among data quality practitioners about the value of aggregate scores. Some consider calculating aggregate scores the ultimate objective of the data quality assessment. Others believe them to be totally meaningless and view the error reports themselves as the main product of data quality assessment. The reason for the disagreement is that aggregate scores are not always defined correctly. In my view, some aggregate scores are meaningless and useless, while others are critically valuable.

For instance, a simple aggregate score for the entire database is usually rather meaningless. We know that 6.3% of all records in the database have some errors. So what? This number does not help me at all if I cannot say whether it is good or bad, and I cannot make any decisions based on this information.

On the other hand, consider an HR database that is used, among other things, to calculate pension benefits. Now, if I can build an aggregate score that says 6.3% of all calculations are probably incorrect because of data quality problems, such a score is very valuable. I can now measure how much it costs the company every year. I can then decide whether or not it makes sense to initiate a data-cleansing project by comparison of its cost with its expected value.

The bottom line is that good aggregate scores are goal driven and allow us to make better decisions and take actions. Poorly designed aggregate scores are just useless numbers. Conversely, detailed error reports are unusable when the volume of errors is so large that the report serves only to discourage and not to enable data quality improvement.

Many scores can be created for a single database. Some can measure data fitness for various purposes; others can indicate quality of various data collection processes. Analysis of aggregate scores answers key data quality questions, such as:

- What is the impact of the errors in your database?

- What are the sources and causes of the errors?

- Where are most of the errors likely to be found?

Let's consider the main categories of aggregate data scores.

12.1.1. Scores Measuring Impact of Bad Data

Data quality is defined as "fitness for the purpose of use." Therefore, data quality should be primarily measured in relation to data usage. For each purpose of use, a specific aggregate score can be designed. Remember that aggregate score is defined as the percentage of good data records among all data records. The score measuring fitness for a specific purpose of use narrows the scope to only relevant records and only considers data quality rules that produce material errors for this particular purpose.

Scores built around data uses provide information on the impact of the bad data. This allows estimating the cost of bad data, evaluating potential ROI of data quality initiatives, and setting correct expectations for data-driven projects.

For example, a human resources database serves many purposes. One of them is tracking health insurance participation. Employees with invalid data related to health insurance plan eligibility and participation will get incorrect coverage. Such errors are very costly, and having 5% rate of employees with incorrect data here is totally unacceptable.

A human resource database may also be used as a source for a newly built data mart about employee education levels. A different subset of data is used for this purpose, and errors are not as critical. The 5% error rate (or may be even 15%) is probably acceptable.

Aggregate scores measuring fitness of data for certain purposes of use are the most valuable of all. Often the entire objective of a data quality assessment project is to calculate one of such scores.

12.1.2. Scores Identifying Sources of Bad Data

Data comes to the database in different ways. Some records are manually entered through various interfaces. Others are electronically delivered from other databases through various interfaces. Aggregate scores based on the data origin provide estimates of the quality of the data obtained from a particular source. Such scores are defined by narrowing down the records to a subset from a common origin. They are critical for identifying sources of bad data and improving data collection processes.

Consider, for instance, a retirement plan administration database. It collects basic indicative data, such as employee addresses and employment status changes, from a human resources system. It also obtains employee and employer contributions amounts from a payroll system. Finally, allocation of the money on each employee's account among the funds comes through manual entry from paper forms or via direct data entry by employees on an intranet. Records of each origin can be identified rather accurately, and aggregate scores can be built separately for these groups of data. These scores will indicate which data collection processes are most at fault. Such knowledge can be put to use immediately to save money by improving the most defective process.

A similar concept involves measuring the quality of the data collected during a specific period of time. Indeed, it is usually important to know if the data errors are mostly historic or were introduced recently. The presence of recent errors indicates a greater need for data collection improvement initiatives. Such measurement can be accomplished by an aggregate score with constraints on the timestamps of the relevant records.

Choice of scores for this category is driven by understanding the processes by which data is collected and updated. While it takes some effort to obtain this information, it offers the most powerful dimension for quality improvement actions – those that move the effort beyond data cleansing to defect prevention. If you learn, for example, that a high frequency of some error types is introduced by a specific department (or system), then you can act upon that knowledge with training, monitoring, incentives, or other tactics. Similarly, by knowing that error rates increase during specific business cycles (due to budgeting or general salary adjustment) you can act to enhance or improve those business processes.

12.1.3. Scores Identifying Location of Bad Data

Errors are usually not distributed uniformly throughout the database. Some tables, for instance, have more errors than others. Scores built for logical subsets of data help us understand distribution of errors in the database. This in its turn is helpful when prioritizing data cleansing initiatives.

Database score simply counts all records in the database and errors found by all data quality rules. While it is rather useless, it is easy to produce and looks good among all other more valuable measures on the data quality scorecard.

Entity scores count all errors in each table. They are easy to produce and understand. A table with a 20% error rate is usually a better candidate for automated data cleansing than a table with a 1% error rate.

Subject population scores count all errors for a particular population of subjects. Such scores are key to understanding overall data quality. For example, employees from different subsidiaries may have drastically different data quality in the human resources system. If 14% of employees from subsidiary A have errors, and then number for subsidiary B is 1%, we certainly have some breakdown in data collection for the former. We now know where the data quality improvement initiative shall start. Also, since data cleansing is often done on the subject level, it is important to identify populations of subject with more data problems.

12.1.4. Record-Level and Subject-Level Scores

Record-level scores measure the percentage of bad data records among all considered records. For example, record-level score for E_STATUS_HISTORY table measures the percentage of good records among all records. Record-level scores give better input in estimates of the magnitude and ROI of the data cleansing initiatives. The IT community also understands them more easily.

Subject-level scores measure the percentage of subjects with one or more bad data records among all considered subjects. Subject-level score for table E_STATUS_HISTORY measures the percentage of employees with no bad employment history data among all employees. Subject-level scores are more suitable when measuring impact of data quality on business processes and when communicating data quality to business users.

The two approaches often yield very different results. Imagine a database with HR data for 10,000 employees. Assume further that the average employee has four records in the E_STATUS_HISTORY table for the total of 40,000 records. If 2,000 employees have one erroneous record each then the subject-level score is a highly disappointing 80% (determined as 8,000 employees without errors divided by the total of 10,000 employees). On the other hand, the record-level score is 95% since we have 38,000 good records out of the total of 40,000 records. While 95% seems like an acceptable quality level, having 20% employees with invalid employment history is hardly acceptable.

In practice, record-level and subject-level scores complement each other. Both should be calculated whenever possible and presented side-by-side on the data quality scorecard.

12.2. SCORE TABULATION PROCESS OVERVIEW

Each aggregate score is defined as a percentage of good data records (and subjects) among all relevant data records (and subjects). For each score, the definitions of "good" and "relevant" data are driven by the purpose for which the score is tabulated. The objective of the first step of score tabulation is, therefore, to define what constitutes "good" and "relevant" data. On the second step we physically count "good" and "relevant" records (and subjects) using the error reports. The basic counts are easy to obtain from the well-designed error catalogue. The difficult part here is making necessary adjustments for data quality rule imperfections. Figure 12-1 outlines the score tabulation process. In the following sections we will discuss the steps in detail.

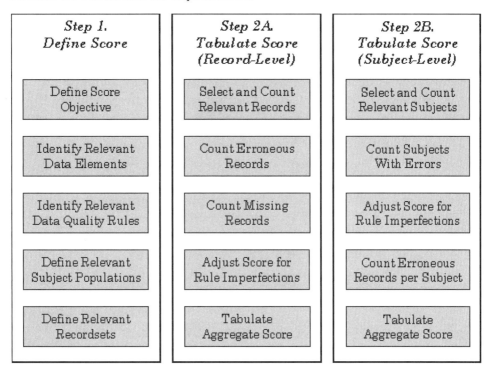

Figure 12-1: Score Tabulation Process

12.3. BUILDING SCORE CATALOGUE

Each score is built for a particular objective, which determines the relevant cast of characters including subject classes, subjects, entities, attributes, recordsets, and data quality rules. All of these definitions must be carefully organized in the score catalogue so they can be used for tabulation and analysis of various scores.

12.3.1. Defining Score Objective

Every score included in the data quality scorecard must be catalogued. The first step is to list it in the main catalogue table – SCORE. For each score we want to provide a descriptive name and a comprehensive description. Optionally each score can be given a unique numeric identifier. I do not find this necessary, as scores are not referenced from many places in the meta data. Table 12-1 illustrates score entry for a simple example, which we will use throughout this chapter.

Aggregate Score #1. *MINING_EMP_PATTERNS*

Definition:

A new HR data-mining project is scheduled. It will use employee dates of birth, hire, and rehire to analyze patterns of age-at-hire for all regular employees of the company. The findings will not be used to make specific decisions about individual employees, but rather to judge changes in historical hiring patterns.

The project intends to use the data stored in summary employment tables. The objective of this aggregate score it to evaluate whether or not quality of these data is adequate for this project. Based on the score, the decision will be made to use another data source, perform partial data cleansing, proceed with inaccurate data, delay, or even abandon the project. It is understood that the data needs not be perfect for all employees. However, a reasonable benchmark of 90% employees with correct data is considered necessary.

Table 12-1: Example of a SCORE Entry

12.3.2. Identifying Relevant Data Elements

Now that we described the score objective, we need to define relevant data elements. Only errors in these data elements will count towards the score. According to the definition given in Table 12-1, the data elements relevant to the project in our example are:

- Employee's original hire date (HireDate in E_EMPLOYEE_INFO)

- Employee's recent rehire date (RehireDate in E_EMPLOYEE_INFO)

- Employee's birth date (BirthDate in E_EMPLOYEE_PROFILE).

Observe that these data elements are stored in separate tables. They can only be used together if the tables are properly joined using the key field EmpID. Thus, we have overall five relevant fields in two tables. These data elements must be logged into SCORE_ATTRIBUTE table in the score catalogue as shown in Figure 12-2.

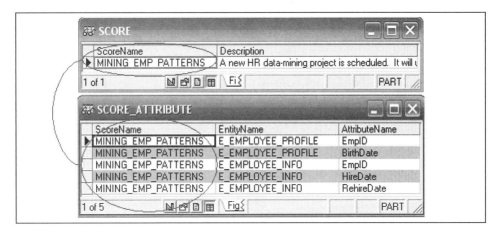

Figure 12-2: Score Catalogue Tracking Relevant Data Elements

12.3.3. Identifying Relevant Data Quality Rules

Not all data quality rules implemented in the course of a data quality assessment project affect the data elements of interest. Thus, only certain errors should be considered when tabulating aggregate scores. The objective of this step is to narrow down the list of relevant data quality rules.

Since the number of rules in a data quality assessment project often reaches several hundreds, it is not immediately clear which rules are relevant for our aggregate score. This is where a well-kept rule catalogue comes in handy. Query 12-1 uses rule domain information stored in the rule catalogue to build the list of all rules that affect one or more of the relevant data elements. If we replace *ScoreName* in the last line of the statement with string *MINING_EMP_PATTERNS*, the query will produce the list of all data quality rules for our example.

```
SELECT   DISTINCT RULE.RuleID, RULE.RuleName, RULE.RuleType
  FROM   SCORE_ATTRIBUTE, RULE_ATTRIBUTE, RULE
 WHERE   SCORE_ATTRIBUTE.EntityName = RULE_ATTRIBUTE.EntityName
   AND   SCORE_ATTRIBUTE.AttributeName = RULE_ATTRIBUTE.AttributeName
   AND   RULE.RuleID = RULE_ATTRIBUTE.RuleID
   AND   SCORE_ATTRIBUTE.ScoreName = ScoreName
```

Query 12-1: List of Relevant Data Quality Rules

This list is a great starting point. However, it is necessary to go through it to confirm that the errors found by each rule are indeed material for the score objective. Since data quality is defined as fitness for the purpose of use, same data element may be considered accurate for one purpose and erroneous for another. This is especially true for such rule types as completeness, retention, currency, and precision. Thus, a rule can affect the data element but be deemed immaterial for the score objective.

Occasionally we have situations when some of the errors found by a rule are material for certain objectives, while other errors are not. A good solution in this case is to create error groups separating errors of each kind. An alternative is to split the rule into two or more groups, each validating data fitness for a specific purpose.

Once we have completed our analysis, the list of relevant data quality rules (and optionally error groups) must be logged in the score catalogue table SCORE_RULE. A portion of the list for our example is shown in Figure 12-3. Notice that I have chosen to keep the ErrorGroup field blank. This indicates that all error groups are relevant.

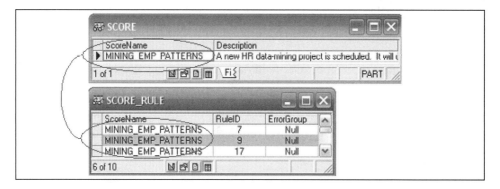

Figure 12-3: Score Catalogue Tracking Relevant Data Quality Rules

12.3.4. Defining Relevant Subject Populations

Now that we identified pertinent data quality rules, the next step is to define records and subjects, which will be counted during score tabulation. We will start from specifying the subject population since it is often used to define relevant records. Also, subject population is obviously directly used for the subject-level score tabulation.

In our example, the definition seems trivial. The subject population includes all past and current regular employees whose data is stored in the HR database. The keyword here is "regular," thus we are not interested in data for temporary employees. More formally these employees can be selected using criteria:

Left ([E_EMPLOYEE_STATUS].[EmployeeType], 1) = 'R'

Figure 12-4 shows this information is logged into SCORE_SUBJECT table in the score catalogue. The reason we need a separate catalogue table rather than adding attributes to SCORE table is because many databases have multiple subject classes. For instance, a general HR database may have data for employees, retirees, and positions. In that case, a single aggregate score can be tabulated separately for various subject classes. This would translate into multiple entries in SCORE_SUBJECT table in the score catalogue, one for each pertinent subject class.

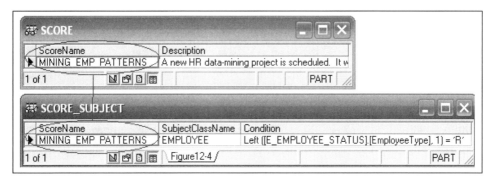

Figure 12-4: Score Catalogue Tracking Relevant Subject Populations

Since we only have one subject class – employees – in our data quality assessment project, and assuming that all the data are dependent on the main employee list stored in table E_EMPLOYEE_PROFILE, we could reference that table directly instead of using the master list. However, I always recommend creating subject master lists, as it makes data quality work much easier.

When the subject selection condition is relatively simple (as in our example), it can be applied on the fly during score tabulation. However, this technique is not efficient and often totally impractical for complex conditions. A better solution is to add a Boolean flag to the subject master list for each aggregate score and populate it either with *True* (for subjects that are pertinent for that score), or *False*. The score condition then simply references the appropriate Boolean field. We will address this issue further in Section 12.6.

The main problem with population conditions is that we are using somewhat inaccurate data to select relevant subject population. The problem is very difficult to deal with since it is of a "chicken-and-egg" type. We are using the condition to measure data quality, but we need quality data to use the condition properly. In truth, the simplest practical approach is to ignore the problem assuming that the data used to evaluate the condition are reasonably accurate.

A more appropriate approach in the spirit of data quality and due diligence is to add a data quality score measuring quality of the data used to evaluate the condition. Thus we would add a score measuring accuracy in determining regular employee population. The score would tell us about the fraction of misidentified regular employees. Now we can simply combine the results of both scores in our data quality scorecard. We will address this issue further in Section 12.6.

12.3.5. Defining Relevant Recordsets

The final part of defining an aggregate score is to specify relevant records. Only these records will be counted during score tabulation. In our example, these include all records in tables E_EMPLOYEE_PROFILE and E_EMPLOYEE_INFO for employees from the selected subject population. We store this information in the score catalogue table SCORE_RECORDSET as shown in Figure 12-5.

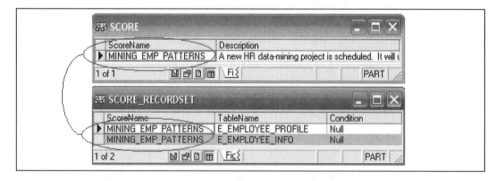

Figure 12-5: Score Catalogue Tracking Relevant Recordsets

The situation when the record selection criteria are simply the pass-through from the subject population constraint is most common. In other words, relevant records are defined as all records in selected tables for pertinent subjects. These conditions can then be enforced by a simple join with the master subject list.

However, more often, relevant records are restricted by some further conditions. For instance, if we used an employment history table for our data-mining project, we would restrict the relevant recordset to only records with actions *HIRE* and *REHIRE*. In this case, we specify conditions for selecting relevant records in field Condition of SCORE_RECORDSET table.

A simple condition can be defined in the "WHERE" clause format and applied on the fly during the score tabulation. More often, however, the conditions are too complex and it is highly ineffective to apply them repetitively inside score tabulation algorithms. A more practical solution is to somehow explicitly mark or list all relevant records before embarking on the score tabulation. We will discuss appropriate techniques shortly in Section 12.4.

12.4. TABULATING RECORD-LEVEL SCORES

We have now defined relevant data quality rules and records. The next step is to count "good" and "bad" records, so we can tabulate the actual record-level score. The overall score is defined as the fraction of "good" records among all records. We can count "good" records by simply eliminating erroneous ones from all relevant records. Further, to get the count of all records, we start with existing relevant records and add missing records, that otherwise would have been relevant. The result is the formula shown in Equation 12-1.

$$\text{Overall score} = \frac{(\text{Count of Relevant Records} - \text{Count of Erroneous Records})}{(\text{Count of Relevant Records} + \text{Count of Missing Records})}$$

Equation 12-1: Record-Level Overall Score

Sometimes it is more convenient to think about missing and erroneous records separately. In order to satisfy this view, we break the Overall Score into two components – Completeness Score and Accuracy Score – shown in Equations 12-2 and 12-3. The product of these two scores equals the Overall Score.

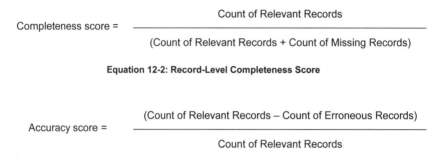

$$\text{Completeness score} = \frac{\text{Count of Relevant Records}}{(\text{Count of Relevant Records} + \text{Count of Missing Records})}$$

Equation 12-2: Record-Level Completeness Score

$$\text{Accuracy score} = \frac{(\text{Count of Relevant Records} - \text{Count of Erroneous Records})}{\text{Count of Relevant Records}}$$

Equation 12-3: Record-Level Accuracy Score

With a perfect set of data quality rules and an absolutely accurate error catalogue, we could obtain necessary counts for these equations using rather simple techniques. In this section, we will demonstrate how it is done. In reality the process is much more complex due to various rule imperfections (discussed in Chapter 11). Algorithms accounting for these imperfections are discussed in the next section. Finally, we will discuss subject-level scores in Section 12.6.

12.4.1. Counting All Relevant Records

The first step is to find and count all relevant records. With explicit queryable conditions for each table (defined in SCORE_RECORDSET table in score catalogue) the counting is rather simple. However, simple conditions are relatively uncommon.

In our example (which is in itself rather trivial) the condition restricts records to those for regular employees only. The regular employees, in their turn, have the first character *R* in EmployeeType field of E_EMPLOYEE_STATUS table. To identify all relevant records in other tables we would need to use a rather complex nested query:

- First-level query builds a list of distinct EmpID values in the records that meet the defined condition in E_EMPLOYEE_STATUS table.

- Second-level query uses this list as a lookup to get counts of records in tables E_EMPLOYEE_PROFILE and E_EMPLOYEE_INFO.

- Third level query adds up these counts.

However, this only takes us halfway home. On the next step of score tabulation, we will need to also count erroneous records among all relevant records. This means we will have to have easy access to the list of all relevant records.

A more practical solution is to somehow mark all relevant records or create a separate list. We can use one of two methods. The least invasive and most effective method is to create a new RECORD_SCORE table and populate it with references to all records from all tables. We could use TableName and RecordID as a method of referencing, the same as we did in ERROR_RECORD table in the error catalogue. This is of great convenience since now we can match erroneous records listed in the error catalogue with references to all data records without having to look into multiple data tables.

Now we simply add Boolean flags to RECORD_SCORE table, one for each score, to indicate whether the records are relevant to the score. These flags are populated once using a query or more complex program and then can be used many times for score tabulation and reporting.

Let's say we added field MiningEmpPatterns to store the flags for the score in our example. We can populate this flag using the nested query described above. Now to count relevant records we use Query 12-2. Say the query returns 10,185. Then 10,185 records altogether are used by the data-mining project and thus are the target population for our aggregate score.

```
SELECT    COUNT (*)
  FROM    RECORD_SCORE
 WHERE    MiningEmpPatterns = True
```

Query 12-2: Count of All Relevant Records Using Record Listing

This method is convenient and provides the best performance. However, it is more difficult to implement when data quality assessment is performed recurrently against a production database. An alternative method is to add flags directly to the actual data tables. Indeed, we could add Boolean field MissingEmpPatterns to each relevant data table and use it directly. This is slightly less efficient for score tabulation but still works splendidly. We will discuss this topic in more detail in Chapter 14.

12.4.2. Counting Erroneous Records

The next step is to count data records with possible errors. These are the records among identified relevant records that violated at least one of the selected data quality rules. If the rules were flawless, we could count such records using a straightforward and quite simple technique. Let's assume that we use the first method to mark relevant records. Then we can easily identify them as having value *True* in MiningEmpPatterns field of RECORD_SCORE table. Now we simply need to go through them one-by-one and check if we have any errors affecting them. Of course, we can determine this by looking in the ERROR_RECORD table in the error catalogue. If we have any errors, we need to further verify that they are found by one of the relevant rules listed in SCORE_RULE table. Any record with a relevant error counts.

Query 12-3 produces the count of potentially erroneous records for the score in our example. Though it seems complex, it really just joins various catalogue tables to assure that we count only relevant records with errors for only relevant rules.

258

```
SELECT    COUNT(DISTINCT ERROR_RECORD.TableName,
          ERROR_RECORD.RecordID)
  FROM    SCORE_RULE, ERROR, ERROR_RECORD, RECORD_SCORE
 WHERE    SCORE_RULE.ScoreName = 'MINING_EMP_PATTERNS'
   AND    SCORE_RULE.RuleID = ERROR.RuleID
   AND    SCORE_RULE.GroupID = ERROR.GroupID
   AND    ERROR.ErrorID = ERROR_RECORD.ErrorID
   AND    ERROR_RECORD.TableName = RECORD_SCORE.TableName
   AND    ERROR_RECORD.RecordID = RECORD_SCORE.RecordID
   AND    RECORD_SCORE.MiningEmpPatterns = True
```

Query 12-3: Count of Potentially Erroneous Records

Say the query returns 2,080, which is the total number of potentially erroneous records relevant to our aggregate score. We now have all the inputs for the Accuracy Score, which equals 79.6% (all but 2,080 records in the target population of 10,185 relevant records violated no relevant rules). In other words, almost 80% of all records that will be used in the data-mining project are guaranteed to be accurate for the purposes of the project. In reality the number is much higher because we are yet to account for rule imperfections (see Section 12.5).

12.4.3. Counting Missing Records

Now we are ready to proceed with the calculation of the Completeness Score. For that we still need to count missing records. This generally is a more difficult task. Indeed, our rules are able to find situations where some records are likely missing, but how do we know that the missing records are relevant to a score at hand? The general answer is that such determination is impossible. However, it can be done in many special cases, and it can be estimated in others.

Let's start from the simplest case with no conditions narrowing down the relevant records. In this case, all missing records are relevant. We could then use Query 12-4 to approximately tabulate the missing record count. Again the query seems rather complex, but it is really a simple join of several catalogue tables, ensuring that we count missing records identified only by relevant rules and only in relevant data tables.

```
SELECT    SUM (ERROR_RECORD_MISSING.MissingCount)
  FROM    SCORE_RULE, SCORE_RECORDSET, ERROR, ERROR_RECORD_MISSING
 WHERE    SCORE_RULE.ScoreName = 'MINING_EMP_PATTERNS'
   AND    SCORE_RULE.RuleID = ERROR.RuleID
   AND    SCORE_RULE.GroupID = ERROR.GroupID
   AND    ERROR.ErrorID = ERROR_RECORD_MISSING.ErrorID
   AND    SCORE_RULE.ScoreName = SCORE_RECORDSET.ScoreName
   AND    ERROR_RECORD_MISSING.TableName = SCORE_RECORDSET.TableName
```

Query 12-4: Count of Missing Records in a Simple Case

This query is not perfectly accurate. It is possible that the same missing record will appear several times, found by several rules. There is nothing we can really do about it except ensure during rule fine-tuning that such situations do not occur. At this point, we can only say that our Completeness Score is conservative, i.e. if anything we slightly overestimate the number of missing records.

For many scores relevant records are restricted by a condition. This is the case in our score example. The good news is that the condition in our example is subject-level, i.e. it restricts relevant employees rather than records for such employees. Such a condition can be incorporated in the missing record count because we have information about the subjects whose records are missing. Indeed, for each error we log the affected subject into the error catalogue table ERROR_SUBJECT. We can now join this table with the master subject list where we flag all relevant subjects and incorporate this additional constraint into the query.

I will not show this monster here for space considerations. While it is quite complex and involves six tables, do not despair. Complex queries are common in data analysis, and computers execute them as easily as the simple ones. I can tell you that I did execute the query in my sample database for kicks, and it returned the number 345. This means that 345 records potentially relevant to our data-mining project are missing.

We can now summarize the results:

- We found the total number of relevant records to be 10,185.

- Of them, 2,080 records might be erroneous.

- In addition, 345 relevant records might be missing.

Based on these counts we can estimate the scores:

- Accuracy Score = (10,185 – 2,080) / 10,185 = 79.8%.

- Completeness Score = 10,185 / (10,185 + 345) = 96.7%.

- Overall Score = (10,185 – 2,080) / (10,185 + 345) = 77.0%.

Now, recall that the acceptable quality benchmark for the data-mining project was set at 90%. Actual data quality seems to be under 80%, way short of the desired level. However, this conclusion is premature. Wait until we adjust the scores for rule imperfections.

12.5. ADJUSTING SCORES FOR RULE IMPERFECTIONS

The counts of erroneous and missing data records we tabulated thus far are really just very conservative upper limits. The actual numbers can be quite different because of various rule imperfections. For instance, consider rule #112 deemed relevant for the score in our example. It compares HireDate with the effective date of the earliest record in employment history. The rule found 1,076 discrepancies. Based on the sample review during rule fine-tuning, we estimated that:

- 10% of these discrepancies are false positives;

- 66% of these discrepancies are due to incorrect employment history; and

- 24% of these discrepancies are caused by erroneous HireDate value.

Since our aggregate score does not care about employment history (and of course since false positives are not errors), the best estimate for the number of relevant errors in rule #112 is 258 (24% of 1,076). This is quite a bit less than the 1,076 we started with.

But how do we incorporate information about all imperfections? It sounds like a totally incomprehensible task, yet there is a simple solution! Well, maybe not truly simple. My friends still tease me for saying at one of my lectures that, "the solution is really intuitive if you have the right kind of intuition." Simple or not, intuitive or not, it is definitely manageable with a reasonable effort.

Let's go back to the method we used in the previous section to count erroneous records. Even though it was done in a single query, you can think of it as a three-step process.

- Start with the list of all records marked as relevant in RECORD_SCORE table.

- Go through the records one-by-one and determine whether or not the error catalogue shows any relevant errors affecting the record.

- Count the records with relevant errors as erroneous.

Now since rules are not flawless, the presence of a rule violation does not guarantee that the record is erroneous. In reality it simply tells us that it could be erroneous with some probability. If we determined such probability, then we could estimate the true total number of erroneous records. We would simply replace step 3 with the following steps:

- For each record affected by one or more relevant errors, determine the probability that the record is truly erroneous.

- Add up the probabilities for all records.

It is truly remarkable, but the technique gives a very robust estimate of the true number of erroneous records!

So how do we determine the probability that a record is erroneous? First let's assume that a record is affected by only one error. The technique is illustrated in Figure 12-6.

We will use various meta data to estimate the probability that the highlighted record #149 for employee #3000 in E_EMPLOYEE_INFO table is erroneous. The record is referenced in the error #1154 identified by rule #112, as can be seen from the error catalogue tables ERROR_RECORD and ERROR. It is deemed relevant because the rule is included in the list of relevant rules for the score at hand.

Of course, the error could be a false positive. During rule fine-tuning we have tried to eliminate false positives, but some certainly persisted. However, we also used sample validation to estimate the percentage of remaining false positives (see Section 10.5). The estimate (0.10 or 10%) is located in the FPProb field of the RULE table, along with false positive probabilities for all other rules. If the estimate is 10% then the probability that the record is erroneous is already down to 90%. We are making progress!

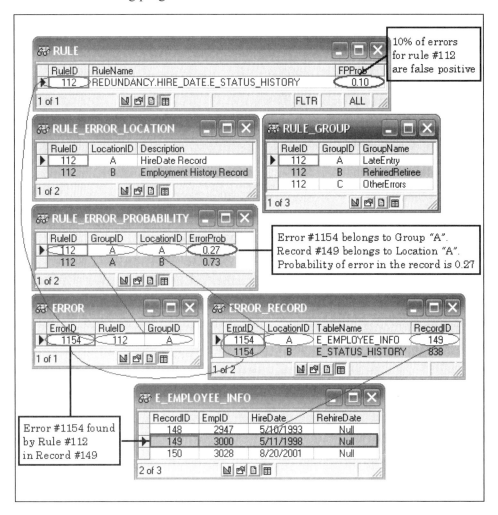

Figure 12-6: Estimating Probability that a Record is Erroneous

The next possible rule imperfection is that the rule that compares data across multiple records may not clearly tell which one is erroneous. Our record may very well be correct, and the one it is compared against is the offender. Luckily we have dealt with this problem, too, during rule fine-tuning. We even created the data structure in the error catalogue to store the probability that a specific record affected by the rule is indeed erroneous (see Sections 11.4 and 11.5). This information is found in the RULE_ERROR_PROBABILITY table. Notice that the probability references error group and error location.

The error #1154 in ERROR table in Figure 12-6 is categorized into error group A (described in RULE_GROUP table as "late data entry"). The record #149 in ERROR_RECORD table is placed into error location A (described in RULE_ERROR_LOCATION table as "HireDate record"). The error probability for this combination is 0.27. Thus, according to the error catalogue record #149 is erroneous with a probability 0.27. Now we multiply 0.27 by the 90% chance the error is not a false positive in the first place and get 24.3%. In other words, the probability that this specific record is erroneous is only roughly 24% despite it being listed as erroneous by rule #112.

We use this number (actually we use the probability 0.243) for score tabulation. It is as if we assume that only 0.243 of the record is erroneous. Statistical techniques do not always match common sense, but they do work! Even though in reality this record is either right or wrong, and so is every other record, our technique will produce the total count of erroneous records very close to the actual. However we cannot tell very accurately which of the records are really erroneous. Of course, the more fine-tuning we do and the more we enhance our rules, the more precise is the identification of errors. So these statistical techniques are less critical once we go to the data cleansing stage.

So far we assumed that the record was affected by only one error. In reality many records will be affected by multiple errors from multiple rules. How do we determine the probability of the record being erroneous in this situation? If the rules were independent, we could use a simple formula for independent probabilities. Say the record is affected by one error with a probability 0.6 and by another error with a probability 0.3. Of course, it is erroneous if either of the errors really affects it. The probability of such an event is 0.72, determined as:

$$1 - (1 - 0.6) * (1 - 0.3)$$

As you see, the probability will increase when more errors possibly affect the record.

Of course in reality rules are not independent. To accommodate for that we could use rather complex mathematical formulas incorporating rule correlations, but it is overkill in practice. Keep in mind that the scores we build are only estimates. A simple relatively accurate method of tabulation is acceptable. So we can assume that if a record is involved in three or more errors then it is erroneous, probabilities aside. Or we can use another similar heuristic technique.

And so we have the method for estimating probabilities that each record is erroneous. We can add up these probabilities and have the total estimate of the number of relevant erroneous records. The last adjustment we must make is for errors missed due to rule imperfections (see Section 10.6). It is quite simple. Say we determined during fine-tuning that 3% of erroneous records in table E_EMPLOYEE_INFO go unnoticed by all rules. Now, assume that we estimated the number of erroneous records (for our score) in this table to be 700 out of the total number of 5,000 records. Of the remaining 4,300 records 3% are likely erroneous, thus we have another 129 missed errors. Then the total estimate for the number of erroneous records is 829. And thus we are done and can produce a rather accurate aggregate score!

A similar procedure can be applied to missing records to determine the estimate of their true number. Recall that missing records are listed in ERROR_RECORD_MISSING table of the error catalogue. Like erroneous records, missing records are assigned to error locations and error groups. Thus the same adjustments can be made to determine that the error is a false positive and that the record is truly missing. This adjustment will produce the probability that a relevant records is missing. Adding up such probabilities yields the estimate for the true number of missing records.

Once we account for rule imperfections, we get a score summary that will look something like this:

- We found the total number of relevant records to be 10,185.

- Of them 2,080 records are affected by possible errors.

- Adjustments for rule imperfection yield the estimate of the true number of erroneous relevant records, which is equal to 829.

- In addition 345 relevant records might be missing.

- Again, adjusting for rule imperfection we get the estimate of the true number of missing relevant records, which is equal to 211.

Based on these counts we can estimate the scores:

Accuracy Score = (10,185 – 829) / 10,185 = 91.9%.

Completeness Score = 10,185 / (10,185 + 211) = 98.0%.

Overall Score = (10,185 – 829) / (10,185 + 211) = 90.0%.

This is much better than the preliminary conservative 77% estimate before the adjustments. The error rate is still rather high but possibly acceptable for the data-mining project.

12.6. TABULATING SUBJECT-LEVEL SCORES

So far we have discussed the tabulation of record-level scores. In practice subject-level scores are often more valuable to the business. For instance, the data-mining project in our example really cares about employees with good data, not simply good records in some relevant tables. In fact, subject-level scores, along with subject-level data analysis and cleansing, are central to the data quality paradigm.

This, of course, does not mean that we wasted time and effort tabulating record-level scores. While subject-level score is more meaningful as an aggregate number, tabulation of record-level scores provides a lot more valuable details about data quality. Indeed, if we chose to try to improve data quality, we would be after specific errors, and those affect specific records. More importantly, subject-level scores build upon the data and techniques for tabulation of the record-level scores.

The formula for subject-level Accuracy Score is given by Equation 12-4.

$$\text{Accuracy score} = \frac{(\text{Count of Relevant Subjects} - \text{Count of Subjects with Errors})}{\text{Count of Relevant Subjects}}$$

Equation 12-4: Subject-Level Accuracy Score

Tabulation of the subject-level score is quite straightforward. Conceptually it is simpler than the record-level score tabulation, I promise! We start with the count of all relevant subjects. Now that one is easy. The right approach is to add a Boolean flag for each score to the master subject list and enter *True* for every relevant subject. Assuming that we created such a field MiningEmpPatterns in EMPLOYEE master list and populated it for all regular employees (according to the subject population definition in the score catalogue), we can use Query 12-5 to get the total count. Say the query returns 5,432. Then the total count of relevant subjects for our data-mining project is 5,432.

```
SELECT    COUNT (*)
  FROM    EMPLOYEE
  WHERE   MiningEmpPatterns = True
```

Query 12-5: Count of Relevant Subjects Using Master List

Now we get to the fun stuff – counting subjects with errors. We start by taking the list of relevant subjects from the master list and joining it with the ERROR_SUBJECT table listing all errors for all subjects. This is why including this table in the error catalogue was so critical! We now get the list of all errors for all subjects in one easy stroke, without having to reverse-engineer it by looking through all errors and matching the records they affect to the subjects. Of course, we need to further narrow down the list of errors by making sure that they belong to relevant data quality rules. Query 12-6 gets us this list for our example. As with many other queries we have shown, it seems complex but really is just a join of several meta data tables. The number of distinct subjects in the list is the initial estimate for the number of subjects with relevant errors.

```
SELECT    EMPLOYEE.SubjectID, ERROR.ErrorID
  FROM    SCORE_RULE, ERROR, ERROR_SUBJECT, EMPLOYEE
  WHERE   SCORE_RULE.ScoreName = 'MINING_EMP_PATTERNS'
    AND   SCORE_RULE.RuleID = ERROR.RuleID
    AND   SCORE_RULE.GroupID = ERROR.GroupID
    AND   ERROR.ErrorID = ERROR_SUBJECT.ErrorID
    AND   ERROR_SUBJECT.SubjectClassName = 'EMPLOYEE'
    AND   ERROR_SUBJECT.SubjectID = EMPLOYEE.SubjectID
    AND   EMPLOYEE.MiningEmpPatterns = True
```

Query 12-6: List of Errors for Relevant Subjects

Unfortunately, this list will include some errors that really should not be included in the score tabulation. One reason is that some errors might affect records that are not relevant for the score. This happens when the relevant records are narrowed down by some condition and thus not all records for each subject are important. Also, this is caused by various rule imperfections, such as false positives.

So now we have to make necessary adjustments. The technique is a bit different from the method we used for the record-level score. For record-level score, we estimated the probability that each relevant <u>record</u> is erroneous. For subject-level score, we estimate probability that each <u>error</u> is really relevant. However, the inside-the-hood mechanics are similar.

Consider an error from the list obtained by Query 12-6. Let's assume for now that it was identified by a rule that has no false positives. How do we determine the probability that the error is relevant? The logic is as follows:

- If the error affects one record and it is a part of the relevant population, then the error is relevant with certainty (probability 1). Of course, we know which records the error affects from ERROR_RECORD table and can check if it is included in our population by cross-referencing it against RECOR_SCORE table, as was discussed in Section 12.4.

- If the error indicates a missing record, then again it is relevant with certainty. In other words, for subject-level score there is no difference between having an erroneous record or missing record among all records for a given subject. In both cases, the subject data has errors.

- If the error affects two or more records and all of them are part of the relevant population, then the error is still relevant with certainty. For instance, consider rule #76 in our example that compares HireDate against BirthDate to see if the age-at-hire is within reasonable limits. A rule violation may not tell us which of the data elements (located in different data tables) are erroneous. However, both records are relevant for our data-mining project. So, regardless of which one is incorrect, we have a problem!

- If the error affects multiple records, one of which is a part of the relevant population while the others are not, then we need to determine probability that the relevant record is indeed erroneous. We do this using the error group and error location information, same as was discussed in the example in Figure 12-6. This probability is the probability that the error is relevant.

- Only in the case when the error affects multiple records, of which more than one but not all are part of the relevant population, does the logic become truly complex. We basically need the probability that at least one of the relevant records is erroneous. This is quite tricky. Fortunately, rules that create such situations are quite rare. So my practical suggestion is to treat them with a heuristic abandon – just say that the error is relevant if it happens to be so convoluted. Of course, we also can try to fine-tune the rule and eliminate the situation.

Well, with that paragraph behind us, what happens if the rule has some false positives? No sweat. Simply take the probability that the error is relevant as determined above and multiply by the probability that it is not a false positive.

Now, having re-disposed of the monster, the next step is to aggregate the results into an estimate of the number of subjects with relevant errors. If 1,000 subjects have one error each, and each error is relevant with probability 0.6, then the best estimate for the number of subjects with errors is 600 (0.6 times 1,000). If the probabilities that the errors are relevant vary, we simply add them all up.

The problem we must contend with is that some subjects have multiple errors. For such subjects we cannot blindly add up the probabilities across errors. Indeed, take a subject that has two errors, both are relevant with probability 0.6. Adding up the numbers gets us 1.2, but the subject cannot have errors with probability 1.2! Assuming that the errors are independent, the true number is 0.84, determined by formula:

$$1 - (1 - 0.6) * (1 - 0.6)$$

And what if the rules are interdependent, as is quite common? The truth is there is not a right answer: the estimate using the above formula is probably still good, as is the assumption that any subject with multiple potential errors can be treated as erroneous with certainty. The bottom line is that we do not want to make calculations too complex.

This is important to most of the calculations I described in this chapter. People often ask me what part of the data quality assessment they can skip for the sake of simplicity and saving resources. I usually respond: "Certainly not rule design, definitely not the good architecture of the error catalogue, and undoubtedly not the implementation of a good interactive dimensional data quality scorecard." On the other hand, we can use the easiest rather than the most efficient methods to implement the rules, skip some portions of rule fine-tuning, and simplify aggregate score tabulation. Eventually, I hope a new generation of future data quality tools will perform advanced technical work and make score tabulation easier.

SUMMARY

In this chapter we have discussed how to define and tabulate aggregate data quality scores, which help make sense out of the jungle of numerous and lengthy error reports. Here is a brief summary of our results.

- Each score aggregates errors identified by the data quality rules into a single number – a percentage of good data records among all target data records. It is possible to build many different aggregate scores by selecting different groups of target data records. Different scores can measure data fitness for various purposes, indicate quality of various data collection processes, and serve many other purposes.

- Record-level scores measure the percentage of bad data records among all considered records. They give better input in estimates of the magnitude and ROI of the data cleansing initiatives. The IT community also understands them more easily.

- Subject-level scores measure the percentage of subjects with one or more bad data records among all considered subjects. They are more suitable when measuring the impact of data quality on business processes and when communicating data quality to business users.

- Each score is built for a particular objective that determines relevant cast of characters including entities, attributes, data quality rules, recordsets, and subject population. All of these definitions must be carefully organized in the score catalogue, so they can be used for tabulation and analysis of various scores.

- Tabulating a score requires identifying and counting all relevant records/subjects as well as the ones with errors. If the rules were flawless, the task would be rather simple and could be accomplished using straightforward queries of meta data from a rule catalogue, error catalogue, and score catalogue.

- The straightforward calculations tend to understate data quality because of various rule imperfections. To produce more accurate estimates we need to account for possible false positives, false negatives, and uncertainty in error location among the errors. This can be accomplished using mathematical techniques of varying complexity. It is important to understand that the calculations can be made infinitely complex in the name of higher accuracy, but no matter what we do they remain estimates only. So some shortcuts in score tabulation are certainly allowed.

- While score tabulation is one of the most complex aspects of data quality assessment, accurate aggregate scores are a critical result of data quality assessment. They help translate data quality assessment results into the cost of bad data, ROI from data quality improvement initiatives, and expectations from the data-driven projects. Thus the effort in accurate score tabulation is not wasted.

Chapter 12 – Measuring Data Quality Scores

CHAPTER 13
DATA QUALITY META DATA WAREHOUSE

In the last four chapters, we have discussed the process of data quality assessment, beginning with the data analysis and design of the data quality rules, through rule implementation and fine-tuning, and up to the building of aggregate data quality scores. Throughout these steps we utilize and create various types of meta data, such as data models and profiles, data quality rules, and error reports. It is important to understand that, regardless of our desire to organize these meta data into an integrated meta data repository, we must contend with their existence; and we must be able to use them with reasonable efficiency. In fact, our success in the data quality assessment largely depends on our ability to efficiently access, analyze, and manipulate these meta data.

I use the term *data quality meta data warehouse* (*DQMDW*) to describe the collection of tools for organization and analysis of all meta data relevant to or produced by the data quality initiatives. *DQMDW* is a very broad concept. It applies to all data quality initiatives, including data quality assessment, ongoing data quality monitoring, data cleansing, and ensuring quality in data integration. In this book, I take a more narrow view of *DQMDW*, specific to data quality assessment. This chapter is made of three sections:

- Section 13.1 provides an overview of the data quality assessment process from the *DQMDW* perspective. We discuss when and how different types of meta data are used and created throughout the data quality assessment process.

- Section 13.2 describes the data quality scorecard – a central product of data quality assessment and the key component of *DQMDW* functionality.

- Section 13.3 discusses other desired functionalities of *DQMDW*, including error analysis, integration with actual data, and general meta data reporting.

13.1. DATA QUALITY ASSESSMENT META DATA

Figure 13-1 shows the content of *DQMDW* for a data quality assessment project. It falls into four broad categories: aggregate meta data, rule meta data, atomic meta data, and general meta data.

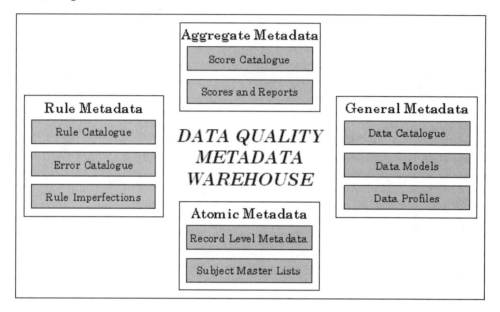

Figure 13-1: *DQMDW* Meta Data Categories

Aggregate meta data provide information about data quality at the highest levels of aggregation. They include definitions and measurements of aggregate scores, as well as other summary data quality reports that form the top layers of the data quality scorecard. Aggregate meta data are the most valuable output of data quality assessment from the perspective of a business user.

Rule meta data comprise all information about data quality rules and the results of their implementation. They include a rule catalogue, an error catalogue, and records of all identified rule imperfections. Rule meta data are the cornerstone of *DQMDW*. They contain all detailed data quality requirements and errors.

Atomic meta data contain information about the quality of each individual record and subject. Whereas *aggregate meta data* take a cumulative view of the data quality, and *rule meta data* perceive data quality as a collection of errors found by various rules, *atomic meta data* track the quality of individual data elements. The atomic meta data are thus at the very bottom of the data quality meta data spectrum.

General meta data describe the content, meaning, and structure of the data itself. These include data catalogues, data models, and data profiles. General meta data are auxiliary to data quality assessment. They also serve many other purposes and are often stored in a general-purpose meta data repository (though unfortunately for many databases they are not stored at all, or at least are rarely kept up-to-date). You may wonder why, then, I include general meta data into *DQMDW*. The fact is that many data quality rules directly validate information described in data catalogues and data models. For instance, attribute domain constraints check valid values; relational integrity rules ensure that the data is compliant with relational data models. Therefore, rule definitions, in a sense, duplicate general meta data. Maintaining partially redundant meta data in separate repositories is inefficient and dangerous. It is much better to integrate general meta data within (or at least with) *DQMDW* and use rule engines to drive the rules off these meta data. In fact, it is worth mentioning that the main purpose of maintaining a general meta data repository with data catalogues, models, and profiles is to ensure proper data use and ultimately information quality. Thus, it is natural to integrate it with other data quality meta data.

In the remainder of this section, we will review the data quality assessment process from the perspective of the data quality meta data model. It will help us understand the importance of an integrated *DQMDW*. Each subsection is dedicated to one of the seven main steps in the data quality assessment process. For every step, we show a picture illustrating its interaction with *DQMDW*. We depict the entire *DQMDW* on each picture for ease of understanding. A dotted line around a meta data category indicates that it will be introduced at a later step. The meta data categories used and/or created during the step are highlighted with shading and arrows.

You can follow the illustrations to see how *DQMDW* is built and used during data quality assessment and how valuable integration of various meta data is. The text supplements the pictures and provides some detail. And, of course, you can always reference one of the prior chapters for the in depth discussion of each step.

13.1.1. Step 1 – Gathering General Meta Data

To begin data quality assessment we must have a good understanding of the structure and architecture of the data. This is common for quality testing of any product – it starts after the materials and dimensions are defined. Therefore, the first step in data quality assessment is gathering general meta data. These meta data fall into two broad categories: data catalogue and data models.

A data catalogue is a collection of basic meta data about data attributes. It includes basic attribute listings, detailed descriptions and usage patterns, and reference information, including valid values and their meanings and default values. A data catalogue is key to understanding the cast of characters in the data quality assessment play.

Data models describe the structure of the data. They fall into four broad categories. Relational data models depict logical relationships between various entities and attributes, and also provide the link between these logical data elements and the physical data architecture. Subject area models define main data subjects – categories of high-level business objects whose data is stored in the database. State-transition models describe the lifecycle of complex state-dependent objects. Temporal models describe the chronological structure of time-dependent data and event histories. Understanding these data models is key to designing data quality rules.

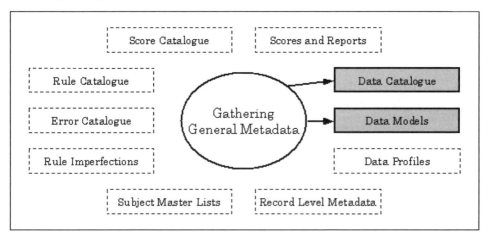

Figure 13-2: Gathering General Meta Data

276

13.1.2. Step 2 – Data Analysis and Profiling

Data catalogues and data models provide theoretical understanding of the data structure. Unfortunately, actual data is often very different from what is theoretically expected. Over time, data models and dictionaries become incomplete, inaccurate, and obsolete. Relying on this information in the design of the data quality rules is careless at best.

To remedy the situation, the second step in data quality assessment is data profiling – the process of examining the data and understanding its <u>actual</u> content and structure. Data analysis and profiling involves numerous techniques, some of which are easy and straightforward while others quite advanced. As a rule of thumb, the more in-depth analysis and profiling we conduct, the easier it is to design a comprehensive set of data quality rules and achieve greater success in data quality assessment. These are some of the key analysis and profiling techniques:

- Attribute profiling examines the values of individual data attributes and yields information about basic aggregate statistics, frequent values, and value distribution for each attribute.

- Relationship profiling is an exercise in identifying entity keys and relationships as well as counting occurrences for each relationship in the data model.

- State-transition model profiling is a collection of techniques for analysis of the lifecycle of state-dependent objects. The result is actual information about the order and duration of states and actions.

- Dependency profiling uses computer programs to look for hidden relationships between attribute values.

- Data gazing is a process of looking at the data and trying to reconstruct the story behind these data. Following the real story helps identify parameters about what might or might not have happened. Once you find that the story behind certain data elements contradicts common sense you can usually come up with data quality rules to catch the disobedient data.

- Investigation of the data models and other meta data is the key to finding complex data quality rules. Redundant and derived attributes can be identified by reading documentation and analyzing the meaning of each entity and attribute. More complex attribute dependencies can be uncovered with a thorough investigation. Anytime the value of one data element restricts acceptable values of another data element, we have the possibility for designing a data quality rule.

Data profiling produces (you guessed it) data profiles. It leads to a more accurate understanding of the data, as well as a more precise data catalogue and data models.

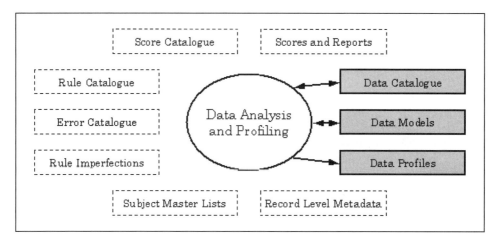

Figure 13-3: Data Analysis and Profiling

13.1.3. Step 3 – Populating Staging Area

Once implemented, the rules will process millions or billions of data pieces in search for potentially erroneous or missing elements. This process may put an unreasonable strain on the production databases that, after all, are already busy doing their daily work. Also, the data structure of operational databases is lacking some components necessary for data quality assessment, but adding attributes to the production tables may be undesirable. Finally, data quality assessment often compares data from multiple heterogeneous databases. Direct access and querying of the data in such a situation is an implementation nightmare.

The simplest solution to these problems is to create a data staging area, replicate the production database into the staging tables, and make necessary structural adjustments. The most important of these adjustments is to add variety of error tracking fields to the data tables. These record level meta data are used to tabulate aggregate data quality scores and track data quality on the atomic level. Another useful adjustment is to create a common record referencing mechanism by adding surrogate RecordID key to all tables. For recurrent data quality assessment, it may be inefficient to create multiple full replicas of the production data in the staging tables. Several alternative structures for the record level meta data can be utilized (see Chapter 14).

In addition to record level meta data, data quality assessment uses subject level meta data, i.e. information about quality of data for individual subjects. This information is critical for measuring the impact of data quality on business processes and to communicate data quality findings to the business users. In order to manage subject level meta data, we must first create lists of all subjects whose data is maintained in the databases – subject master lists. We can then add a variety of data quality tracking fields to these master lists. Obviously the staging area is the natural location to manage subject master lists.

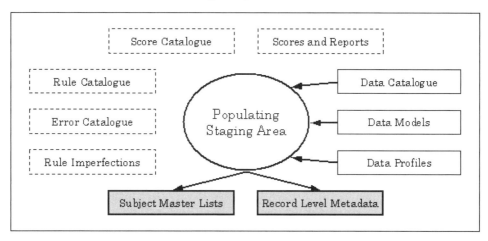

Figure 13-4: Populating Staging Area

13.1.4. Step 4 – Designing Data Quality Rules

Armed with a good understanding of the data, we can proceed to the design of the data quality rules – various constraints on valid data values and relationships that can be checked using computer programs. These data quality rules are the main tool of data quality assessment. It is the conscious, systematic making and applying of data quality rules that turns barbaric data hackers into modern data quality professionals.

Rule design is a meticulous process described in detail in Part II of this book. A typical data quality assessment project requires hundreds of rules from various categories, including attribute domain constraints, relational integrity rules, rules for historical data and event histories, rules for state-dependent objects, and various miscellaneous attribute dependency constraints.

Rule design relies on the information found in the data models and data profiles. This is why it is so critical to have streamlined access to these general meta data during data quality assessment.

The important part of the rule design process is to organize the rules into a comprehensive rule catalogue. Thus we have another critical component of the meta data model.

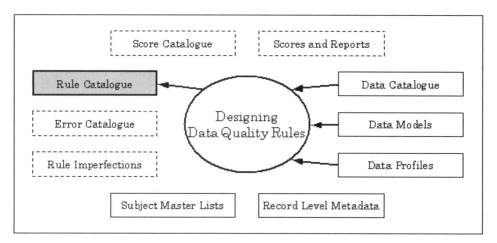

Figure 13-5: Designing Data Quality Rules

13.1.5. Step 5 – Implementing Data Quality Rules

With a comprehensive rule catalogue and a convenient staging area, we are ready to implement the rules and identify data errors. This process largely involves rule coding using a combination of tools, SQL queries, stored procedures, and more complex programs.

The main purpose of this step is to produce a comprehensive error catalogue. While on the surface it seems trivial to just produce various error reports, the task proves quite challenging. A good error catalogue must support the following functionality:

- Aggregate, filter, and sort errors across various dimensions, such as data elements, data quality rules, and subject populations.

- Identify overlaps and correlations between errors for different rules.

- Identify data records and subjects affected by a particular error or a group of errors.

- Identify all errors for a particular data record, subject, or a set of records.

This functionality can only be achieved if the error catalogue stores all error reports in a relational structure and provides a link between errors, rules that identify them, and the erroneous data records themselves. The error catalogue is a cornerstone of *DQMDW*.

Many data quality rules directly validate the constraints placed on the data by the data models or in the data catalogue. Therefore, an efficient data quality rule engine must have direct run-time access to these meta data. We have an important vote for integrating the general meta data repository with (or better within) *DQMDW*.

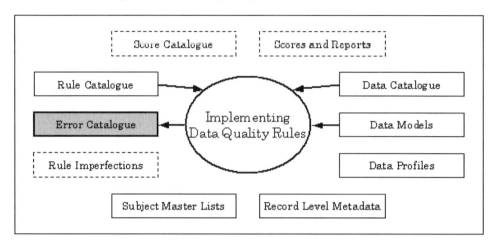

Figure 13-6: Implementing Data Quality Rules

13.1.6. Step 6 – Fine-Tuning Data Quality Rules

Data quality assessment relies on our ability to use data quality rules to accurately identify all data errors. However, it is very difficult to design perfect data quality rules. The ones we come up with will often fail to spot some erroneous records and falsely accuse others. They may not tell you which data element is erroneous even when the error is identified, or they may identify the same error in many different ways. Error reports produced by such rules tend to suffer from the same malady as the data itself – poor quality.

In order to save our data quality assessment efforts from imminent doom, we must maximize the accuracy of error reports. This is accomplished through the process of rule fine-tuning. Rule fine-tuning relies largely on manual verification of the sample data and comparison of the results with the errors identified by the data quality rules. The discrepancies are addressed through rule redesign, error grouping, and other techniques. Any rule imperfections that cannot be eliminated must at least be understood and accounted for in the data quality scorecard.

Of course, the ability to access, manipulate, and analyze error reports is key to the success of rule fine-tuning. However, it is equally important to have the ability to access, manipulate, and analyze data profiles and other general meta data. This is another vote for integration of a general meta data repository with *DQMDW*.

Rule fine-tuning plays a dual role from the meta data perspective. On one hand, it produces and a comprehensive list of rule imperfections, which are used to enhance the rules and improve the accuracy of the error catalogue. On the other hand, it quantifies residual rule imperfections, including percentages of false positives among errors identified by each rule, probabilities of errors by location and error group for rules comparing multiple data elements, and estimates for the number of errors missed by all rules. These are important ingredients of the data quality meta data.

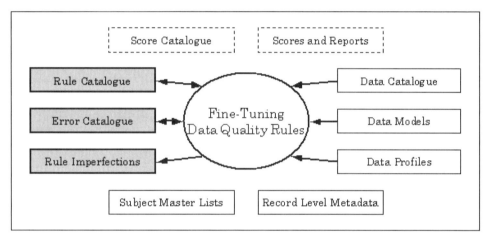

Figure 13-7: Fine-Tuning Data Quality Rules

13.1.7. Step 7 – Tabulating Aggregate Scores

Error reports produced by data quality rules provide detailed information about data quality. While extremely valuable, these error reports are overwhelming in volume and complexity. Aggregate scores help make sense out of the jungle of the numerous and lengthy error reports. They provide high-level estimates of the data quality. Each score aggregates errors identified by the data quality rules into a single number – a percentage of good data records among all target data records.

By selecting different groups of target data records, we can create many aggregate scores for a single database. Well-designed scores are goal driven and allow us to make better decisions and take actions. For instance, they can measure data fitness for various purposes or indicate quality of data collection processes. From the perspective of understanding the data quality and its impact on the business, aggregate scores are they key piece of data quality meta data.

To produce a meaningful and valuable aggregate score we must fully understand its purpose. For any given purpose, not all data are important and not all errors are material. Thus, in order to tabulate aggregate scores, we need to identify relevant data elements, data quality rules, recordsets, and subject populations. All of this information is stored in the score catalogue.

Once a score is defined, we proceed to tabulate it. First we use information from the rule catalogue, error catalogue, and score catalogue to evaluate quality of individual data records and subjects, thus producing atomic data quality meta data. Then we use various mathematical and statistical techniques to properly aggregate these atomic meta data into the aggregate scores and reports.

The aggregate scores and reports are the final ingredient in the ultimate product of the data quality assessment – interactive dimensional data quality scorecard. The reader can see how all data quality meta data comes together in an integrated *DQMDW*. Indeed, over the last two steps we used every piece of data quality meta data together.

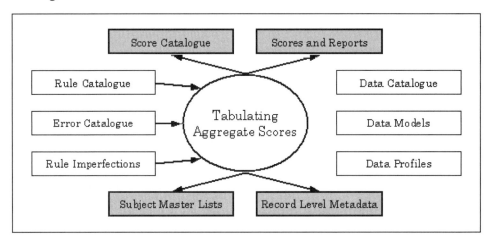

Figure 13-8: Tabulating Aggregate Scores

13.2. DATA QUALITY SCORECARD

And now we welcome the ultimate result of our craftsmanship – the data quality scorecard. ***Data quality scorecard*** is the central product of the data quality assessment project. It provides comprehensive information about data quality and allows both aggregated analysis and detailed drill-downs. A well-designed data quality scorecard is the key to understanding how well the data supports various data-driven projects. It is also critical for making good decisions about data quality initiatives.

In other words, a data quality scorecard is what data quality assessment is all about. We can spend months designing, implementing, and fine-tuning data quality rules. We can build a neat rule catalogue and extensive error catalogue. But without a data quality scorecard, all we have are raw materials. No amount of firewood will make you warm in the winter unless you can make a decent fire.

As the name suggests, a data quality scorecard presents data quality scores. However, this is only on the surface; the data quality scorecard is a lot more. Unfortunately, many data quality assessment projects invest time and effort in designing and implementing data quality rules and building error reports but stop there. Some go one more step and estimate some aggregate scores, mostly for reporting to the management. But the really important step that exponentially increases the value of data quality assessment is to build the data quality scorecard that is not just a report, but a valuable analytical tool. Of all the time and money investments in the data quality assessment, this one has highest ROI.

Figure 13-9 represents the data quality scorecard as an information pyramid. At the top level are aggregate scores; at the bottom level is information about data quality of individual data records. In the middle are various score decompositions and error reports allowing us to analyze and summarize data quality across various dimensions and for different objectives. A data quality scorecard integrates data quality meta data with general meta data and actual data itself. It brings together all components of *DQMDW* and is undoubtedly its most important function. In one word – it is a marvelous result of a well-done data quality assessment job.

Figure 13-9: Data Quality Scorecard Information Pyramid

13.2.1. Score Summary

For one database we can have many different aggregate scores. In fact, it is desirable to have many scores measuring different facets of the data quality. It allows us to measure costs of the bad data and potential ROI of data quality improvement initiatives.

At the top level, a data quality scorecard shows various aggregate scores. Table 13-1 illustrates the idea. For each score, completeness and accuracy metrics are shown along with subject-level metrics for all relevant subject classes. In general, a database may have multiple subject classes, and thus a given score can have multiple subject-level metrics on the right side of the table.

Score Name	Completeness Score	Accuracy Score	Overall Score	Subject Level Score
MINING_EMP_PATTERNS	98.0%	91.9%	90.0%	81.1%
COMP_DATA	96.4%	84.5%	81.5%	77.5%
EDU_COMPLIANCE	83.3%	97.5%	81.2%	86.4%

Table 13-1: Top Level of Data Quality Scorecard

13.2.2. Score Decompositions

Next layer in the data quality scorecard is composed of various score decompositions, which show contributions of different components to the data quality. Table 13-2 illustrates an example of score decomposition along the data table dimension. It demonstrates how aggregate score *MINING_EMP_PATTERNS* is comprised from sub-scores for two individual data tables, E_EMPLOYEE_PROFILE and E_EMPLOYEE_INFO.

	EMPLOYEE PROFILE	EMPLOYEE INFO	TOTAL
All Target Records	5,198	4,987	10,185
Records Affected by Errors	114	1,966	2,080
Erroneous Records	97	732	829
Missing Records	0	211	211
Completeness Score	100.0%	95.9%	98.0%
Accuracy Score	98.1%	85.3%	91.9%
Overall Score	98.1%	81.6%	90.0%

Table 13-2: Score Decomposition along Data Table Dimension

It is clear from this point of view that the records in E_EMPLOYEE_INFO table have many more problems than those in E_EMPLOYEE_PROFILE. Indeed, the profile records are nearly perfect with no missing data and less than 2% errors; while employment dates are missing for over 200 employees, and another 700+ have erroneous data. We can immediately see where the heart of the problem is.

A variety of decompositions are possible along several main dimensions, including:

- Decompositions across data elements show contribution to the aggregate score by errors for different entities or attributes (see example above).

- Decompositions across data quality rules show contributions to the aggregate score by errors identified by different rules (e.g. rules of different types).

- Decompositions across subject populations show contributions to the aggregate score by errors for different groups of subjects (e.g. employees from different subsidiaries).

- Decompositions across record subsets show contributions to the aggregate score by errors in different groups of records (e.g. more recent vs. older records).

13.2.3. Intermediate Error Reports

The level of detail obtained through various score decompositions is most certainly enough to understand where most data quality problems come from. However, if we want to investigate data quality further, more drill-downs are necessary. The next step would be to produce various reports of individual errors that contribute to the score (or sub-score) tabulation. These reports can be filtered and sorted in various ways to better understand the causes, nature, and magnitude of the data problems.

For example, Figure 13-10 shows an error listing for rule #112, which matches original hire date (stored in HireDate field of E_EMPLOYEE_INFO table) against the effective date of the earliest record in the employment history. It lists all 1,076 discrepancies. For each of them, the report indicates EmpID for the employee whose data are incorrect and also shows the two dates that are supposed to match.

	RuleID	ErrorID	EmpID	Msg
▶	112	26445	12268	8/23/1978 vs 4/17/1978
	112	26446	2945	2/28/1986 vs 2/1/1982
	112	26448	808	8/2/1987 vs 9/9/1987
	112	26450	4247	9/20/1956 vs 6/25/1956
	112	26455	726	6/11/1951 vs 6/29/1952
	112	26459	6558	2/29/1960 vs 10/20/1960
	112	26461	4542	4/29/1968 vs 1/8/1968
	112	26462	2169	5/11/1970 vs 9/7/1970
	112	26463	6004	11/12/1998 vs 11/9/1998
	112	26465	5750	5/15/1972 vs 6/18/1971
	112	26467	2571	1/31/1994 vs 9/7/1993
	112	26471	8644	9/5/2000 vs 8/5/1974

Record: 1 of 1076

Figure 13-10: Listing of Errors Found by Rule #112

In addition to error reports (such as the report shown in Figure 13-10), we could look at the actual erroneous data. This, of course, assumes that *DQMDW* is fully integrated with actual production data (or staging data). Erroneous record listings can be obtained by joining the error catalogue tables with data tables. This is illustrated in Figure 13-11, which contains a report of the same errors found by rule #112 but in the form of actual listings of affected data records. Side-by-side comparison of the two affected tables gives more detail since it allows us to see all data in the erroneous records. It helps locate and correct individual errors.

ErroneousRecordsByRule : Select Query

	ErrorID	HireDate	RehireDate	TermDate
▶	26445	8/23/1978		
	26446	2/28/1986		
	26448	8/2/1987	9/9/1987	
	26450	9/20/1956		10/7/2001
	26455	6/11/1951	6/29/1952	
	26459	2/29/1960	9/11/2000	
	26461	4/29/1968		
	26462	5/11/1970	9/7/1970	
	26463	11/12/1998		8/4/2001
	26465	5/15/1972		

Record: 1 of 1076

ErroneousRecordsByRule : Select Query

	ErrorID	EffDate	StateCode	ActionCode
	26445	4/17/1978	A	HIRE
▶	26446	2/1/1982	A	HIRE
	26448	9/9/1987	A	HIRE
	26450	6/25/1956	A	HIRE
	26455	6/29/1952	A	HIRE
	26459	10/20/1960	A	HIRE
	26461	1/8/1968	A	HIRE
	26462	9/7/1970	A	HIRE
	26463	11/9/1998	A	HIRE
	26465	6/18/1971	A	HIRE

Record: 2 of 1076

Figure 13-11: Listing of Records Affected by Rule #112

13.2.4. Atomic Level Information

At the very bottom of the data quality scorecard pyramid are reports showing the quality of individual target records or subjects. These atomic level data reports identify records and subjects affected by errors and even show the probability that each of them is erroneous.

Figure 13-12 contains a portion of such a listing. It shows three records from the target population in E_EMPLOYEE_INFO table. Along with the data it provides error probability for the aggregate score *MINING_EMP_PATTERNS*. The first record has error probability 1.00, meaning it is erroneous with certainty. The second record has error probability 0.24 meaning that it is affected by one or more errors but is rather unlikely to be erroneous. A more likely scenario is that the rule compares it with another data element that is indeed erroneous. Finally, the last record has error probability 0.00, meaning it was not affected by any identified errors. If we looked at the complete listing of all records and added up all error probabilities, the result would yield the Accuracy Score (with a minor adjustment for possibly missing errors).

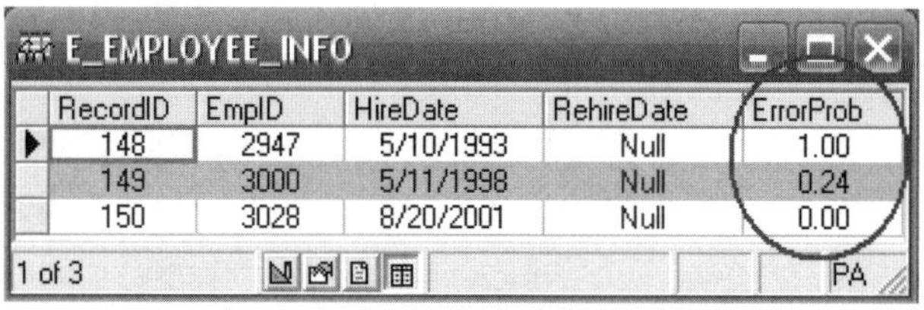

RecordID	EmplD	HireDate	RehireDate	ErrorProb
148	2947	5/10/1993	Null	1.00
149	3000	5/11/1998	Null	0.24
150	3028	8/20/2001	Null	0.00

Figure 13-12: Atomic Level Data Quality Report

Of course, if we are in the error investigation mode, it is useful to be able to set up various filters on the record list. It would also help to drill down further and see which errors by which rules affect a particular record. Thus, if we drilled-down the record #149 from Figure 13-10, we would see that it is affected by a single rule #112, which compares HireDate field against the effective date of the earliest record in employment history. We would further learn that 10% of errors found by the rule are deemed false positives; and of the remaining errors HireDate is expected to be erroneous in only 27% of cases, while employment history record is incorrect in 73% of cases.

The atomic layer completes the data quality scorecard pyramid. As the reader can see, the pyramid starts from the aggregate scores and demonstrates how they were obtained, which portions of the data have most problems, and eventually which individual records contributed to the observed error level.

13.2.5. Miscellaneous Definitions

The reports throughout the data quality scorecard reference scores, data elements, and data quality rules. It is very useful to have direct access to the definitions of these components.

For example, for each score in the data quality scorecard, it is useful to have a drill-down to the score description. It provides all information from the score catalogue including score objective, relevant data elements, data quality rules, subjects, and records. This is illustrated in Table 13-3.

Score Name	MINING_EMP_PATTERNS
Score Objective	A new HR data-mining project is scheduled. It will use employee dates of birth, hire, and rehire to analyze patterns of age-at-hire for all regular employees of the company. The objective of this aggregate score is to evaluate whether or not quality of these data is adequate for this project.
Relevant Data Elements	E_EMPLOYEE_PROFILE.EMP_ID E_EMPLOYEE_PROFILE.BIRTH_DATE E_EMPLOYEE_INFO.EMP_ID E_EMPLOYEE_INFO.HIRE_DATE E_EMPLOYEE_INFO.REHIRE_DATE
Relevant Rules	Rule #7 PK.E_EMPLOYEE_PROFILE Rule #9 PK.E_EMPLOYEE_INFO Rule #17 PK.E_EMPLOYEE_INFO Rule #21 REL_OPT.E_EMPLOYEE_INFO
Relevant Subjects	Subject Class EMPLOYEE: Left (E_EMPLOYEE_STATUS.EmployeeType, 1) = 'R'
Relevant Records	General filter - records for relevant subjects only E_EMPLOYEE_PROFILE – no specific filter E_EMPLOYEE_INFO – no specific filter

Table 13-3: Score Definition

Further drill-downs could provide detailed information about each of the relevant data elements (obtained from the data catalogue and data profiles) and data quality rules (found in the rule catalogue). Another drill-down would allow us to see the list of all relevant subjects (gathered from the master subject list). Also, if *DQMDW* is fully integrated with actual data, a drill-down would allow us to see listings of relevant data records.

13.3. OTHER DQMDW FUNCTIONS AND REPORTS

Having an integrated *DQMDW* allows us to perform data quality analysis with high efficiency. Of course, the data quality scorecard is the main analytical tool. However, it is often desirable to produce various ad-hoc reports in the course of data quality analysis. In this section, we will discuss the main categories of such reports.

An error catalogue contains endless listings of errors. Analysis of the errors requires the ability to organize and aggregate them across various dimensions. The most common aggregations are:

- Aggregation by data quality rules, which shows how many violations of each rule are found

- Aggregation by data elements, which shows how many errors are found in various tables or for various attributes

- Aggregation by subject populations, which shows what groups of subjects have more error-prone data

- Aggregation by subjects, which shows how many errors affect each particular subject and how many different data elements are erroneous

- Aggregation by data records, which shows the erroneous records and how many errors from how many rules affect each record

Besides varying the aggregation dimension we can also choose what to aggregate. Indeed we can count errors themselves, erroneous records, or subjects with errors.

Figure 13-13 shows a portion of the summary error report aggregated by data quality rules. Here we aggregate errors across the rules. The report can be easily built by querying the rule catalogue and the error catalogue. For each rule, the report lists identifier, name, type, and the number of rule violations. We see eight identity rules, five reference rules, four cardinal rules, and three domain constraints.

Most rules found some errors, with rules #3, #7, #21, and #32 identifying rather significant problem areas. For instance, rule #7 found 3,601 errors, meaning that table E_PAY_RATE_HISTORY has that many situations with two or more records sharing the same EmpID and EffDate. On the other hand, several rules in the list do not find any errors.

RuleID	RuleName	Rule Type	ErrorCount
1	PK.E_EMPLOYEE_PROFILE	Identity	0
2	UK.E_EMPLOYEE_PROFILE.SSN	Identity	2
3	UK.E_EMPLOYEE_PROFILE.NAME	Identity	280
4	PK.E_EMPLOYEE_INFO	Identity	47
5	PK.E_EMPLOYEE_STATUS	Identity	0
6	PK.E_STATUS_HISTORY	Identity	5
7	PK.E_PAY_RATE_HISTORY	Identity	3601
8	PK.E_PAY_SPECIAL_HISTORY	Identity	7
11	FK.E_EMPLOYEE_INFO	Reference	3
12	FK.E_EMPLOYEE_STATUS	Reference	2
13	FK.E_STATUS_HISTORY	Reference	6
14	FK.E_PAY_RATE_HISTORY	Reference	16
15	FK.E_PAY_SPECIAL_HISTORY	Reference	4
21	REL_OPT.E_EMPLOYEE_INFO	Cardinal	3450
22	REL_OPT.E_EMPLOYEE_STATUS	Cardinal	0
23	REL_OPT.E_STATUS_HISTORY	Cardinal	33
24	REL_OPT.E_PAY_RATE_HISTORY	Cardinal	4
31	DOMAIN.E_EMPLOYEE_PROFILE.GENDER	Domain	2
32	DOMAIN.E_EMPLOYEE_PROFILE.BIRTH_DATE	Domain	283
41	DOMAIN.E_EMPLOYEE_INFO.HIRE_DATE	Domain	99

Record: 1 of 71

Figure 13-13: Errors Aggregated by Data Quality Rules

Drill-down capabilities of *DQMDW* are very important. The idea is that for any portion of a summary error report, a detailed error listing can be generated and further filtered down and/or sorted by various criteria.

The error listings are a step towards analysis of the errors on the atomic level. Integration of *DQMDW* with actual data allows us to generate many useful atomic level error reports. Below are some examples.

- List of data records affected by a particular data problem or a group of data problems

- List of all errors that affect a particular record or a group of records

- List of all data records and data errors for a particular subject presented in an integrated subject browser

For instance, a simple join of the error catalogue with an actual data table would produce the list of <u>all</u> potentially erroneous records in that particular table, rather than just errors found by a particular rule. Such reports will list each record several times if it happens to be affected by multiple errors. The listing can now be filtered and sorted by either the data values or across the rules, thus giving more flexibility to error analysis.

Atomic level error reports can even be made available to some of the data users. This allows the users to judge quality of the records before making any decisions based on the data. It is a dream application of *DQMDW*.

SUMMARY

In this chapter we discussed the content and functionality of the data quality meta data warehouse (*DQMDW*). Here are the key conclusions:

- *DQMDW* is a collection of tools for organization and analysis of all meta data relevant to or produced by the data quality initiatives. Meta data used in a data quality assessment projects falls into four broad categories: aggregate meta data, rule meta data, atomic meta data, and general meta data. Integration of all the meta data into an efficient *DQMDW* is critical to the ultimate value of data quality assessment.

- A data quality scorecard is the central product of the data quality assessment project. It provides comprehensive information about data quality and allows both aggregated analysis and detailed drill-downs. It is not just a report but also a valuable tool for data quality analysis.

- Having an integrated DQMDW allows us to perform data quality analysis with high efficiency. There are many useful meta data reports that can be generated. Error summary reports aggregate errors across various dimensions. For any portion of a summary report, a detailed error listing can be generated and further filtered down and/or sorted by various criteria. These error listings are a step towards analysis of the errors on the atomic level. Integration of *DQMDW* with actual data allows us to generate many useful atomic level error reports.

CHAPTER 14
RECURRENT DATA QUALITY ASSESSMENT

Assessment is key to understanding data quality. The data quality scorecard provides comprehensive information about data fitness for various purposes. Assuming that some flaws are discovered, the next step is to initiate a data quality improvement program, including data cleansing and enhancement of data collection processes. The question then becomes, how do we measure the success of such programs? Without a clear way to show data quality improvements, it is impossible to understand the value of the program, analyze its shortcomings, and make enhancements. The solution is to institute a recurrent data quality assessment, whereas data quality will be reevaluated periodically to show the progress.

Another aspect of data quality is that it may be acceptable today but may quickly deteriorate over time. Recurrent data quality assessment allows us to establish quality benchmarks, monitor trends, and identify new causes of data problems.

On the surface recurrent data quality assessment is trivial. We simply need to re-run the established process periodically and observe the results. In practice challenges abound. This chapter presents a comprehensive treatment of the problems and solutions for recurrent data quality assessment.

- Section 14-1 outlines the basic approach to recurrent assessment. It shows how to make adjustments to data quality rules to account for changes in data structure, as well as how to build a dynamic data quality scorecard.

- Section 14-2 shows how to monitor data quality on the atomic level. It describes mechanisms for comparison of error catalogues produced by consecutive assessment runs.

- Section 14-3 outlines mechanisms for adding time dimension to the data quality meta data warehouse, which is necessary to analyze data quality trends over many assessment runs.

- Section 14-4 discusses techniques for performing assessment against production data directly, bypassing data staging area.

14.1. BASICS OF RECURRENT DATA QUALITY ASSESSMENT

Let's say we would like to check the quality of data in a particular database every six months. The first time we execute assessment exactly as was discussed thus far in this book. We bring the data to the staging area; go through data analysis and profiling; design, implement, and fine-tune data quality rules; populate the data quality meta data warehouse; and build the data quality scorecard. The next time we want to run the assessment all we need to do is backup the staging area and *DQMDW*, wipe out the error catalogue, reload the most recent data dump back to the staging area, and rerun all data quality rules. This procedure will produce the new data quality scorecard quickly and with practically no extra work.

Of course, the reality is somewhat more complex. First of all, this approach assumes that the rules will successfully apply to the new data dump. This requires careful rule design. We must avoid relying on temporal data characteristics. For instance, data currency rules cannot use constant date 1/1/2006, but instead must use a function returning first day of the current year. In general, any dynamic rule parameters must be consolidated in a separate function or a database table that can be updated before each run.

Even properly designed rules will decay and produce wrong results (or even fail outright) when the data structure changes between assessment runs or when the business rules that are the basis of data quality rules change. Therefore, blind re-execution is likely to create many problems. The solution is to perform comparative analysis of the data between the dumps. This includes a simple comparison of the data structure and a rather advanced comparison of data profiles. Fortunately, data profile comparison can be largely automated. I recommend writing a program that runs through all aspects of the profiles and identifies any significant changes for further review. For instance, value frequencies can be easily contrasted, and any change of more than 15% can be deemed significant. I also like to look for new or disappearing values and large changes in aggregate statistics (such as mean or standard deviation). Similarly, relational profiles, state-transition profiles, and other data profile components must be compared.

Once we find any changes in data structure, it is necessary to understand how they impact data quality rules. We can narrow down the list of possibly impacted rules by selecting only those whose rule domain includes affected attributes. After that it is strictly a manual analytical process. We need to understand the nature of the changes to the data structure and then review the rule catalogue and decide whether or not the rules will still work properly. Some rules always must be fine-tuned before each assessment run.

Once we are comfortable that the rules will work adequately, we can execute them and build the new data quality scorecard. The next step is to analyze the changes in the results. The things to compare are aggregate scores and score decompositions, as well as summary error counts by rule. Generally speaking, any significant change must be analyzed and explained. Sometimes the analysis will indicate that data quality has changed. This is exactly the result we are looking for in setting up recurrent data quality assessment. Hopefully, the data quality has improved. Otherwise, if data quality has deteriorated, our findings can be used to identify means for future improvements. Another possibility is that data quality did not really change, but some changes to the data require further modification of the rules. While we try to catch all such situations through a priori comparative data profiling, some will always slip through the cracks and get caught on the back end of the assessment run.

One more challenge to address is that some new errors might have been introduced into the data that are not caught by any of the existing rules. The only solution here is additional manual data review and rule fine-tuning. Ideally we want to utilize the findings of data users in the course of their normal work between the assessment runs, since many data problems are caught on a daily basis in the trenches. This will save unnecessary extra manual data verification. To do so we must create a process by virtue of which all data quality problems found by the data users are reported.

Assuming that we overcame all the obstacles, we now have the second data quality snapshot. We can repeat the procedure to create such snapshots regularly. While we lose the details of each assessment run when we repopulate data staging area and error catalogue, the summary results can be maintained and integrated into a dynamic data quality report. We can definitely add time dimension to the data quality scorecard summary and score decomposition layers. This affords a high-level view of data quality trends. Table 14-1 illustrates a dynamic scorecard summary from three consecutive assessment runs.

Score Name	Comple-teness Score	Accuracy Score	Overall Score	Subject Level Score
MINING_EMP_PATTERNS	98.0% 98.4% 98.7%	91.9% 89.6% 87.4%	90.0% 88.2% 86.3%	81.1% 79.5% 77.9%
COMP_DATA	96.4% 96.4% 96.3%	84.5% 84.8% 84.4%	81.5% 81.7% 81.3%	77.5% 77.6% 77.4%
EDU_COMPLIANCE	83.3% 92.4% 94.5%	97.5% 98.6% 99.0%	81.2% 91.1% 93.6%	86.4% 94.7% 96.4%

Table 14-1: Trends in Data Quality Scores

We can see from Table 14-1 that the quality of the data used in the data-mining project (*MINING_EMP_PATTERNS* score) has deteriorated, even though fewer data records are missing. This is a cause of concern and indicates a systematically failing data collection process. On the other hand, data quality for education compliance reporting (*EDU_COMPLIANCE* score) significantly improved, probably as a result of a data-cleansing project. Note that any significant improvement in data quality must be analyzed and explained. In absence of a data quality improvement initiative, such a result may be indicative of a flaw in data quality rules.

14.2. DATA QUALITY CHANGES ON ATOMIC LEVEL

Sometimes it is useful to be able to identify changes in data quality on the atomic level. In other words, we may want to know which errors were fixed (or just somehow disappeared) and which new errors were introduced. In order to do this we must compare the error reports produced by consecutive assessment runs.

The simplest method is to have each rule generate comprehensive error messages that uniquely identify the errors. Recall that we store custom error messages in the main ERROR table of the error catalogue and have complete flexibility as to the message structure and content. We can then run a simple comparison and identify all error messages from the previous run that are no longer present in the last run, as well as all new messages that mysteriously showed up in the last run. The next step is to use error report drill-downs to identify the nature of the changes.

The main technical difficulty with this approach is the need to build messages that uniquely identify the errors. This proves rather tricky for many rules. For instance, even in the case of a simple attribute domain constraint, the message must include the unique record key along with the erroneous attribute value. For rules comparing multiple records, storing complete error identification in the message may be practically impossible.

Even if we can overcome the technical challenge, there remains a serious analytical inconvenience. Comparison of the error messages tells us which errors changed, but not which records have been fixed or contaminated. Indeed, though errors reference actual data records (in ERROR_RECORD table of the error catalogue), we execute recurrent data quality assessment against different copies of the data in the staging area. Thus, there is no clear method of determining whether or not some errors in two assessment runs actually affected the same record.

A more comprehensive solution is to ensure a unique system for data referencing. This can be done on two levels. On the subject level, we simply need to maintain persistent master subject lists. When we reload the staging area with the next data dump, instead of creating a new master subject list we simply match new data to the existing subjects and only add new subjects. For extra convenience, we can mark all subjects present in a given assessment run with a Boolean flag.

With a persistent master subject list, tracking error dynamics is rather straightforward. The easiest method is to build and compare subject-by-rule status matrices. Each matrix has subjects in rows, rules in columns, and a yes/no flag in the intersections indicating whether or not an error was identified by a specific rule for a specific subject. Status matrices are easy to populate based on error catalogue table ERROR_SUBJECT. Superimposing matrices for consequent runs provide lists of all changes in subject data quality.

This is illustrated in Table 14-2 showing portions of two superimposed subject status matrices. For each subject the top row of flags corresponds to the results of the previous run, while the bottom row shows the results of the following run. Highlighted flags indicate error changes. For instance, subject #1 had an error found by rule #14 in the original assessment run, which was not found by the second run. Instead, rule #42 identified a new error. Further, subject #2 had no errors in the original assessment run, but now has an error found by rule #35; subject #3 had an error in rule #20, but has no errors in the new run. Of course, the matrices need not be compared manually. Instead, a simple query can identify and report all discrepancies for further analysis.

| | 1   2   3   4   5 |
	12345678901234567890123456789012345678901
Subject #1	NNNYNNNNNNNNNYNNNNNNNNNNNYNNNNNNNNNNNNNNNNNNNNNNNN NNNYNNNNNNNNNNNNNNNNNNNNNNYNNNNNNNNNNNNNNNYNNNNNNNNN
Subject #2	NNNNNNNNNNNNNNNNNNNNNNNNNNNNNNNNNNNNNNNNNNNNNNNNN NNNNNNNNNNNNNNNNNNNNNNNNNNNNNNNNNNNNYNNNNNNNNNNNNNNNN
Subject #3	NNNNNNNNNNNNNNNNNNNNNNNNYNNNNNNNNNNNNNNNNNNNNNNNNN NNNNNNNNNNNNNNNNNNNNNNNNNNNNNNNNNNNNNNNNNNNNNNNNNN

Table 14-2: Comparison of Status Matrices

Subject level comparison is useful but still does not provide information about data quality changes on the most atomic level – individual records. The ability to easily identify individual records with new errors would be invaluable for ongoing data quality management. Of course, every time we execute data quality assessment the error catalogue lists references to all erroneous records in ERROR_RECORD table. Furthermore, we add data quality meta data fields to all tables and populate them during score tabulation so that we can track the quality of each record. So what is the big deal? Can't we just match this information? The problem is that when we load the data to a staging area, we populate artificial surrogate key RecordID for easy referencing of all records. If the key values are created independently for each assessment run, then the same record may be referenced differently, and straightforward matching is impossible.

A possible solution is to ensure that the records retain their RecordID from run to run by matching record keys during data load into the staging area. However this still does not distinguish between records that did not change at all among runs and records that retained their keys but had changes in some non-key attributes. A more comprehensive solution is to create a record-matching table, which would map RecordID values across assessment runs. We can populate it by matching records based on their actual primary key values and add flags indicating which non-key attributes have changed. This second method is preferable; although, it requires more overhead in storage and querying.

14.3. ADDING TIME DIMENSION TO DQMDW

In order to analyze data quality changes on the atomic level, we must have access to *DQMDW* and staging area data for subsequent assessment runs. If we are only interested in data quality comparison between the last and current assessment runs, it may be easier to just keep two separate databases. However, if we want to have access to the entire history of data quality on the atomic level, it is time to think about adding time dimension to *DQMDW*, and possibly even to the staging area.

Adding time dimension to *DQMDW* is straightforward. First we introduce a concept of assessment run and give it a unique identifier and timestamp. Then we add this run identifier to the ERROR table. Now we can maintain error listings for any number of runs within the error catalogue. Of course, the size of the error catalogue will grow linearly over time. In theory this size increase can be minimized if we utilize the fact that many errors repeat from run to run. Therefore, rather than duplicating the error in the next run, we can somehow mark it as a repeating offender. While this method is technically possible (I have actually tried it), it creates many inconveniences and technical difficulties. I would not recommend it unless error catalogue size gets completely out of hand.

Of course, now that we have added time dimension to the error catalogue, we also should add time dimension to the rule catalogue to accommodate for the changes in rule design. Indeed, as we mentioned before, some rules always change between assessment runs due to fine-tuning or to reflect changes in data structure and data quality requirements. For example, attribute domains often change as new value codes are added or old ones stop being used. Data currency, retention, granularity, precision, and completeness requirements often change when new data uses are introduced. In order to make an intelligent comparison of the data quality assessment results, we must know which rules have changed and how exactly they were modified.

Rule versioning provides the means for storage, maintenance, and access to the history of rule changes. In its simplest form, rule version information can be maintained as a series of time-stamped free-flow comments in the rule listing. It can be stored in the Informal Description attribute or in an additional Versions attribute. Table 14-3 illustrates the point for a simple attribute domain constraint. It shows that the rule was changed twice over three years. Each entry indicates the date of change, initials of the person who made the change, and the nature of the change.

Rule #1. *DOMAIN.E_STATUS.EMP_TYPE*

Formal Definition:

[E_EMPLOYEE_STATUS].[EmployeeType] In ('O', 'RF', 'RP', 'TF', 'TP')

Informal Description:

Employee type must either be *O* ("occasional") or consist of exactly two characters, with the first one as *R* ("regular") or *T* ("temporary") and the second one as *F* ("full-time") or *P* ("part-time"). All other values are invalid.

Versions:

01/15/2004. ABM. Original rule version introduced.

11/05/2005. ABM. New code *O* ("occasional") added.

05/23/2006. OPM. All 3-digit codes (*RF1*, *RF2*, *RF3*, and *RF4*) eliminated.

Table 14-3: Simple Rule Version History

304

This technique works well when rule changes are only of interest for general inquiries. For example, if you look back at the results of the data quality assessment performed in May 2005 and find the error report for rule #1 puzzling, you can always check the version of the rule used at the time. However, it takes manual effort to figure it out. When rules are volatile (which is typical for databases with volatile data structure and uses), it is preferable to be able to query version information automatically. A simple solution is to add RULE_VERSION table to the rule catalogue. Table 14-4 shows possible structure of this table.

Attribute Name	Attribute Description
Rule Identifier (PK)	Reference to the rule identifier in RULE entity
Version Number (PK)	Sequential number of the rule version
Effective Date	Date when the rule version was first introduced
End Date	Last date when the rule version was used
Rule Name	Rule name
Formal Definition	Unambiguous rule definition using standard templates
Informal Description	Natural language description for a non-technical user

Table 14-4: Structure of RULE_VERSION Table

The RULE_VERSION table largely replicates the main RULE table of the rule catalogue, but adds version number and the effective rule timeframe. While it takes some extra effort to maintain, the new table can be queried to identify the exact state of each rule at any point in time. If it is desirable to maintain rule domain, error groups, and rule parameters for each version, then we simply replace entity RULE with RULE_VERSION and add VersionNumber to all other tables in the rule catalogue.

Of course, the rule versioning mechanism can be made even more sophisticated. You can build your own or utilize existing version-control software packages. In my experience, going beyond the simple design of Table 14-4 is only justifiable for enterprise-wide recurring data quality assessment initiatives. Luckily, in that case you are likely to have broader IT support of the project and can choose an adequate sophisticated solution.

Once we have added time dimension to error catalogue and rule catalogue, we are definitely better off adding time dimension to the data models, and especially data profiles. This is extremely valuable for the analysis in data quality trends.

The final step, of course, is adding time dimension to the data in the staging area and to the atomic level data quality meta data. The straightforward solution is to combine data from different snapshots used in individual assessment runs, and to add a run identifier to all records. This is really easy but will result in unlimited growth of the staging area. If the database is not huge, runs are infrequent, and only some recent history is of interest; then undoubtedly this solution is the best. Otherwise, some space management is in order. We can save space if we do not duplicate records that do not change between runs. Since in large databases the majority of records are often historical and rarely (if ever) change, this method will control the size of staging area very efficiently. Even more advanced techniques are plausible, including rather sophisticated audit trail mechanisms, but they are out of scope of this book. We will address these techniques more in the "Data Integration" volume of this series when we discuss the architecture of an information integration hub.

14.4. EXECUTING ASSESSMENT RUNS AGAINST PRODUCTION DATA

When data quality assessment is done on a regular basis and if the target database contains large volumes of data, we may have to run the rules directly against the production database rather then replicating it to the staging area. This creates additional challenges.

The first common mistake is to execute assessment against production data from the beginning. This is highly undesirable. While recurrent execution of data quality rules can put a mild strain on the production database, the process of rule implementation and fine-tuning will drive database administrators to a nervous breakdown, or at least motivate them to resist the data quality assessment project. Regardless of the long-term plans, we must start project implementation and complete the first run in a staging area. Once the process is up and running, we can re-point the rules to the production data.

The main challenge now is that we are stuck with the actual structure of the database and do not have homogeneous surrogate key RecordID in all tables. In absence of the surrogate key, we are forced to reference records by their actual primary key (or any unique key). For instance, erroneous records in table E_EMPLOYEE_PROFILE must be referenced by its primary key field EmpID. For the table E_PAYCHECK we would be using its composite primary key made of fields EmpID and EffDate.

Two approaches can be used to reference records by the actual primary key. The most straightforward method is to replace the numeric attribute RecordID in the ERROR_RECORD table with a text attribute KeyValues. We can use it to store the key value(s) for each referenced record. This presents no problems for tables with simple keys but is more difficult for ones with composite keys. In the latter case, we must store key values in a comma-separated string or a similar format, such as {114585; 11/15/2006} for a record from table E_PAYCHECK.

This method is simple to use and saves space in the error catalogue but makes error reporting cumbersome. Indeed, even the simplest report listing all erroneous records in a data table requires joining the data table with the ERROR_RECORD. Such a join is rather difficult for tables with composite keys. More importantly, performance of such a join will be unsatisfactory even for relatively small error counts.

An alternative method is to create homogeneous surrogate keys and then use intermediate lookup tables to match these surrogate keys with actual primary keys. For instance, we can create new intermediate table E_PAYCHECK_KEY in the staging area and populate it with three attributes: RecordID, EmpID, and EffDate. The first one is the surrogate key field, while the last two fields reference actual primary key of E_PAYCHECK table. Now we can use RecordID to reference erroneous records in the error catalogue, disregarding the fact that this surrogate key is not physically located in the E_PAYCHECK table.

Of course, we are now faced with the challenge of populating the key lookup tables. This is not as easy as it seems. We cannot simply repopulate it every time we want to run data quality assessment. Had we done that, the same actual records would be assigned different keys at different times and thus erroneous records identified in a past run would not be properly referenced. Also, it may not be advisable to create a new copy of the lookup table for each data quality assessment run, as it would result in a rapid expansion of the staging area.

The solution is to create lookup key records only for the erroneous actual records and only the first time an error in the record is found. This logic can be programmed in the error catalogue engine. Say we are executing a rule and found an error affecting E_PAYCHECK record with key {*114585; 11/15/2006*}. Before registering it, error catalogue engine would try to locate record with this key in the E_PAYCHECK_KEY table. If the record does not exist, it is created and given a new unique value of the surrogate key RecordID, otherwise the RecordID of the existing record is obtained. This RecordID is registered in the ERROR_RECORD.

Obviously this method requires the error catalogue to be a rather sophisticated object, rather than just a passive data storage. Also, it adds processing time to rule validation, which may be undesirable when a data quality assessment is performed frequently and against the production database. The alternative is to temporarily store composite key values in the ERROR_RECORD table and then periodically process the newly accumulated references and create appropriate surrogate key records. In my personal experience, this second alternative is more cumbersome and subject to many technical challenges. I strongly prefer to create lookup key records on the fly during rule validation.

I must say that frequent data quality assessment against a production database is technically and technologically rather challenging. There is no simple solution. In fact, there is no right solution, rather many options exist; and the best one depends on the dynamics of the data. Fortunately, situations that require such a complex solution are rare. If you happen to find yourself faced with this challenge, maybe it is not enough to read this book, and you really need the maestro himself. Just send me an e-mail. I love data quality challenges!

SUMMARY

Ongoing data quality monitoring requires recurrent data quality assessment. The first time we execute recurrent assessment exactly as discussed in the first 13 chapters of this book. The consecutive assessment runs require additional procedures and techniques.

- Data quality rules decay and produce wrong results when the data structure changes between assessment runs. The solution is to perform comparative analysis and profiling of the data between the dumps. Once we find any changes in data structure it is necessary to understand how they impact data quality rules. Some rules always must be fine-tuned before each assessment run.

- Every time we want to run the assessment all we need to do is wipe out the error catalogue, reload the most recent data dump back to the staging area, and fine-tune and rerun all data quality rules. Each rerun creates a data quality meta data snapshot. While we lose the details of each assessment run when we repopulate the data staging area and error catalogue, the summary results can be maintained and integrated into a dynamic data quality scorecard report. This affords a high-level view of data quality trends.

- Sometimes it is useful to be able to identify changes in data quality on the atomic level. The simplest method is to have each rule generate comprehensive error messages, which uniquely identify the errors. We can then run a simple comparison and identify all error messages from the previous run that are no longer present in the last run, as well as all new messages that appeared in the last run.

- A more comprehensive solution is to ensure a unique system for data referencing. On the subject level, we simply need to maintain persistent master subject lists. On the record level, we can create a record-matching table, which would map RecordID values across runs. Alternatively, we can ensure that the records retain their RecordID from run to run by matching the old value during data load into the staging area.

- In order to analyze data quality changes on the atomic level, we must have access to *DQMDW* and staging area data for subsequent assessment runs. If we are only interested in data quality comparison between the last and current assessment runs, it may be easier to just keep two separate databases. However, if we want to have access to the entire history of data quality on the atomic level, we must add time dimension to *DQMDW*.

- When data quality assessment is done on a regular basis and if the target database contains large volumes of data, we may have to run the rules directly against the production database rather than replicating it to the staging area. Frequent data quality assessment against production database is technically and technologically very challenging. There is no simple solution. In fact, there is no right solution, rather many options exist; and the best one depends on the dynamics of the data.

APPENDIX & INDEX

APPENDIX – CHARTS AND TABLES

In this appendix I provide a few charts with a pictorial overview of some topics from this book. The first five diagrams categorize data quality rules, followed by the diagram listing strategies for rule design.

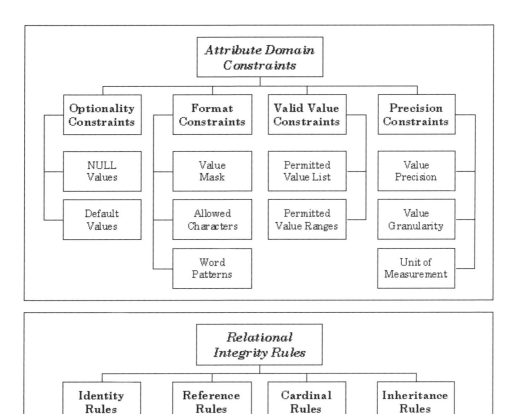

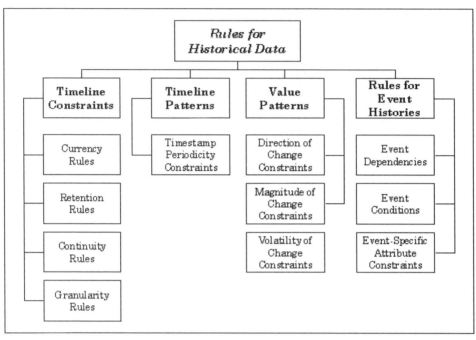

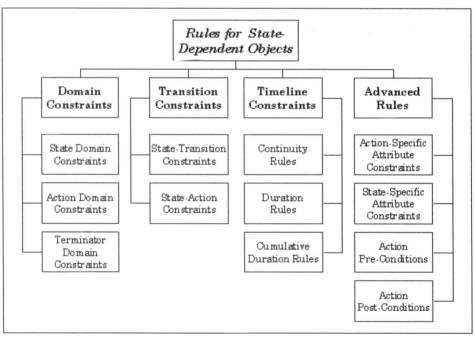

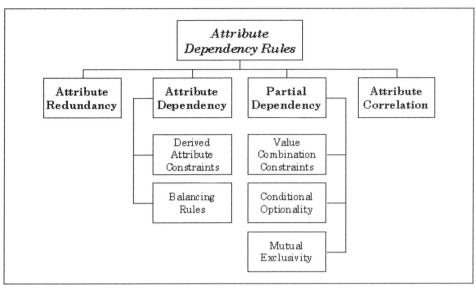

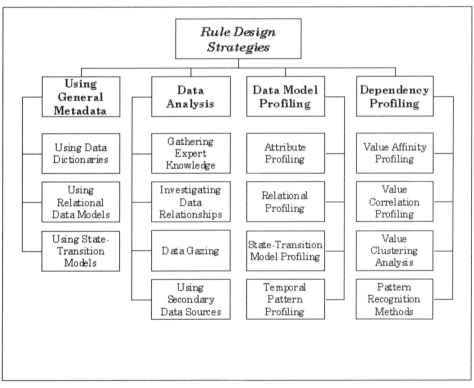

The final diagram presents core parts of the data quality assessment meta data model.

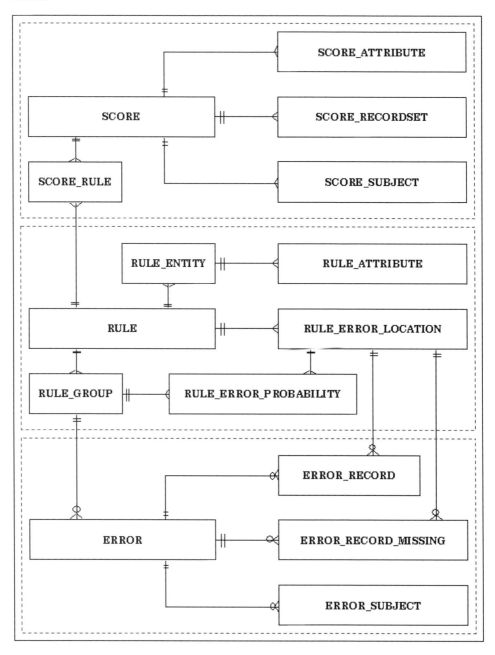